Data Structures
for Programmers

Data Structures for Programmers

Milton Rosenstein, Ph.D.
New York Institute of Technology
Old Westbury, New York

WILEY

A WILEY-INTERSCIENCE PUBLICATION
JOHN WILEY & SONS
New York • Chichester • Brisbane • Toronto • Singapore

Library of Congress Cataloging in Publication Data:

Rosenstein, Milton.
Data structures for programmers.

"A Wiley-Interscience publication."
Bibliography: p.
1. Data structures (Computer science) I. Title.

QA76.9.D35R67 1988 005.7'3 88-262
ISBN 0-471-63520-0

Printed in the United States of America

10 9 8 7 6 5 4 3 2 1

To my wife Rebecca,
heart and bedrock of my being.

Preface

This text is the product of five years of teaching data structures to students who, at first, could see no use for it. In those early days when it was strictly a graduate course, data structures was taught as an end-in-itself. The various data structures were formally described and applied in lengthy unstructured programs or algorithms, that were often beyond students' ability to comprehend and always beyond their ability to create. In those days, *teaching* data structures to these students was more an exercise in intimidation than education.

I think that this was also true for the teacher. How hard I worked to unravel those huge monolithic programs and how carefully I tried to present them to the class, measuring every word, watching every face for signs of puzzlement and despair and, usually vainly, for a bright glimmer of understanding. And how rarely did I succeed; one misstep, a moment of uncertainty or lack of clarity on my part was always enough to topple my often shaky pedagogic edifice and cloud the eyes of my audience.

Actually the students were right. The data structures course in those days was primarily background for compilers. Only in the pursuit of compiler theory would students finally find meaningful applications for the stacks, queues, lists, arrays, trees, lattices, and more, which were previously dizzily paraded before them.

Meanwhile, ordinary programming proceeded untouched by compiler theory. Programming remained a seat-of-the-pants creative art. Programs were unstructured, and ingenious algorithms were generated mainly by revelation. Data structures and program engineering, apparently, had little to offer people who only wanted to write useful, task-oriented programs instead of compilers. Most students sensed this.

Over the years, we teachers have begun to learn what we have been trying to teach others. A true appreciation of the crucial role of data structuring in the creation of algorithms and the absolute practical necessity of structured programming, has begun to emerge. Data structures are now understood as the raw material from which algorithms are built. A course in data structures is now recognized as an essential course in creating algorithms. Composing algorithms without a background in data structures is akin to designing electronic equipment without a knowledge of mathematics. Structured programming has also assumed its rightful throne. We realize now that unstructured programming produces Frankenstein monsters, difficult to comprehend, communicate, debug, or verify. Each day software breakdowns demonstrate anew that these massive, monolithic programs can no longer be tolerated.

This book is my contribution to the growth of understanding and appreciation of the role of data structuring and structured programming in task-oriented programming. It reflects at least five years of satisfaction on my part and on the part of my students that something of immense utility has been taught and learned.

I have attempted to write a text that is practically oriented but theoretically sound. The data structures covered are those that have immediate and practical application. Each data structure is described in straightforward language shorn of unnecessary (though impressive) complications. The goal, kept firmly in mind, is to apply these structures to programming, not to wallow in their complexities. Therefore once described, they are immediately put to use in a variety of useful and practical applications. I have spared the reader those little bits of procedures and programs, endemic to existing texts, that leave readers in midair, unable to realize actual programs without a lot more work. Every topic is carried to the level at which it can be used by the reader. These applications are complete and fully detailed. They include databases, syntax checkers, scheduling and inventory programs, tests for isomorphism and subisomorphism, searching and sorting, infix-to-polish transformations, spelling and symbolic equation checkers, language extension by adding new operators, digital gate circuit analysis, and more. I am somewhat proud of these algorithms and programs. They are mostly original and, I trust, convincingly demonstrate the utility of data structuring.

I have aimed this work at any and all who write programs, be they students, hobbyists, or professional programmers. This book is appropriate for a single semester data structure course in a computer science program or in any technical school that teaches programming. It also lies within the ken of any persistent and perspicacious reader with a passion for programming. To make this work compatible with the backgrounds of such a broad spectrum of readers, I have written every program and procedure in both BASIC and Pascal and have fully annotated and explained each one. The ability to compose programs in either language is the only required background. BASIC is the primary language of micro users, but Pascal is popular at present in most colleges. Using both bridges the gap between the two languages and encourages the BASIC fan to learn Pascal and vice versa. This gap is virtually eliminated by the SBASIC, used of necessity in the latter half of the text.

Although this text bears my name, it is the work of many people: those colleagues and writers of other texts from whom I learned and upon whose work I built; my students whose bright and questioning minds forced me to clarify many an incompletely understood concept; Dr. Philip Kantrowitz, now deceased, who acted as mentor to me and so many other authors; my two daughters Louise and Amy, whose faith sustained my own, and my wife Rebecca, whose mind and heart are the true source of this book and of every other thing I accomplish.

MILTON ROSENSTEIN PH.D.

New York Institute of Technology

Contents

1 Introduction

1.1 MOTIVATIONS

All programming starts with the creation of a set of simple steps that will permit the computer to accomplish its task. This set, called an *algorithm,* predetermines the nature of the program. A poor or inappropriate algorithm will lead to a long, awkward program that is difficult to understand, debug, or verify. A happy choice may lead to a concise and simple program that practically writes itself. Clearly, this first step is the most crucial one.

Yet, most programmers give insufficient thought to the choice or creation of the algorithm. It is for them an art, not a science. Their algorithms arise from some creative intuitive process or are taken from a book. They know of no criteria with which to evaluate algorithms, and consequently they tend to seize upon the first one that seems to fit their needs. They are, therefore, apt to accept an inappropriate one as readily as a good one.

The creation of algorithms need not be an intuitive art. There exists a well-developed area of knowledge called *Program Engineering* that can provide us with valuable guides and procedures for programming, in general, and especially powerful ones for the creation of algorithms. These procedures work. They make algorithm creation less an art and more a science. They are useful. Moreover, they can be learned by anyone willing to expend a modest effort.

Program Engineering informs us that data structures are fundamental elements in algorithm creation and that the selection of a data structure is the crucial decision that predetermines the program. It holds that a correctly chosen (appropriate) data structure leads easily to the formulation of a concise and efficient algorithm. If we choose a poor (inappropriate) one, we are in heavy trouble. Not that we will be unable to formulate an algorithm and complete the task. Unfortunately, we probably will be able to do so, but the resulting program will be unnecessarily long and difficult to understand, debug, and verify. In the next section we learn why this is true.

1.1.1 The What and Why of Data Structures

Data is the raw material on which a program works. It may be numbers, character strings, or combinations of both. It may be the output of an analog-to-digital converter that is sampling an electronic signal. It may be a stream of bits read off a punched tape, a magnetic tape, or a disk. It may be the output of a modem that is converting audible beeps and whistles out of a telephone into computer-readable form. It may be, and often is, the output of keyboard manipulations.

The function of all programs can be simply defined in terms of the input data. The program must process the data and transform it from its initial form to some desired target form. For example, consider a simple program designed to add numbers and to output the sum. We may say that this program transforms a stream of numbers (*data*) into a sum (*target*). A more sophisticated program such as an accounting program may be viewed as transforming business data into a spreadsheet display of debits and credits.

Is there any value in defining programs in this way? For one thing, it makes us think of a program as a tool or a set of tools used to transform raw material into a final form. Anyone who has built anything knows that the difficulty associated with a task depends on the kind of raw material you start with. Constructing a wooden table is easy if you start with a kit. All you have to do is to put it together. It is harder if you start with wood from the lumberyard. Even there, if you can use a sheet of plywood for the top, the job is simpler than gluing up narrow strips of wood. It is a poor mechanic, indeed, who does not carefully consider the properties and form of his raw material before beginning a job.

The same considerations apply to intellectual tasks. The form or structure of the raw material (data) critically affects the difficulty of the task. For example, consider a mathematical problem calling for the multiplication of two numbers. This would seem to be a simple problem, so let's try it. Multiply the following two numbers:

$$\text{LXVII} \times \text{CLXIV} = ?$$

This problem is not so easy after all. Multiplication of roman numerals is not simple. However, if the data had been given in a different form, say, in the arabic numerals,

$$67 \times 164 = ?$$

the task would have been easy. Note that both tasks are identical, the multiplication of two numbers representing the same quantities. It is clear that the difficulty of a task depends critically on the form of the raw material—in this case, the data.

These examples can be proliferated without end. If you have believed that difficulty is a function of the intended task or problem, you should now rethink the matter. Clearly, a task can not be difficult and easy at the same time. Yet, our previous example appears to be just that. In this example, the difficulty of the task is almost entirely dependent on the form of the data. Difficulty, then, cannot be a characteristic of the task but must, instead, depend on how we approach the task.

These lessons apply to programming as well. A programming task cannot be rated in terms of difficulty. A thoughtless, ill-considered approach can generate a long, hard-to-understand and harder-to-debug program. Another approach may accomplish the same task with a short, concise, easily understood program that debugs effortlessly. If this lesson is really learned, long-winded programs will be viewed with doubt and suspicion rather than shown off as proof of the accomplishment of a difficult task.

The organization of the data on which the program operates is clearly one of the most important factors affecting program development. It is the raw material that crucially controls the program. Concise, efficient programming certainly depends on the way the data is organized. The programmer who fully realizes this fact has taken a giant stride toward superior programming.

Substitute *structured* for *organized,* and you have defined the term *data structure.* A physical structure has form. It is composed of recognizable elements joined in some coherent way. A data structure is no different. As we shall see, it too is composed of elements united by some coherent rule. The plural, *data structures,* refers to the many ways in which data can be organized.

These ways have been carefully studied and well analyzed. Most of them arose out of a pressing need in the development of compilers. These huge programs must use up as little computer memory as possible. This means they must be as concise as possible. Also, they must operate as quickly as possible and must be as error-free as possible. Conventional seat-of-the-pants programming would not suffice. Therefore, the most advanced techniques of program engineering had to be used—among them, data structuring.

1.2 SOME DATA STRUCTURES

It is time to look at some specific data structures so that we can see what they are and how they serve the programmer. We will take a cursory view, so we will have no space for details. That will come later. Our purpose is to provide a glimpse into a storehouse of information that is guaranteed to improve the reader's programming skills.

1.2.1 The Table and the Multiply-Linked List

The well-known table format is a data structure. The data elements (numbers and/or strings) are organized into rows and columns. Generally, each row refers to a single item. Each column refers to a single characteristic of the item. Figure 1.1 displays a table.

The table organization facilitates certain operations. We can easily sum the quantity column and determine how many items are on hand. Likewise, we can sum the price column and determine the total value. If we wish to find the price of a particular item, we can scan down the first column until we find the item and then move horizontally along the row to the price column. (This procedure is expedited if the items are entered in alphabetical order.) The table has many useful properties. This accounts for its popularity.

There are operations that are not facilitated by the table. If we arrange the items in alphabetical order, we cannot at the same time arrange the prices in ascending or descending numerical order. Consequently, when it is easy to find any item, it will not be easy to find the highest- or lowest- or second-highest-priced item. This problem could be overcome by setting up another table in which the items are ordered by price, but this begins to get cumbersome and wastes memory. If we wish to order items on the basis of more than one characteristic, the table structure is clearly inappropriate.

We begin to catch a glimpse of the crucial importance of using the right data structure.

Suppose we have many items defined by name, price, number-in-stock, etc. We need to select a desired item and then to print out its name together with its price, number, etc. An algorithm for this is obvious. Arrange the items by name in alphabetical order in table form. Given the name of an item, search the first column until it is either found or passed by alphabetically. If it is found, print out the entire row. If it is bypassed, print out "not in stock." The table is clearly appropriate to this task. We may take as proof the fact that the algorithm is straightforward and immediately apparent.

Our next task appears to be more demanding. (If we did not realize that difficulty is not a characteristic of tasks, we might indeed think it is more *difficult.*)

ITEM	PRICE	QUANTITY ON HAND	REORDER FLAG
pins	$5/gross	200 gross	50 gross
hooks	$1/dozen	300 dozen	50 dozen
eyes	$3/gross	50 gross	50 gross
locks	$2/unit	500 units	100 units

Figure 1.1 Table.

In addition to selecting items by name, our client also wants to pick out items on the basis of price, number-in-stock, last reorder date, and other associated data. Our client wishes to be able to select highest price, second- or third-highest price, and likewise for number-in-stock and reorder dates.

If we stayed with the preceding table, we would be in trouble. Our algorithm would no longer be so obvious nor so simple. We might, given *price* as the search factor, reorder the table on the basis of price and then search it. Given *number-in-stock,* we could again reorder the table, and so on. Surely we could write a program based on this algorithm, but it would be a mistake to do so.

There is another data structure called a *multiply-linked list* (to be studied later) that can handle this task more efficiently. This data structure permits the programmer to establish a *list* of items plus all associated data, that is simultaneously ordered for all entries. This structure could be set up once and left alone. An ordered search could be conducted for any element in the list. The resulting program would be concise and easy to understand and to debug. It would also run faster than the table program.

1.2.2 The Digraph

The digraph is a data structure that looks like a flat Tinker Toy assembly. Drawn on paper, it consists of a series of small circles (*nodes*) connected by lines (*links*). The circles represent items and the lines represent relations between items. For example, the data—station A connects to station D, station B connects to station C and station C connects to station A—would be represented as a digraph by Figure 1.2.

Figure 1.2 provides obvious algorithms that answer questions concerning connections. Can I go from station A to station C in one stop? If not, what stations must I pass through? Can I go from station B to station D without passing through station A? The first question is answered by seeing if there is a link between A and C. If not, trace through and record the links you must pass through to get from A to C. The second question is also answered by traversing the drawing. (Later, we shall learn how to support this action on the computer.)

Suppose you had the seemingly complex task of writing a program to provide railroad information. You could simply enter the entire train schedule into the computer in the tabular form in which it is usually found and rely on your inge-

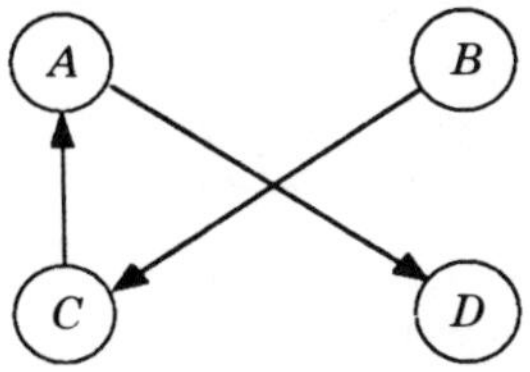

Figure 1.2 Station connection digraph.

nuity to answer questions about it. Unfortunately, you could probably complete the program, but it would be longer and more complicated than the railroad it serves. When we study digraphs, you will be astonished by how readily they generate simple, straightforward algorithms that will solve all tasks involving connections.

1.2.3 The Binary Tree

The binary tree also consists of nodes connected by links, the nodes representing items and the links representing relations. However, the binary tree differs from the digraph and bears a closer resemblance to a real tree. There is one entrance into the structure. It is through the *root* node. This node may branch out to one or two subnodes below. In turn, each subnode may branch out to one or two subnodes, and so on. Figure 1.3 displays a binary tree.

The binary tree has many remarkable applications. It is the most efficient search structure. Items in a tree can be found in a fraction of the time required for a list or a table. When a left link is given a different meaning than a right link, the tree takes on a shape. It can then be used for pattern recognition, and therefore it has application in speech and handwriting recognition. There are other important applications of the binary tree. These will be studied later.

1.2.4 Other Data Structures

Other data structures include the multidimensional array, the recursive digraph, the adjacency matrix, the singly- and doubly-linked lists, the multiway tree, the hedge, the indexed tree, the forest, and the lattice. This list is by no means exhaustive because new structures are always possible. Each structure serves a unique purpose, simplifying and expediting the creation of new algorithms. Therefore, a working knowledge of these data structures significantly extends the programmer's ability to create algorithms. Moreover, these al-

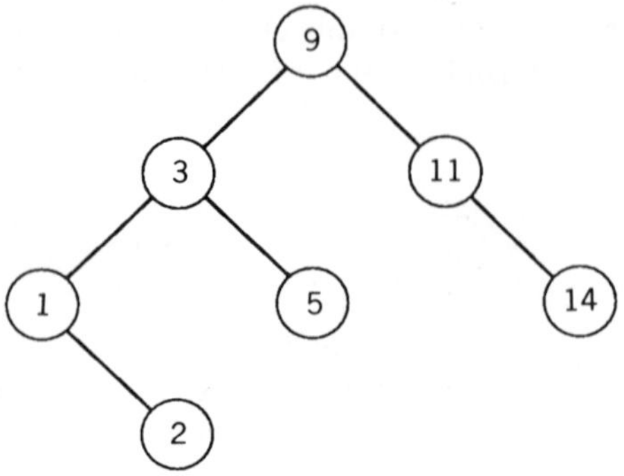

Figure 1.3 Binary tree.

gorithms are always simple and direct, and they lead to concise, understandable, and consequently easily debugged programs.

1.3 TOP-DOWN PROGRAMMING, MODULARIZATION, AND DATA STRUCTURES

The clarity of a program can be judged in part by the time required to debug it. The greater the debugging time, the more incomprehensible the program. Lengthy debugging is a sure indication that the algorithm is uncertain and difficult to understand and, as a result, the program is long and unclear. A good program is a clear program that consequently is easily debugged.

Judged by these standards, what can we say about most professional programs when the industry expects only ten lines of debugged code per day from professional programmers? What can be said about the end product of those programmers, professional or otherwise, who as a matter of course expect to spend more hours debugging a program than writing it?

To be fair, we must admit that the ten-line-per-day standard does not apply to very short programs but to long ones. No programmer would expect to spend eight hours debugging a ten-line program. The standard applies to the case where a programmer spends two weeks writing a lengthy, complicated program and then is forced to spend 20 weeks debugging it. At this writing, this is considered both acceptable and normal.

Program Engineering suggests that we exploit the fact that short programs require very little debugging whereas long ones require a lot of debugging. Why not then break a long program into several short ones? That way each short program can be debugged separately and then joined to form the long program. Programs are modularized (segmented) by writing appropriate sections as subprograms and joining them by a main, or *calling,* program. Experience has demonstrated that this procedure saves time and improves the product. Programs constructed according to these principles are called *structured programs.* Figure 1.4 shows a sample structured program format.

Another Program Engineering procedure (*top-down programming*) also depends on modularization. Top-down programming is a technique for planning and writing a program. It approaches program composition as globally as possible, seeking an overview of the entire job. Subsequently, the job is sectioned repeatedly on the basis of some rationale until the terminal stage, the operating program, is reached. This procedure conforms to the typical hierarchal structure of industry. Therefore, it works particularly well for large programming endeavors—where the person in charge must apportion the work to lieutenants who in turn must further delegate responsibilities. It is also an excellent procedure for the individual programmer since it proceeds from an initial overview of the task and guides the programmer to further division of the effort. Figure 1.5 shows a typical top-down programming procedure.

Modularization and top-down programming require that the programming

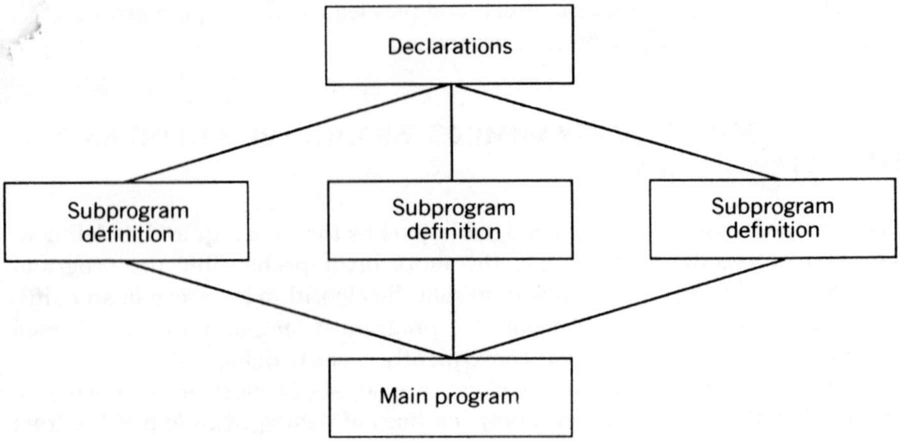

Figure 1.4 Sample structured program format.

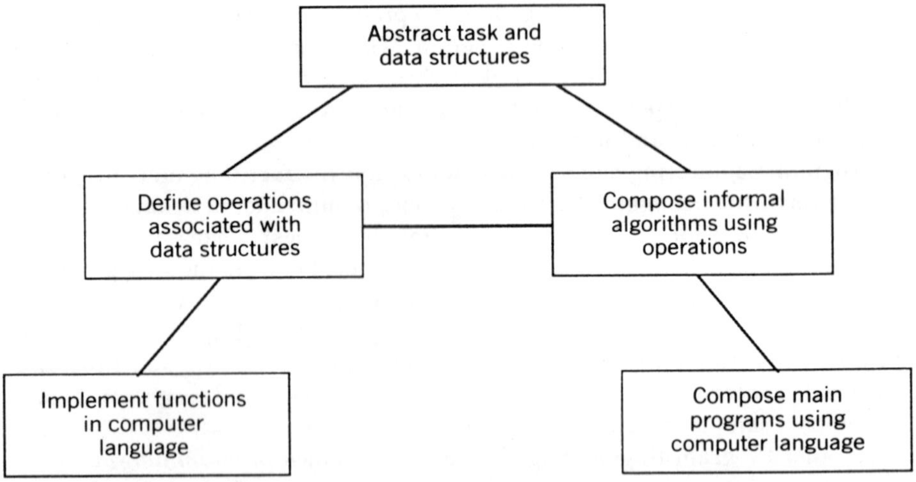

Figure 1.5 Example of top-down program planning.

procedure be sectioned, but neither approach provides a rationale for sectioning. Modularization by itself does not necessarily lead to a superior program. Sectioning a program into smaller units can produce a poorer program if the sectioning is done unintelligently. Neither does following the top-down procedure guarantee that the chosen planning stages will expedite and improve the planning process. Here, too, a poor choice can confuse the entire process. Both procedures depend on an appropriate sectioning rationale if they are to work effectively.

Data structuring provides an effective sectioning rationale for both modularization and top-down programming. We shall see that to choose an optimum algorithm, we must first determine the structure of the task and match the data structure to it. The selection of a data structure provides a good first level for the top-down approach. Each data structure carries along a set of operations that are appropriate to the data structure. Using only these operations, the programmer must compose an informal algorithm. The ease with which this algorithm is composed tests the appropriateness of the selected data structure. The informal algorithm is a good second-level tier for the top-down procedure and provides an overview of the program. Finally, the algorithm must be implemented in some computer language as subprograms and united by a main program. These steps provide the final tier. All these procedures provide a practical basis for modularization and division of work. (These procedures will require extension for programs employing multiple algorithms.)

1.4 WHAT THIS MEANS TO PROGRAMMERS

Most of us do not program for a living. We may write programs for use in other serious efforts such as scientific research, management of a business, or some educational purpose, or we may simply be exploring the potentials of computer applications as a hobby. Regardless of motivation, all of us are interested in producing superior programs, in reducing the time required, and in extending our ability to create algorithms. A working knowledge of Program Engineering will help.

REVIEW QUESTIONS

1.1 Compose an algorithm to sort three-letter words into an alphabetical order based on all three letters. Describe and analyze the thought process associated with this task.

1.2 Provide some examples of a task that is difficult when approached one way and easy, another way.

1.3 Use a table structure containing *item, price,* and *number-in-stock* to compose an algorithm that will permit selecting any item, the first-, second-, and third-highest price and number-in-stock. Is this algorithm straightforward or complicated? How will this work for extremely large tables?

1.4 Represent the following airline connection information as a data structure (draw structure): city A links to city D and city F, city G links to city A and city D, city D links to city A, city F and city G.

1.5 You head a team of programmers writing a program to verify checks prior to cashing. The checks must undergo some tests before action is taken. Tests might include: Is there an account? Is the account overdrawn? Does it contain enough to satisfy the check? Establish a top-down procedure to organize the work of your team.

2 The *N*-Dimensional Array

2.1 STRUCTURE AND REPRESENTATION

An *array* is a collection of items arranged in some pattern. The items may be either numbers or strings (a string is a sequence of characters) but usually not both. The pattern may be a simple one-dimensional sequence of elements. For example,

1 3 24 12 or Joe Paul Peter Sam

This is often called a *vector*. The pattern (or *structure*) may be a two-dimensional rectangular grouping. For example,

(a)

1	3	5	2
5	2	7	0

(b)

−5	2	0	1	0
0	2	1	3	0
3	−1	2	4	2

(c)

4	3
5	2
3	2
4	3

or

(d)

Paul	John	Pete
Hal	Sam	Paul
Ed	Joe	Bill

or

(e)

Now	is	the	time
for	all	good	men
to	come	to	the
aid	of	their	country

This is called a *matrix* (*matrices* is the plural). The pattern may have three, four, five, or more dimensions. In general these multidimensional structures are called *n-dimensional* matrices, where n represents any number.

The general one-dimensional array (**A**) can be represented by

$$\mathbf{A} = a_1 \quad a_2 \quad a_3 \quad \cdots\cdots \quad a_k$$

where "......" represents additional terms and a_k represents the last term. **A** is the name of the array, a_1, a_2, etc., are the *elements* of the array, and the subscripts 1 through k are called *indexes* (singular is *index*). **A** has 1 row and k columns. The column to which an element belongs is given by the index. For example, element a_5 is in column 5.

The general two-dimensional array is given by

$$\mathbf{A} = \begin{array}{lllll} a_{1,1} & a_{1,2} & a_{1,3} & \cdots\cdots & a_{1,k} \\ a_{2,1} & a_{2,2} & a_{2,3} & \cdots\cdots & a_{2,k} \\ a_{3,1} & a_{3,2} & \cdots & \cdots\cdots & a_{3,k} \\ a_{4,1} & \cdots & \cdots & \cdots\cdots & a_{4,k} \\ \cdots & \cdots & \cdots & \cdots\cdots & \cdots \\ \cdots & \cdots & \cdots & \cdots\cdots & \cdots \\ a_{n,1} & a_{n,2} & \cdots & \cdots\cdots & a_{n,k} \end{array}$$

where the first index of element a represents the row in which the element is found and the second index represents the column. For example, the element $a_{3,6}$ is located in row 3, column 6. The array shown has n rows and k columns. It is described as a two-dimensional $n \times k$ array.

Three-dimensional matrices can be represented geometrically by taking the first index as the row, the second as the column, and the third as a position in space above the page. Dimensions beyond this are impossible to represent or visualize in any simple geometrical way.

2.1.1 Another Representation

Instead of interpreting the indexes as the coordinates of a point (element) within a set of orthogonal (mutually perpendicular) axes, let them simply indicate the location of (directions to) an element. In the first case (orthogonal axes), we encounter difficulty beyond three dimensions because we cannot visualize anything beyond three-dimensional geometric space. However, we have all had a lot of experience with specifications of the locations of things. We know they can be complex and number more than three. For example, the location of Empire State Building is given by

Country	USA
City	New York
Borough	Manhattan
Street	34th
Address	125

Five items are required here. If we consider the *Empire State Building* to be an element (ESB) in an n-dimensional array and the indexes as specifying its location, then the element (ESB) is defined by

$$\mathrm{ESB}_{\mathrm{USA,\ New\ York,\ Manhattan,\ 34,\ 125}}$$

and it is an element in a five-dimensional matrix.

A filing system provides a fine representation of an n-dimensional array. Suppose we have a filing system containing single-word items. The system consists of items in lines, lines on pages, pages in drawers, drawers in cabinets, and cabinets in groups. Each item needs six location specifications: group, cabinet, drawer, page, line, and position in line (column). If the entire filing system is the array (**I**), any item (i) within it is defined by $i_{i,j,k,l,m,n}$, where i is the group number, j is the cabinet number, k is the drawer number, l is the page number, m is the line number, and n is the column number. **I** is a six-dimensional matrix.

2.2 MATCHING DATA STRUCTURE TO TASK

Throughout this book we shall assert that the data structure best suited to a task is one that matches the structure of the task. The filing system provides a good illustration of what this means. Note how easily and efficiently the data in the filing system is transferred to the n-dimensional array, and vice versa. This is a good indication of the kinship of the two structures. Note that the same operations—finding an item (or a block of items), retrieving or deleting it (or them), or adding an item (or a block of items)—are simple and natural to both structures. Generalized directions for filing, deleting, and retrieving that apply to both structures at once could easily be written. These two measures, efficiency of data transfer and similarity of basic operations, are the assurance of similarity of structure.

2.3 IMPLEMENTING THE N-DIMENSIONAL ARRAY

FORTRAN, Pascal, PL1, and other similar languages support multidimensional arrays directly, but this is not true for BASIC. Most versions of BASIC support only one- and two-dimensional arrays. However, it is almost always the case that any language can be modified or extended to include the features of others. BASIC is easily extended to include multidimensional arrays.

All arrays are contained in memory as vectors (one-dimensional arrays) plus information that permits the computer to reconstruct the array when it is called. For example, the two-dimensional array

$$\mathbf{A} = \begin{matrix} a_{1,1} & a_{1,2} & a_{1,3} & a_{1,4} \\ a_{2,1} & a_{2,2} & a_{2,3} & a_{2,4} \\ a_{3,1} & a_{3,2} & a_{3,3} & a_{3,4} \end{matrix} = \begin{matrix} 2 & 4 & 0 & 1 \\ 3 & 0 & 1 & 0 \\ 5 & 7 & 3 & 4 \end{matrix}$$

may be stored in memory as

$$\mathbf{B} = \begin{matrix} b_1 & b_2 & b_3 & b_4 & b_5 & b_6 & b_7 & b_8 & b_9 & b_{10} & b_{11} & b_{12} \\ 2 & 4 & 0 & 1 & 3 & 0 & 1 & 0 & 5 & 7 & 3 & 4 \end{matrix}$$

plus the equation

$$a(i, k) = b(C(i - 1) + k) \qquad (2.1)$$

where items within parenthesis are subscripts representing indexes and C is the number of columns in **B**. The computer returns the element $a_{i,k}$ by transforming it into the equivalent element (b_k) using Eq. (2.1). This is illustrated in Example 2.1.

EXAMPLE 2.1

Find the value of the elements $a_{1,4}$, $a_{2,3}$, and $a_{3,4}$ when **A** is stored in memory as **B** plus Eq. (2.1) with $C = 4$.

1. $a(1, 4) = b(4 \times (1 - 1) + 4) = b(4) = 1$
2. $a(2, 3) = b(4 \times (2 - 1) + 3) = b(7) = 1$
3. $a(3, 4) = b(4 \times (3 - 1) + 4) = b(12) = 4$

A three-dimensional array is stored in computer memory as a vector plus the equation

$$a(i, j, k) = b(J_{max} \times K_{max} \times (i - 1) + K_{max} \times (j - 1) + k) \qquad (2.2)$$

where J_{max} is the maximum size of the second index (j) and K_{max} is the maximum size of the k index. For example, suppose we had three pages each containing two rows and three columns of numbers. This data can be represented as a three-dimensional array (**A**), where the element $a_{i,j,k}$ is located on page i, row j, and column k. **A** could be displayed by placing each page side by side as follows:

Page 1	Page 2	Page 3
2 1 4	0 2 3	3 0 5
6 2 0	1 4 2	2 1 7

Within computer memory this is stored as the vector **B**:

$$\mathbf{B} = 2\ 1\ 4\ 6\ 2\ 0\ 0\ 2\ 3\ 1\ 4\ 2\ 3\ 0\ 5\ 2\ 1\ 7$$

plus Eq. (2.2), where $J_{\max} = 2$ and $K_{\max} = 3$. Example 2.2 shows how this works.

EXAMPLE 2.2

Find the values of the elements $a_{1,2,3}$, $a_{2,1,2}$, and $a_{3,2,1}$.

1. $a(1, 2, 3) = b(2 \times 3 \times (1 - 1) + 3 \times (2 - 1) + 3) = b(6) = 0$
2. $a(2, 1, 2) = b(2 \times 3 \times (2 - 1) + 3 \times (1 - 1) + 2) = b(8) = 2$
3. $a(3, 2, 1) = b(2 \times 3 \times (3 - 1) + 3 \times (2 - 1) + 1) = b(16) = 2$

These results may be extended by induction. For example a four-dimensional array with elements $a_{i,j,k,l}$ would use the transformation

$$a(i, j, k, l) = b(J_{\max}K_{\max}L_{\max}(i - 1) + K_{\max}L_{\max}(j - 1) + L_{\max}(k - 1) + l)$$

2.3.1 Implementation in BASIC

The vector-to-n-dimensional transformation is easily supported in BASIC by the *user-defined function.* For example, to set up and operate on the three-dimensional array of Example 2.2, define the user function

```
10 FNA(I,J,K) = JMAX * KMAX * (I-1) + KMAX * (J-1) + K
```

where JMAX and KMAX are assigned the values 2 and 3 respectively. Input vector **B** is dimensioned by

```
20 DIM B(18)
```

The statement

```
30 PRINT B(FNA(2,1,3))
```

will output the value 3 because FNA(2,1,3)=$2 * 3 * (2-1) + 3 * (1-1) + 3 = 9$ and $B(9) = 3$.
The statement

```
40 W = B(FNA(2,1,3) + B(FNA(3,2,1)
```

will place the value 5 in W because $B(FNA(2,1,3) = 3$ and $FNA(3,2,1) = 2 * 3 * (3-1) + 3 * (2-1) + 1 = 16$ and $B(16) = 2$.
The statements

```
50  FOR I = 1 TO 3
60   FOR J = 1 TO 2
70    FOR K = 1 TO 3
80     IF B(FNA(I,J,K)) > 2 THEN PRINT B(FNA(I,J,K))
90    NEXT K
100  NEXT J
110 NEXT I
```

will scan the array and print all numbers greater than 2.

These examples demonstrate the ease with which n-dimensional arrays can be implemented and used in BASIC.

2.4 APPLICATIONS OF THE N-DIMENSIONAL ARRAY

Because the n-dimensional array has a structure similar to a filing system, it is appropriate for the same uses. We have mentioned some—filing, retrieving, and deleting—but there are many others. Essentially, a filing system is a database, and it supports all database operations. Therefore, the n-dimensional array is the appropriate data structure for a database. Databases are usually very large and cannot be accommodated in core memory. Therefore, they must be stored on disks as files. Since the file structure is similar to a one-dimensional matrix, the transformation procedure described for BASIC must be used for all languages.

Database operations, whether manual or computerized, include entering, deleting, and changing data. In addition, there are more sophisticated information-retrieval operations that involve conditional search. Finding all people who live in their own homes in the northeast region of the United States and who earn over $20,000 per year is one example. We shall see how simple and obvious the algorithms for these operations are, once we have organized the data into an n-dimensional array.

2.4.1 Structure of a Sample Database

Suppose we need a database for a state motor vehicle department. The data is organized as follows:

Level 1	Year of manufacture: 1984 through 1985
Level 2	Make: manufacturer's name: five makes
Level 3	Folder: 26 folders
Level 4	Rows: there is one page per folder, each holding a maximum of 40 rows (lines)
Level 5	Columns: there are three columns on the page. Column 1 contains the owner's name; column 2, the social security number; and column 3, the license string

This data can be encompassed in a five-dimensional array ($MV(i, j, k, l, m)$). Index i specifies the year the vehicle was manufactured. (In a manual system, i directs the user to one of two cabinets.) Index j encompasses the various makes of vehicles. (In a manual system, it directs the user to one of five drawers in a specified cabinet.) Index k identifies each folder. (In a manual system, it might represent looking for the first letter of the last name of the owner.) Index l identifies the line on the page (row) that contains the owner's name and associated data. Index m identifies the column.

2.4.2 Implementing the Database

Figure 2.1 shows this database implemented in a BASIC program. (Note in Figure 2.1 the line below line 340 is a continuation of that line.) Figure 2.2 shows the PASCAL implementation. Both programs are interesting and worthy of close study. They illustrate the programming techniques advocated in this text and some of their advantages.

Program Structure

The Pascal program (Figure 2.2) qualifies as a *structured* program. The program is modularized into six subprograms called *functions* and *procedures.* These may be composed and debugged separately. They may also be saved in a library and reused as desired. These subprograms are called by a short and simple main program. This excellent structure is the direct result of using Pascal and is not remarkable. It is indeed required by the language. This is one of the major advantages of using Pascal.

The BASIC program (Figure 2.1) is also structured, and this is remarkable. BASIC neither requires nor encourages this kind of structure. Compare this program against the BASIC programs encountered in the various computer magazines. These are usually monolithic (not modularized) and virtually lacking in clear-cut structure. They must be debugged and saved in their entirety. Few if any are entitled to be called *structured.*

```
10 REM DATA BASE PROGRAM: DBASE1
20  REM ==================================================================
30 REM              DECLARATIONS AND FUNCTIONS
40  IM=2: JM=5: KM=26: LM=40:MB=3: 'MAX VALUES OF MATRIX
50  DEF FNA(I,J,K,L,M)=JM*KM*LM*MB*(I-1)+KM*LM*MB*(J-1)+LM*MB*(K-1)+MB*(L-1)+M
60  OPEN "R",#1,"B:DBASE",10 'OPENS RANDOM FILE-RECORD SIZE 10 BYTES
70  FIELD #1, 10 AS  F$  'ALLOCATES SPACE IN RANDOM BUFFER FOR VARIABLE
80    GOTO  430            BYPASSES SUBPROGRAMS
90   REM SUBPROGRAMS
110    REM SUBPROGRAM PUTFILE, FILES DATA
120     LSET F$=A$  'MOVES DATA INTO RANDOM BUFFER
130     CODE% = FNA(II,JJ,KK,LL,MM) 'SETS RECORD POSITION
140    PUT #1, CODE%  'PLACES DATA IN RECORD AT CODE% INTO BUFFER
150   RETURN
160    REM SUBPROGRAM GETFILE RETRIEVES DATA
170     CODE% = FNA(II,JJ,KK,LL,MM)   'SETS RECORD POSITION
180     GET #1, CODE%  'PLACES DATA IN RECORD AT CODE% INTO BUFFER
190    RETURN
200    REM SUBPROGRAM LOCATION DATA
210     PRINT " YEAR, MAKE, FOLDER NO.,  ROW  AND COLUMN NO.IF KNOWN"
220     PRINT " AND DATA STRING. ENTER 0  WHERE INDICES ARE  UNKNOWN"
230     PRINT " AND EMPTY STRING WHEN DATA IS UNKNOWN."
240     INPUT I,J,K,L,M,A$
250       FOR P=LEN(A$)+1 TO 10:A$=A$+" ":NEXT P
260    RETURN
270   REM SUBPROGRAM RETGET, RETRIEVES AND FILES DATA
280    GOSUB 200  'CALLS SUBPROGRAM LOCATION
290    IF I=0 THEN FOR II=1 TO 2 ELSE II = I
300     IF J=0 THEN FOR JJ = 1 TO 5 ELSE JJ=J
310      IF K=0 THEN FOR KK = 1 TO 26 ELSE KK=K
320       IF L=0 THEN FOR LL = 1 TO 40 ELSE LL = L
330        IF M=0 THEN FOR MM= 1 TO 3 ELSE MM=M
340         IF S=1 THEN GOSUB 160:PRINT F$:INPUT "ENTER Y/N";E$:
            IF E$="N" THEN RETURN ELSE GOSUB 110:RETURN
350         IF S=2 THEN GOSUB 160: IF F$=A$ OR A$="          " THEN RETURN
360        IF M=0 THEN NEXT MM
370       IF L=0 THEN NEXT LL
380      IF K=0 THEN NEXT KK
390     IF J=0 THEN NEXT JJ
400    IF I=0 THEN NEXT II
410   RETURN
420 REM =================================================================
430 REM MAIN PROGRAM
440 REM SELECT OPERATION
450  PRINT "SELECT OPERATION. 1: INSERT, CHANGE OR DELETE DATA."
460  PRINT "                  2: RETRIEVE DATA"
470  PRINT "                  3: QUIT"
480   INPUT S
490   IF S=3 THEN 530
500   GOSUB 270
510   IF S=1 THEN PRINT A$ " FILED AT "II;JJ;KK;LL;MM: GOTO 450
520   IF S=2 THEN PRINT F$"("II;JJ;KK;LL;MM")": GOTO 450
530  END
```

Figure 2.1 BASIC database program.

Figure 2.2 Pascal database program.

```
PROGRAM Database(input,output);
  (DECLARATIONS AND PROCEDURES)
    LABEL AGAIN;
    TYPE
      Datum = STRING[10]; Dta =  RECORD item:Datum END;
    CONST (SETS INTEGER CONSTANTS)
      IM:INTEGER=2;JM:INTEGER=5;KM:INTEGER=26;LM:INTEGER=40;MB:INTEGER=3;
    VAR      I,J,K,L,M,P,S,II,JJ,KK,LL,MM,TT:INTEGER; (SETS VARIABLES)
        dd,item:datum;du, dt:Dta;et:CHAR;
        NI,NJ,NK,NL,NM:INTEGER;
        Dbase1:FILE OF Dta; (Defines DBASE FILE)
     FUNCTION Transform(I,J,K,L,M:INTEGER):INTEGER;
     BEGIN (DEFINES FUNCTION THAT TRANSFORMS FROM VECTOR TO MATRIX)
        Transform := JM*KM*LM*MB*(I-1)+KM*LM*MB*(J-1)+LM*MB*(K-1)+MB*(L-1)+M;
     END;
    PROCEDURE FILLBLANKS(VAR ps:datum); (MAKES ALL DATA SAME LENGTH)
     BEGIN
       FOR P:=LENGTH(ps) to 10 do ps:=ps+' ';
     END;
    PROCEDURE PUTFILE; (FILES DATA)
      BEGIN
       TT:=TRANSFORM(II,JJ,KK,LL,MM); (TRANSFORMS MATRIX LOC. TO VECTOR LOC)
       RESET(DBASE1);
       SEEK(dbase1,TT); (LOCATES POSITION)
       WRITE(dbase1,dt); (ENTERS DATA INTO FILE)
      END;
    PROCEDURE GETFILE;
       BEGIN
        TT:=TRANSFORM(II,JJ,KK,LL,MM);
        RESET(DBASE1); (SETS POINTER TO BEGINNING OF FILE)
        SEEK(dbase1,TT); (LOCATES POSITION)
        READ(DBASE1,Du); (READS DATA FROM FILE)
        END;
    PROCEDURE LOCATION; (ASKS USER FOR DESIRED DATA)
      BEGIN
        WRITELN('YEAR, MAKE, FOLDER NO.,  ROW  AND  COLUMN IF KNOWN');
        WRITELN('AND DATA STRING. ENTER 0 WHERE INDICES ARE UNKNOWN');
        WRITELN('AND EMPTY STRING WHEN DATA IS UNKNOWN.');
        READLN(I,J,K,L,M,dd);
        FILLBLANKS(dd);dt.item :=dd;
      END;
    PROCEDURE RETGET; (RETRIEVES AND FILES DATA)
      LABEL RETURN;
      BEGIN
        LOCATION; (CALLS LOCATION)
        NI:=2;NJ:=5;NK:=26;NL:=40;NM:=3; (ESTABLISHES LOOPING CONDITIONS)
        IF I<>0 THEN NI:=I ELSE I:=1;
        IF K<>0 THEN NJ:=J ELSE J:=1;
        IF J<>0 THEN NK:=K ELSE K:=1;
        IF L<>0 THEN NL:=L ELSE L:=1;
        IF M<>0 THEN NM:=M ELSE M:=1;
     FOR II:=I TO NI DO  (FINDS MATRIX LOCATION FOR READING OR FILING DATA)
          FOR JJ:=J TO NJ DO
           FOR KK:=K TO NK DO
            FOR LL:=L TO NL DO
             FOR MM:=M TO NM DO
              BEGIN (READS OR FILES DATA AT PROPER LOCATION)
               IF S=1 THEN BEGIN GETFILE;WRITELN(DU.ITEM);
                 WRITELN('ENTER? Y/N');READLN(et);if et='Y' THEN
                 PUTFILE  ELSE GOTO RETURN;END;
```

Figure 2.2 *(Continued)*

```
                IF S=2 THEN BEGIN GETFILE;IF (du.ITEM=dd) OR
                  (dd ='            ') THEN GOTO RETURN;END;
                END;
RETURN:END;

{MAIN PROGRAM, SELECTS DESIRED OPERATION AND CALLS PROCEDURES}
 BEGIN
 ASSIGN(DBASE1,'B:DBASE2');
AGAIN: WRITELN('SELECT OPERATION 1. INSERT, CHANGE OR DELETE DATUM');
       WRITELN('                 2. RETRIEVE DATUM');
       WRITELN('                 3. QUIT');
 READLN(S);
 IF S=1 THEN BEGIN RETGET; WRITELN(DT.ITEM,' FILED AT ','(',II,JJ,KK,LL,MM,')');
   GOTO AGAIN;END; {VERIFIES FILING}
 IF S=2 THEN BEGIN  RETGET;WRITELN(du.ITEM,'(',II,JJ,KK,LL,MM,')');
   GOTO AGAIN;END; {DISPLAYS RETRIEVED ITEM}
END.
```

Although BASIC does not encourage good structuring, Figure 2.1 shows that it does not preclude it. Once the techniques of structuring have been learned, they can be applied to programming in any language. The BASIC program of Figure 2.1 consequently has been modularized. Each subprogram (subroutine or function) can be debugged separately and saved for further use, thus simplifying debugging. The subprograms are called by a simple, concise main program. The program is therefore as structured as its Pascal counterpart.

The Data Structure

The heart of these programs resides in the subprogram *RETGET*. This short subprogram allows the user to file an item in any cell of the database, to retrieve it, or to change it. It permits a search for any item, using whatever location information is known, however incomplete. For example, if we know the year and column of an item but do not know the make of the car or the folder number, we can find the exact location of the item (say, a license plate) and then determine the make, the manufacturer, the owner's name and social security number. These operations are illustrated in the following example.

EXAMPLE 2.3

Perform the following operations on the database of Section 2.4.1

(a) File entries into the database of Section 2.4.1. (b) Change license plate number in one row. (c) Determine owner's name from license plate number. (d) Find all owners with license plates beginning with the letter *A*.

(a and b) On RUN the program displays the MENU

```
SELECT OPERATION. 1: INSERT, CHANGE OR DELETE DATA
                  2: RETRIEVE DATA
                  3: QUIT
```

To enter owner's name, input 1.
Program calls LOCATION and displays

```
YEAR, MAKE, FOLDER NO., ROW AND COLUMN IF KNOWN

AND DATA STRING. ENTER 0 WHERE INDEXES ARE UNKNOWN

AND EMPTY STRING WHEN DATA STRING IS UNKNOWN.
```

To file owner's name—for example, Barton John at year 1, make 2, folder 2, row 1 and; column 1—enter

```
1, 2, 2, 1, 1, "BARTON JOHN"
```

The program displays the existing entry at the specified location plus the location. If, for example, there were no existing previous entry, the display would show

```
(1 2 2 1 1) ENTER Y/N
```

If the file had been previously filled with the empty indication "EEEEEEE," the program would display

```
EEEEEEE (1 2 2 1 1) ENTER Y/N
```

If the file had contained the entry "Bush James" at this location, the display would be

```
BUSH JAMES (1 2 2 1 1) ENTER Y/N
```

If the user wishes to overwrite this with "Barton John," he enters Y. The program files the entry at the specified location and verifies this by displaying

```
BARTON JOHN FILED AT (1 2 2 1 1)
```

If the user does not wish to enter the item, he enters N, and the entry is aborted. After entry, the SELECT OPERATION menu is displayed. This same operation is repeated for columns 2 and 3 to fill a row. Changing an entry is accomplished in the same way. To change a license plate string in column 3, enter

```
1, 2, 2, 1, 3, "AWN344-52"
```

Respond Y to the "ENTER Y/N" prompt and the entry is made.
(c) To locate an unknown entry at an incompletely known location given another

entry in the row, choose 2 from the SELECT menu. Then, in response to the location-entry question, enter the correct index number for the known locations and 0's for the unknown. Also enter the known item. To find the owner of license plate QRS232-34 when the year = 2, the folder = 3, and the column = 3, enter

```
2, 0, 3, 0, 3, "QRS232-34"
```

The program will search column 3 in all rows within folder 3 for all makes in year 2 until the "QRS232-34 is found. It will then display this string and its location. For example,

```
QRS232-34(2 3 2 2 3)
```

To find the owner's name, the user selects 2: RETRIEVES DATA and enters

```
2, 3, 2, 2, 1, ""
```

The program retrieves the owner's name at this location and displays the result.

Although the program is *bare bones*, it is clearly extremely flexible and easily modified for more complicated actions such as the conditional search required by (d). We do this for the BASIC program.

(d) Make the following modifications

```
Add    355 IF S=3 THEN GOSUB 160:IF LEFT$(F$,1)=LEFT$(A$,1)
           THEN RETURN
       465  PRINT "          3: CONDITIONAL SEARCH: FIRST
            CHARACTER"
CHANGE 470 PRINT"             4: QUIT"
        490 IF S=4 THEN 530
```

In response to the location prompt, enter

```
0, 0, 0, 0, 3, "A"
```

The program will search the database, looking only at the first letter in column 3, and return the location of the first license plate, beginning with *A*. The user can then use this location to read column 1, the owner's name. Increment the line number by 1, and continue this search. Most likely this operation will be made automatic. We leave this as a project for the reader.

The flexibility of *RETGET* is a product of the five-dimensional matrix. If this data structure had not been selected, the subprogram would probably have been much longer and more complicated. The time spent in considering and choosing the appropriate data structure has been, in this case, richly rewarded. This is always the case.

Once the appropriate data structure has been selected, the algorithm is almost obvious. To search through the entire database for a specified entry, iterate (loop) through each index, comparing each entry against the specified one. To search for a specified entry when the location is partially known, iterate only through the unknown indexes. To enter, retrieve, or change an entry at a known location, do not iterate but go directly to the specified location.

The BASIC program RETGET accomplishes this controlled iteration by using conditional iteration. For example, if I = 0 (line 290), the outermost loop is iterated and II (the outermost index) iterates from 1 to 2. If I is not zero, then the ELSE applies, and II does not iterate. Instead, it is given the value of I. Therefore, if location of I were known to be 2, the outermost index would be set at this value. If I were not known and set at 0, the outermost index would iterate. Other indexes act in the same way. Note that to prevent a NEXT WITHOUT FOR error, the NEXT statements must also be made conditional.

The Pascal RETGET requires a slightly different approach. The first five IF statements determine whether iteration will occur or, if not, will set the value of the index. For example, if I is not known and set at zero, the ELSE applies and I is set at 1. I is also used as the lower limit of the outermost loop. Therefore, in this loop, II will iterate from 1 to NI (NI = 2). If I is known, the IF statement will apply and NI will be set equal to I. I is the lower limit, and NI is the upper limit of the loop. Therefore, the loop will iterate only once, and II will assume the value I.

The other subprograms are straightforward and conventional, or have been discussed. The function TRANSFORM converts the five-dimensional matrix to a file location. FILLBLANKS converts every entry to a ten-character string. This is required to evaluate string equality in Pascal and usually in BASIC. PUTFILE and GETFILE file and retrieve data strings in the database file. LOCATION displays requests for the necessary location data.

2.5 TOP-DOWN DESIGN

These programs were composed in accordance with the principles of top-down design. The *n*-dimensional data structure was selected because it closely matches the database or filing system structure. Then, the following informal, natural language algorithm was formulated using this data structure and its attendant operations:

> Establish a five-dimensional matrix as the database with conditional looping. Transform matrix to a vector for random disk file operation. To enter, retrieve, or change data at a known location, enter the location indexes plus the data string if it is known. If data string is unknown, enter the empty string. For completely specified locations, the program accesses matrix directly. For partially or unspecified locations, conditional looping operates to iterate through unknown indexes.

This informal algorithm gives a simple overview of the whole program and acts to guide further work. Notice that the structure is first established. Then, the algorithm is described in terms of the operations appropriate to the structure. In this case, the appropriate matrix operations are accessing, entering, changing, or retrieving.

The algorithm is used to modularize the program. We need to transform matrix locations to vector locations (TRANSFORM), to enter location and string data (LOCATION), to enter and retrieve data from a file (PUTFILE and GETFILE), and to access and search the matrix (RETGET).

The next step in the top-down procedure requires some decisions about how to proceed. Should the subprograms be developed using flowcharts or a pseudocode, or directly in a chosen language? What language should be used to implement the program? If the work is to be done by a team, how should it be divided?

These decisions can be based on the way the program has been modularized. If the subprograms appear to be simple and straightforward, they can be directly written in the chosen language. If not, then a flowchart or a pseudocode is helpful. The best language to use is the one that most directly supports the chosen data structure. In a team effort, individuals or groups should be assigned one or more subprograms.

In our case, the subprograms appear to be straightforward and short. The most complicated one, RETGET, is familiar to me. Therefore, the subprograms were composed directly in BASIC and Pascal. These languages were used because they are widespread and support vectors and random files. Each subprogram was entered and debugged separately. Since the longest one, RETGET, contains 20 lines in BASIC and about 20 statements in Pascal, the subprograms were quickly debugged, and saved separately for future use.

2.6 SUMMARY

The n-dimensional matrix is the appropriate data structure for programming tasks involving databases. It can be easily implemented in any language that supports vectors. Databases are usually too large to be retained in core memory. They are therefore almost always stored on disks. Disk files are vector structured. Therefore, the n-dimensional matrix must be transformed into vector form for disk storage and retrieval but remain in n-dimensional form for program operation. The choice of the n-dimensional matrix suggests a simple and flexible algorithm that is easily modularized and implemented in a concise structured programs. This is equally true for BASIC as for Pascal. Also the algorithm expedites top-down programming of the task.

PROGRAMMING PROJECTS

2.1 Expand the database program to support input and output of complete lines (records) containing owner's name, social security number, and license string.

2.2 Change the database program so that the 26 folders are in alphabetical (lexical) order, A through Z.

2.3 Modify the database program so that for new records the owner's name will be placed in the appropriate folder in column 1 of the first available empty line.

2.4 Reduce the dimensions of the database program so that the matrix is small enough to be retained in core. Write a version that is core based. Compare the response time of this program to the disk-based version. Do this for both floppy and hard disks, if possible. Comment.

2.5 Modify the original database program so that instead of accessing the disk for each cycle, large portions of the disk are read into core before being searched. What effect does this have on program response time?

2.6 Modify the original database program so that it will conduct an automatic conditional search.

3 The Digraph

3.1 CONNECTIONS

There is a popular song that goes, "The foot bone's connected to the leg bone, the leg bone's connected to the thigh bone," and so on. This ditty makes the important point that connections (*relations*) between things are an essential aspect of reality—some say the most important aspect—and that a true understanding depends on grasping these connections.

Certainly, this is true for a large class of computer tasks concerned with relations and connections. For example, those that answer such questions as: Does *A* connect to, or relate to, or follow, or derive from, or lead to *B*, and so on? Also, for more global questions such as: Do the internal connections or relations of structure *A* coincide with structure *B*, and if not, how do they differ? Does structure *A* contain a specified set of internal relations? Although at present these questions may appear to be abstract, we will see that they apply to useful and realistic tasks.

3.2 THE STRUCTURE OF THE DIGRAPH

The *digraph* (directed graph) is the data structure of choice for all tasks involving connections. Figure 3.1 gives a representation of a digraph. As shown, it consists of small circles or any closed shape (*nodes*) connected by directed lines (*links*). The nodes represent the elements, the things connected, and the links represent the connections, the relations between elements. The nodes may stand for anything desired: data records, trains, products, algebraic variables, nouns,

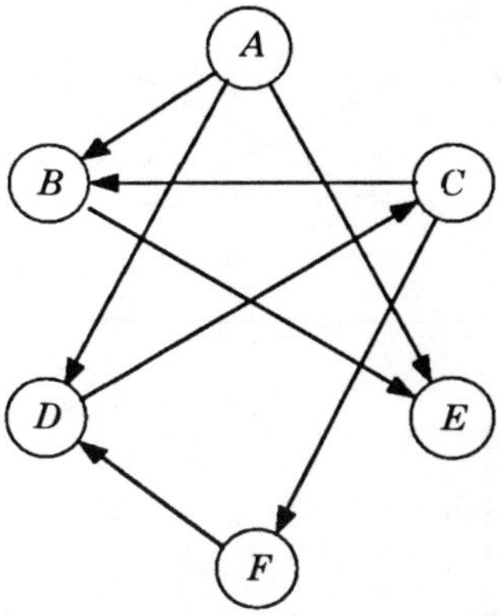

Figure 3.1 Digraph representation.

places, etc. However, they are always treated as *things.* The links signify the relations between these things. Their interpretations can range from simple physical connection to abstract analytic and mathematical relations. For example, the set of relations "product *A* sells better than product *B* and *C*, product *D* sells better than *B* and not as well as *C*" is represented by Figure 3.2. The relation "sells better than" is represented as a unidirectional (*directed*) link.

Figure 3.3 represents the more abstract set of relations "can be derived from." The nodes of the figure represent algebraic expressions. A connection means that one expression can be directly derived from the other nodes that connect (point) to it.

Links can be made to represent quantitative as well as qualitative relations by attaching *weights* to them. These structures are called *weighted digraphs.* They are extremely useful for handling symbolic equations, for representing *word*-generating systems, for representing signal flow graphs, and so on. These applications lie beyond the scope of this text, but the astute programmer can pursue

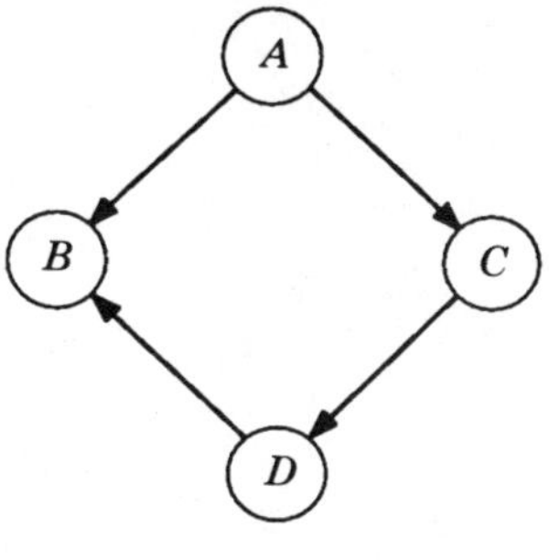

Figure 3.2 Digraph: "sells better than."

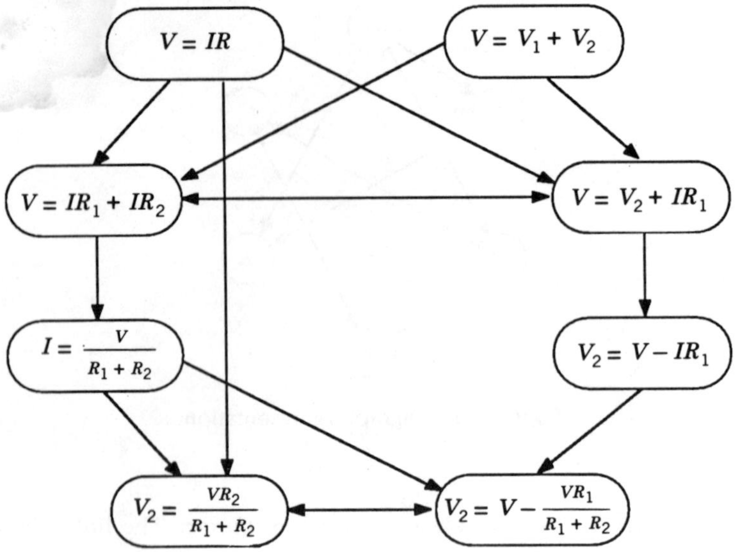

Figure 3.3 Digraph: "can be directly derived from."

this topic independently. Figure 3.4 is the digraph representation of the set of simultaneous equations

$$\begin{aligned} x_1 &= ax_0 + dx_2 \\ x_2 &= bx_0 + cx_1 + ex_2 \\ x_3 &= fx_1 + gx_2 \end{aligned} \tag{3.1}$$

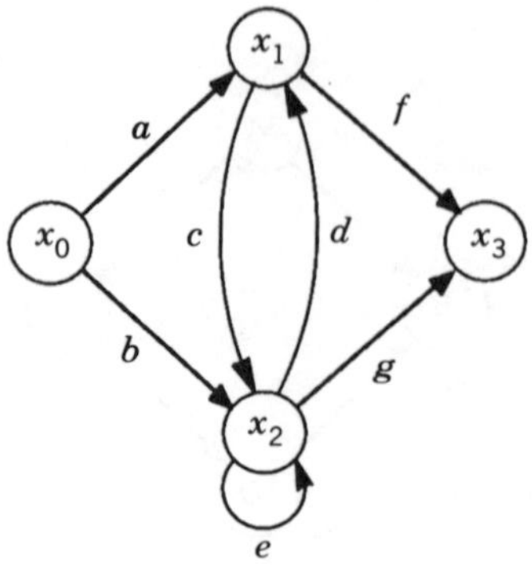

Figure 3.4 Weighted digraph.

where the link connecting x_0 to x_1 weighted a, means that $x_1 = ax_0$ plus the contribution of any other links directed at x_0.

A link that relates a node to itself is called a *sling*. Many such relations exist; for example, "equal to," "is contained in," "is an element of the same set," and so on. Figure 3.4 contains a sling signifying that one of the terms of x_2 is ex_2.

In Figure 3.5 the links represents the relation "can be concatenated with" or "joined to." By repeated traversal of the sling, the digraph generates an open-ended set of *words* of the form *xy*, *xxy*, *xxxxy*, and so on.

3.3 IMPLEMENTATION

The representation of the digraph as circles connected by lines (diagrammatic digraph) is congenial to the human mind, but not to the computer. The computer requires a numerical and more mathematical representation. This is provided by a structure called the *adjacency matrix.*

The adjacency matrix is a square matrix (the number of columns equals the number of rows). The rows and columns are given the same designations and represent the nodes of the digraph. A one at the intersection of a row and column means that a link connects the node designated by the row to that designated by the column. A zero means that no such link exists. The adjacency matrix is implemented in the computer as a square 2-dimensional array of one's and zero's. Figure 3.6 displays some diagrammatic digraphs and their adjacency matrix representations.

The weighted digraph is implemented in the computer as a square two-dimensional array (weighted adjacency matrix), containing either numerical elements of any value or string constants. The weighted adjacency matrix for Figure 3.4 is shown in Figure 3.7.

3.3.1 Digraphs and Matrix Algebra

Matrix algebra is a well-developed branch of mathematics. It is an algebra that operates on two-dimensional arrays rather than on the simple numbers of ordinary algebra. It is defined for addition, subtraction, two kinds of multiplication, and other operations. After we have reviewed the four specified operations, we shall see that they have interesting and useful applications in programming.

Addition, subtraction, and *outer multiplication* are analogous to ordinary number operations. Matrix **A** is added to matrix **B** to give matrix **C** by adding

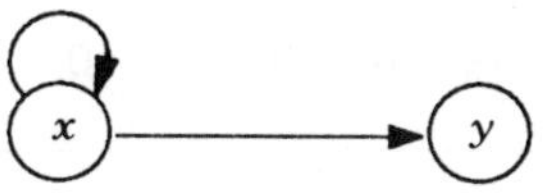

Figure 3.5 Digraph with sling.

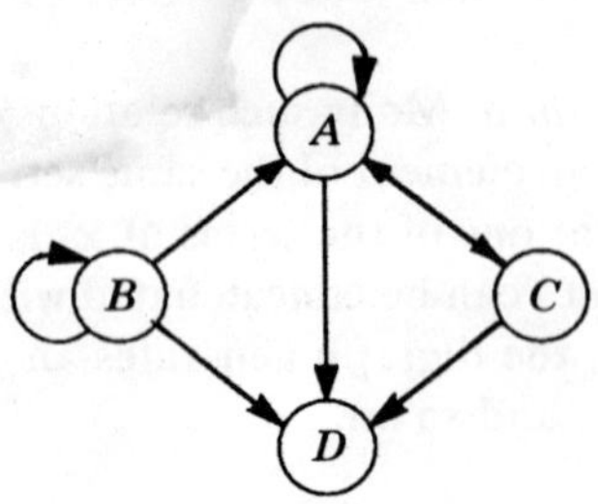

	A	B	C	D
A	1	0	1	1
B	1	1	0	1
C	1	0	0	1
D	0	0	0	0

(a)

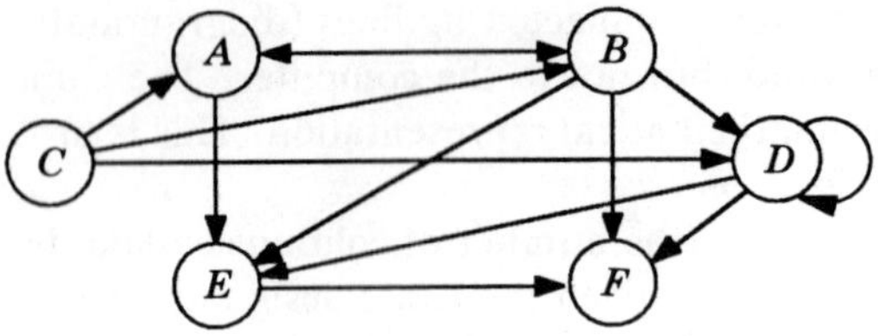

	A	B	C	D	E	F
A	0	1	0	0	1	0
B	1	0	0	1	1	1
C	1	1	0	1	0	0
D	0	0	0	1	1	1
E	0	0	0	0	0	1
F	0	0	0	0	0	0

(b)

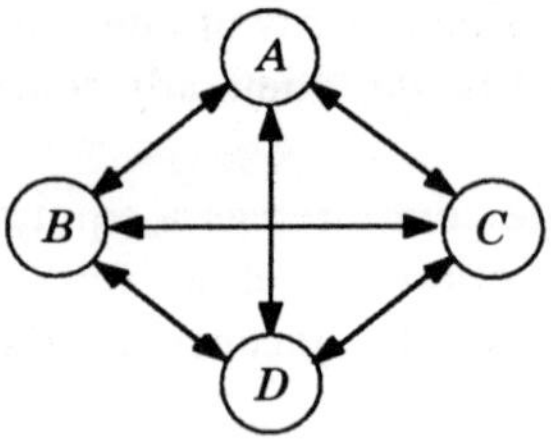

	A	B	C	D
A	0	1	1	1
B	1	0	1	1
C	1	1	0	1
D	1	1	1	0

(c)

Figure 3.6 Digraphs and their adjacency matrices.

	x_0	x_1	x_2	x_3
x_0	0	a	b	0
x_1	0	0	c	f
x_2	0	d	e	g
x_3	0	0	0	0

Figure 3.7 Digraph for Figure 3.4.

each element of **A** to the corresponding element of **B**. This can be expressed analytically by

$$c(i, j) = a(i, j) + b(i, j) \tag{3.2}$$

where $c(i, j)$ is any element of **C** and i and j, the respective row and column indexes, range over the entire matrix. Subtraction can be considered addition with the sign of the second matrix reversed. This is given by

$$c(i, j) = a(i, j) - b(i, j) \tag{3.3}$$

In outer multiplication, each element of **A** is multiplied by the corresponding element of **B**. This is given by

$$c(i, j) = a(i, j) \times b(i, j) \tag{3.4}$$

Since the indexes i and j must match in all operations, addition, subtraction, and outer multiplication require that all involved matrices be of the same order (have the same number of rows and columns). Example 3.1 illustrates these operations.

EXAMPLE 3.1

Given two matrices **A** and **B**, where

$$\mathbf{A} = \begin{matrix} 1 & 0 & 3 & 2 \\ 2 & -2 & 2 & 0 \\ 0 & 1 & 1 & 0 \\ 3 & 1 & 0 & -1 \end{matrix} \qquad \mathbf{B} = \begin{matrix} 2 & 3 & 4 & 0 \\ 0 & 1 & -2 & 3 \\ 4 & 2 & 0 & 1 \\ 1 & 0 & 2 & 0 \end{matrix}$$

find (a) = **C** = **A** + **B**, (b) **C** = **A** − **B**, and (c) **C** = **A** × **B**.

(a)

$$\mathbf{C} = \begin{matrix} 1+2 & 0+3 & 3+4 & 2+0 \\ 2+0 & -2+1 & 2-2 & 0+3 \\ 0+4 & 1+2 & 1+0 & 0+1 \\ 3+1 & 1+0 & 0+2 & -1+0 \end{matrix} = \begin{matrix} 3 & 3 & 7 & 2 \\ 2 & -1 & 0 & 3 \\ 4 & 3 & 1 & 1 \\ 4 & 1 & 2 & -1 \end{matrix}$$

(b) Subtracting $b(i, j)$ from $a(i, j)$ [or adding $a(i, j) + -b(i, j)$] gives

$$\mathbf{C} = \begin{matrix} 1-2 & 0-3 & 3-4 & 2-0 \\ 2-0 & -2-1 & 2+2 & 0-3 \\ 0-4 & 1-2 & 1-0 & 0-1 \\ 3-1 & 1-0 & 0-2 & -1-0 \end{matrix} = \begin{matrix} -1 & -3 & -1 & 2 \\ 2 & -3 & 4 & -3 \\ -4 & -1 & 1 & -1 \\ 2 & 1 & -2 & -1 \end{matrix}$$

(c) Multiplying **A** by **B** (outer multiplication) gives

$$\mathbf{C} = \begin{matrix} 1\times 2 & 0\times 3 & 3\times 4 & 2\times 0 \\ 2\times 0 & -2\times 1 & 2\times -2 & 0\times 3 \\ 0\times 4 & 1\times 2 & 1\times 0 & 0\times 1 \\ 3\times 1 & 1\times 0 & 0\times 2 & -1\times 0 \end{matrix} = \begin{matrix} 2 & 0 & 12 & 0 \\ 0 & -2 & -4 & 0 \\ 0 & 2 & 0 & 0 \\ 3 & 0 & 0 & 0 \end{matrix}$$

All the operations are easily implemented on the computer when needed. However, it is good practice to prepare subprograms for each operation so that they may be called as required. This, in effect, extends the language so that it handles matrix algebra directly. Figure 3.8 does this for BASIC and Pascal.

Inner Multiplication

Inner multiplication is peculiar to matrix algebra and has no analog in ordinary algebra. It is best introduced by an example.

EXAMPLE 3.2

Perform inner multiplication for the matrices **A** and **B**, where

$$\mathbf{A} = \begin{matrix} 2 & 3 & 1 & 0 \\ 3 & 0 & 1 & 2 \\ 0 & 1 & 3 & 1 \end{matrix} \qquad \mathbf{B} = \begin{matrix} 2 & 0 \\ 0 & 1 \\ 4 & 2 \\ 3 & 1 \end{matrix}$$

The first element in row 1 of **C** ($c(1, 1)$) is given by

$$c(1, 1) = a(1, 1)b(1, 1) + a(1, 2)b(2, 1) + a(1, 3)b(3, 1) + a(1, 4)b(4, 1)$$

or

$$c(1, 1) = 2 \times 2 + 3 \times 0 + 1 \times 4 + 0 \times 3 = 8$$

```
2000 REM SUBROUTINE MAT-ADD, MATRIX ADDITION
2010 REM MAT Z = MAT X + MAT Y
2020  FOR I= 1 TO N
2030    FOR J=1 TO N
2040      Z(I,J) = X(I,J) + Y(I,J)
2050  NEXT J,I
2060 RETURN

2100 REM SUBROUTINE MAT-SUB,MATRIX SUBTRACTION
2110 REM MAT Z = MAT X - MAT Y
2120  FOR I= 1 TO N
2130    FOR J=1 TO N
2140      Z(I,J) = X(I,J) -    Y(I,J)
2150  NEXT J,I
2160 RETURN

2200 REM SUBROUTINE MAT-MULT, MATRIX OUTER MULTIPLICATION
2210 REM MAT Z = MAT X * MAT Y
2220   FOR I = 1 TO N
2230    FOR J = 1 TO N
2240      Z(I,J) = X(I,J) * Y(I,J)
2250   NEXT J,I
2260 RETURN
```

(a)

```
PROCEDURE MatAdd;
  BEGIN
   FOR I := 1 TO N DO FOR J := 1 TO N DO Z[I,J] :=X[I,J] + Y[I,J];
 END;

 PROCEDURE MatSub;
  BEGIN
   FOR I := 1 TO N DO FOR J := 1 TO N DO Z[I,J] :=X[I,J] - Y[I,J];
 END;

 PROCEDURE MatMult;
  BEGIN
   FOR I := 1 TO N DO FOR J := 1 TO N DO Z[I,J] :=X[I,J] * Y[I,J];
 END;
```

(b)

Figure 3.8 Matrix operations: (a) BASIC; (b) Pascal.

The second element in row 1 of **C** ($c(1, 2)$) is given by

$$c(1, 2) = a(1, 1)b(1, 2) + a(1, 2)b(2, 2) + a(1, 3)b(3, 2) + a(1, 4)b(4, 2)$$

or

$$c(1, 2) = 2 \times 0 + 3 \times 1 + 1 \times 2 + 0 \times 1 = 5$$

The first element in row 2 of **C** ($c(2, 1)$) is given by

$$c(2, 1) = a(2, 1)b(1, 1) + a(2, 2)b(2, 1) + a(2, 3)b(3, 1) + a(2, 4)b(4, 1)$$

or

$$c(2, 1) = 3 \times 2 + 0 \times 0 + 1 \times 4 + 2 \times 3 = 16$$

The second element in row 2 of **C** ($c(2, 2)$) is given by

$$c(2, 2) = a(2, 1)b(1, 2) + a(2, 2)b(2, 2) + a(2, 3)b(3, 2) + a(2, 4)b(4, 2)$$

or

$$c(2, 2) = 3 \times 0 + 0 \times 1 + 1 \times 2 + 2 \times 1 = 4$$

The pattern should now be apparent. To find $c(1, 1)$, multiply each element in the first row of **A** by each corresponding element in the first column of **B**, and sum the results. To find $c(1, 2)$, multiply each element in the first row of **A** by each corresponding element in the second column of **B**, and sum the results. To find $c(2, 1)$, multiply each element in the second row of **B** by the corresponding elements in the first column of **B**, and sum the results, and so on. The general expression for the process is given by

$$c(i, j) = \sum_{k=1}^{n} a(i, k)b(k, j) \tag{3.4}$$

where k varies from 1 to n and $n =$ the number of columns in **A** or the number of rows in **B**. (The Greek letter sigma (Σ) means that each term generated as k goes from 1 to n is summed as a running total. For the matrices, given $n = 4$, so that $c(1, 1)$ is computed using (3.4) by

$$c(1, 1) = a(1, 1)b(1, 1) + a(1, 2)b(2, 1) + a(1, 3)b(3, 1) + a(1, 4)b(4, 1)$$

as required. Applying this procedure to matrices **A** and **B** gives

$$\mathbf{C} = \begin{matrix} 8 & 5 \\ 16 & 4 \\ 15 & 8 \end{matrix}$$

Some conditions are made evident by Example 3.2. First, multiplication is only possible when the number of columns in the first matrix equals the number of rows in the second. Second, the resultant matrix has the same number of rows as the first matrix and the same number of columns as the second. Third, inner multiplication is not commutative, meaning that **A** $\times$ **B** does not necessarily equal **B** $\times$ **A**. In fact, though **A** $\times$ **B** may be possible, **B** $\times$ **A** may not. However since adjacency matrices are always square, **A** and **B** must be of the same order, **C** will also be of this order, and **A** $\times$ **B** equals **B** $\times$ **A**. Figure 3.9 gives BASIC and Pascal subprograms for inner multiplication.

```
3000 REM SUBROUTINE INMULT, INNER MATRIX MULTIPLICATION
3010 REM MAT Z = MAT X . MAT Y
3020  FOR I = 1 TO N
3030   FOR J = 1 TO N
3040    SUM = 0
3050     FOR K = 1 TO N 'STARTS ROW-COLUMN COMPUTATIONS
3060       SUM  =  SUM + X(I,K) * Y(K,J) 'ADDS PRODUCTS  OF  ROW-COLUMN OPERATIONS
3070     NEXT K
3075    Z(I,J)= SUM 'ASSIGNS SUM TO MATRIX Z
3080  NEXT J,I
3090 RETURN
```

(a)

```
PROCEDURE InMult; {INNER MATRIX MULTIPLICATION}
  BEGIN
    FOR I := 1 TO N DO FOR K := 1 TO N DO
        BEGIN
          Sum := 0;
          {BEGINS ROW-COLUMN COMPUTATIONS AND ADDS RESULTS}
          FOR J := 1 TO N DO Sum := Sum + X[I,J] * X[J,K];
          Z[I,K] := Sum; {PLACES RESULT OF EACH ROW-COLUMN COMPUTATION IN Z}
        END;
  END;
```

(b)

Figure 3.9 Matrix inner multiplication: (a) BASIC; (b) Pascal.

3.3.2 Digraph Algebra

When matrices are restricted to adjacency and weighted adjacency matrices representing digraphs, matrix algebra becomes a digraph algebra. Under these conditions, matrix algebra operations translate into unique and useful digraph operations. In turn, these digraph operations simplify many programming tasks.

The digraph transformations generated by the digraph algebra operations—addition, subtraction, and outer multiplication—are shown in Figures 3.10, 3.11, and 3.12. The figures show two digraphs (**A** and **B**) their adjacency matrix representations and the effect of the various matrix operations on the resultant digraph (**C**).

In Figure 3.10 the two adjacency matrices (**A** and **B**) are added and every resulting nonzero element is set equal to 1. This ensures that the results of adding two adjacency matrices will remain an adjacency matrix (or that the addition of digraphs will always generate another digraph). The new adjacency matrix is transformed into a digraph diagram. This, we see, contains all the links of both digraphs.

An application to transportation systems is evident. Given the task of combining two or more transportation systems, represent each system as an adja-

Digraph 1

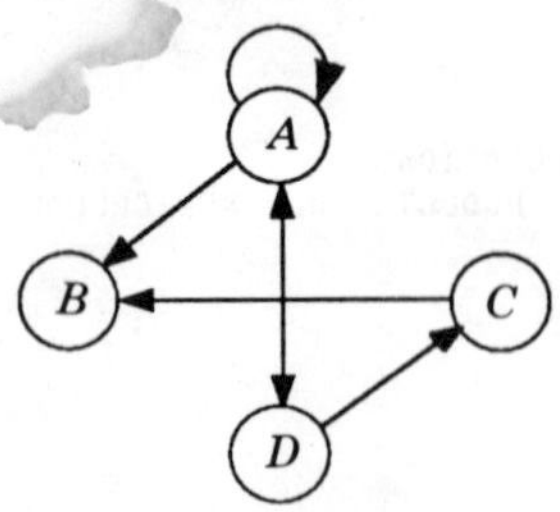

Digraph 2

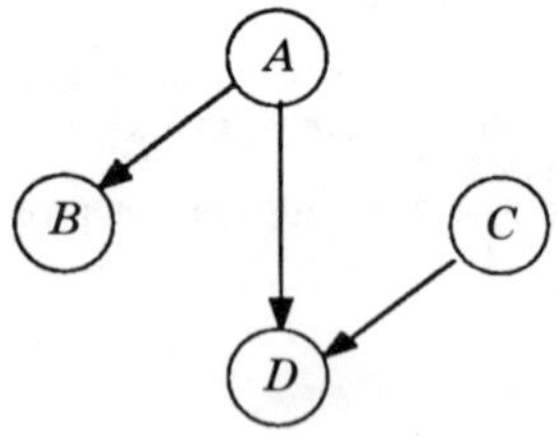

Matrix 1

	A	B	C	D
A	1	1	0	1
B	0	0	0	0
C	0	1	0	0
D	1	0	1	0

Matrix 2

	A	B	C	D
A	0	1	0	1
B	0	0	0	0
C	0	0	0	1
D	0	0	0	0

Matrix 1 + Matrix 2

	A	B	C	D
A	1	1	0	1
B	0	0	0	0
C	0	1	0	1
D	1	0	1	0

Digraph 1 + Digraph 2

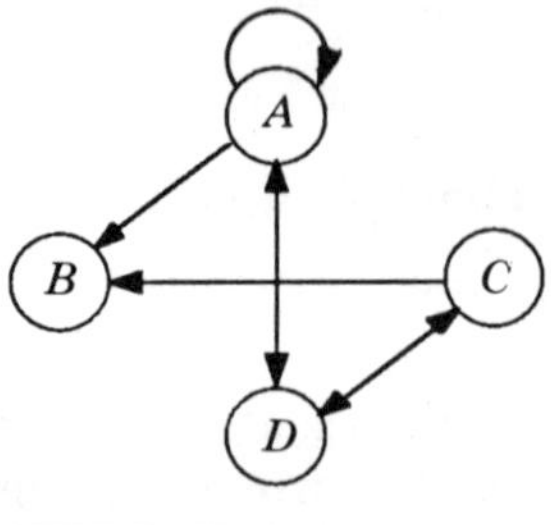

Figure 3.10 Results of adding adjacency matrices.

cency matrix and perform matrix addition as required. Suppose we had to evaluate the increase in connections arising from this combination. Compare the new number of links against the number in each of the original systems. Summing the one's in each matrix gives the number of links.

Figure 3.11 shows the results of subtracting one adjacency matrix from another and transforming all nonzero values to one. We see that matrix subtraction generates a digraph (**C**) in which all links common to **A** and **B** are eliminated.

Subtraction exposes the differences between digraphs. A digraph without links (an adjacency matrix with all elements equal to 0) is generated when **A** and

Digraph 1

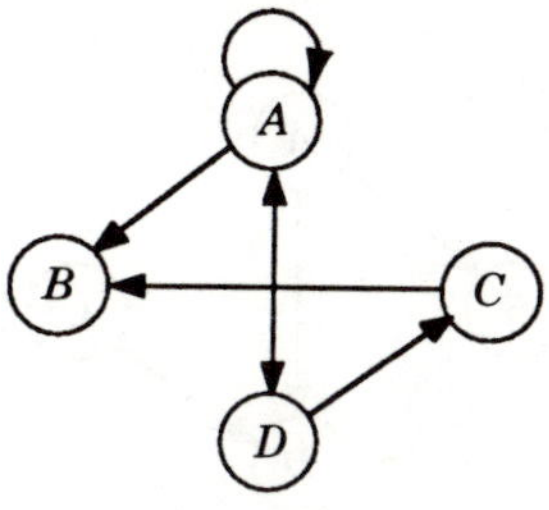

Digraph 2

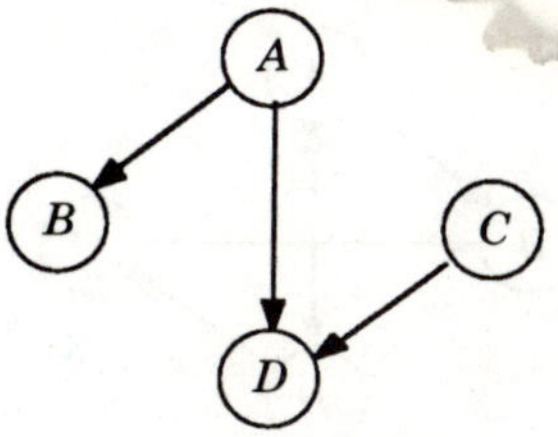

Matrix 1

	A	B	C	D
A	1	1	0	1
B	0	0	0	0
C	0	1	0	0
D	1	0	1	0

Matrix 2

	A	B	C	D
A	0	1	0	1
B	0	0	0	0
C	0	0	0	1
D	0	0	0	0

Matrix 1 − Matrix 2

	A	B	C	D
A	1	0	0	0
B	0	0	0	0
C	0	1	0	1
D	1	0	1	0

Digraph 1 – Digraph 2

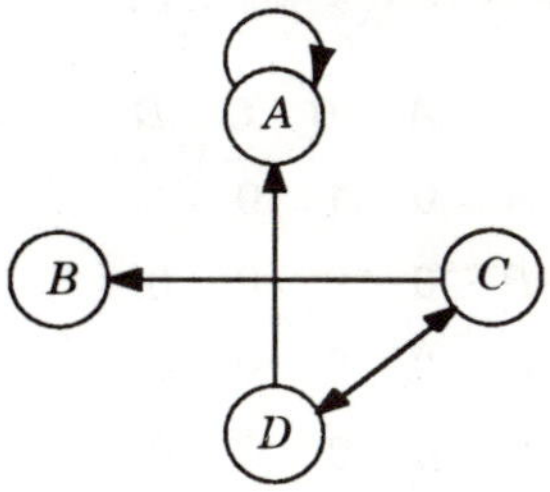

Figure 3.11 Results of subtracting adjacency matrices.

B are identical. Otherwise, **C** contains only links not common to **A** and **B**. Subtraction can be used to determine the difference between two structures.

Figure 3.12 illustrates the results of outer-multiplying two adjacency matrices. After multiplication all nonzero elements in the result are set to 1, so that the matrix is transformed into a digraph. Only links common to **A** and **B** are retained in **C**. Applications include finding similarities in disparate structures, finding similarities in patterns within a structure, and finding patterns within a structure that survive transformations.

Repeated inner multiplication of the adjacency matrix of a digraph by itself has unexpected significance for digraphs. Figure 3.13*b* shows that $\mathbf{A} \cdot \mathbf{A}(\mathbf{A}^2)$

Digraph 1

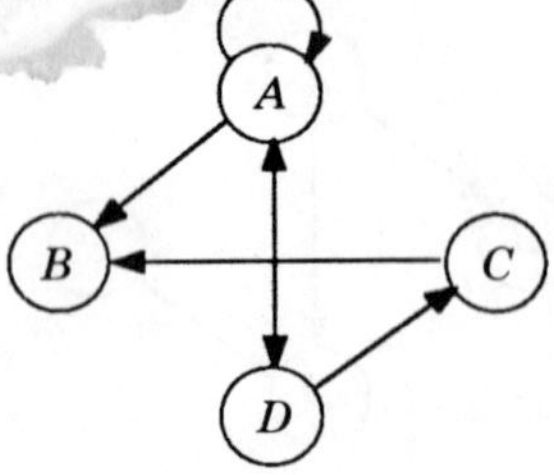

Digraph 2

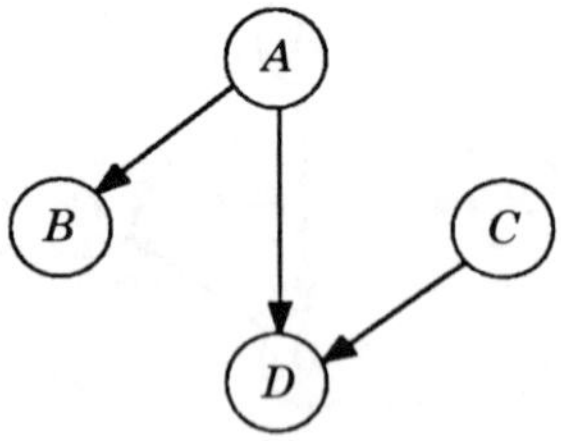

Matrix 1

	A	B	C	D
A	1	1	0	1
B	0	0	0	0
C	0	1	0	0
D	1	0	1	0

Matrix 2

	A	B	C	D
A	0	1	0	1
B	0	0	0	0
C	0	0	0	1
D	0	0	0	0

Matrix 1 × Matrix 2

	A	B	C	D
A	0	1	0	1
B	0	0	0	0
C	0	0	0	0
D	0	0	0	0

Digraph 1 × Digraph 2

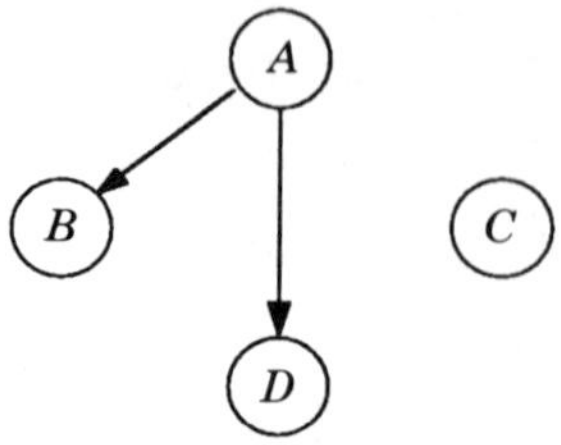

Figure 3.12 Results of outer multiplication on adjacency matrices.

represents a digraph in which each direct link means "there is a path of length 2" between the two nodes. The weight of the link gives the number of such paths. For example, the $\mathbf{A}^2$ digraph reveals that there are two paths of length 2 in $\mathbf{A}$ from node A to node D. The two paths are, first, A to A via the sling then to D and, then, A to B to D. $\mathbf{A}^3(\mathbf{A} \cdot \mathbf{A} \cdot \mathbf{A})$ generates a weighted digraph in which each link gives the number of paths of length 3 between nodes (Figure 3.13*c*). $\mathbf{A}^4$ does the same for paths of length 4 (Figure 3.13*d*).

The *path matrix* is a useful derivative of this process. When an adjacency matrix is raised from $\mathbf{A}$ to $\mathbf{A}^n$, where n is the number of nodes, when all matrices are added together and every nonzero element set to 1, a path matrix is gener-

Figure 3.13 Repeated inner multiplication.

Digraph A

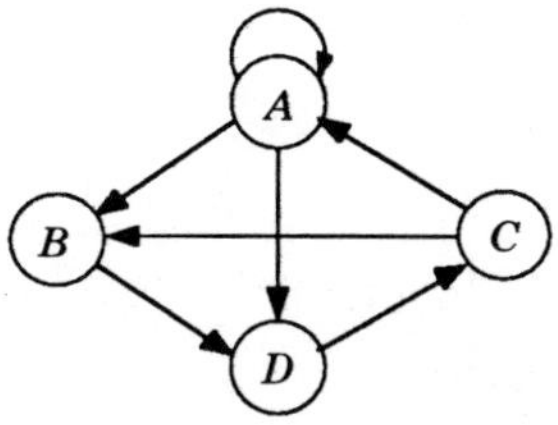

Matrix A

	A	B	C	D
A	1	1	0	1
B	0	0	0	1
C	1	1	0	0
D	0	0	1	0

(a)

Paths of length 2

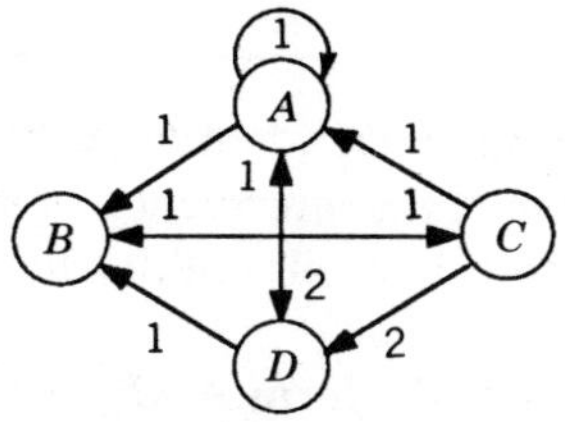

$\mathbf{A} \cdot \mathbf{A} = \mathbf{A}^2$

	A	B	C	D
A	1	1	1	2
B	0	0	1	0
C	1	1	0	2
D	1	1	0	0

(b)

Paths of length 3

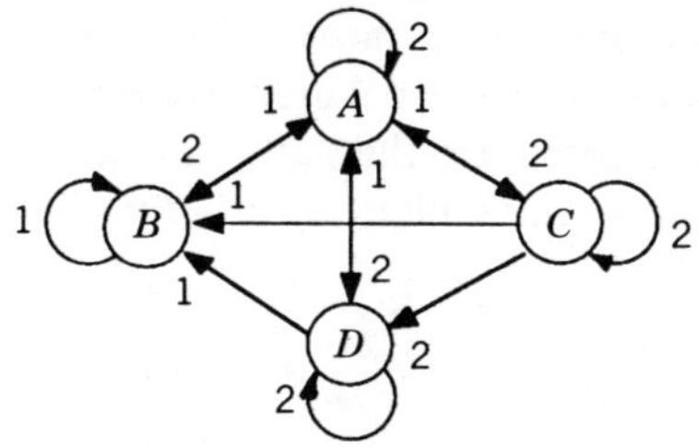

$\mathbf{A} \cdot \mathbf{A} \cdot \mathbf{A} = \mathbf{A}^3$

	A	B	C	D
A	2	2	2	2
B	1	1	0	0
C	1	1	2	2
D	1	1	0	2

(c)

Paths of length 4

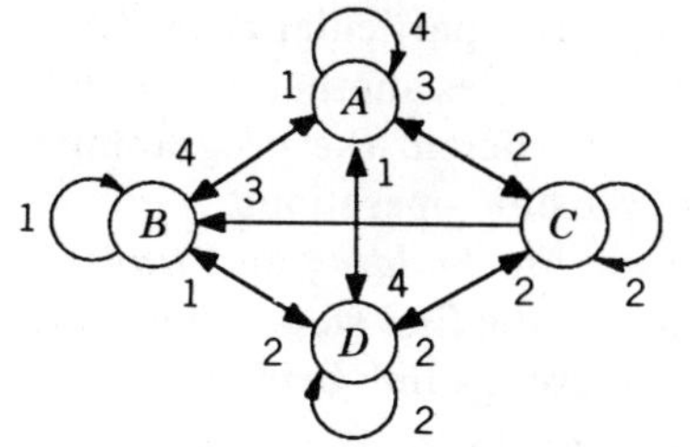

$\mathbf{A} \cdot \mathbf{A} \cdot \mathbf{A} \cdot \mathbf{A} = \mathbf{A}^4$

	A	B	C	D
A	4	4	2	4
B	1	1	0	2
C	3	3	2	2
D	1	1	2	2

(d)

Figure 3.13 *(Continued)*

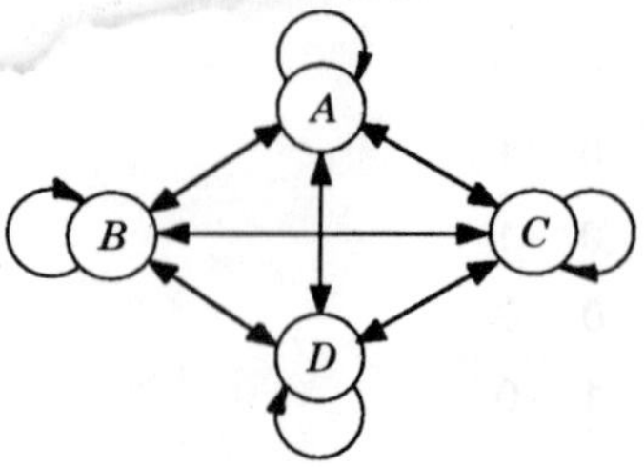

$\mathbf{A} + \mathbf{A}^2 + \mathbf{A}^3 + \mathbf{A}^4$,
if $a(ij) \langle\rangle 0$, $a(i, j) = 1$
for all i, j

	A	B	C	D
A	1	1	1	1
B	1	1	1	1
C	1	1	1	1
D	1	1	1	1

(e)

ated. The path matrix represents a digraph in which the links identify paths of unspecified lengths between nodes. For example, a one at the intersection of row *A*, column *C* means a path exists between nodes *A* and *C* but tells nothing about its path length (Figure 3.13*e*).

Applications abound. Given a large amount of data of the form *A r B*, *A r C*, *F r A*, *F r C*, etc., where *r* represents any given relation or connection. If, for example, the nodes represent telephones, *r* would represent "connect to." The task might be to verify that every phone could be reached from every other one. If the nodes were cities connected by airlines, the task would be to verify connections between all cities. If the nodes were equations and *r* meant "derivable from," the task might be to see if all the equations formed a coherent set (each equation derivable from every other one). For all cases, form the path matrix. If all elements are 1, all nodes are reachable from and can reach every other node.

3.4 OPERATIONS

Each data structure entails a set of fundamental operations. Algorithms associated with a data structure must be created by the action of these operations on the structure. Algorithm creation is simplified because the number and scope of possible operations is reduced, usually to a very few. If a particular data structure does not easily yield an algorithm, the programmer tries another data structure. Contrast this with the unstructured approach wherein the programmer must create an algorithm from a very large set of possible operations.

The most fundamental operations on the digraph are *building* and *traversing*. Building the data structure from data is of course the first step. After that, we do little more than traverse the digraph to see if there is a link between nodes. This fundamental step generates many other operations. For example, questions as to which nodes connect to a given node, which nodes lie in the path between two nodes, whether there is a connection regardless of path length between two nodes, and other similar questions, can be readily answered.

3.4.1 Building the Digraph

Building the digraph on the computer level means establishing the adjacency matrix. This is efficiently accomplished by setting up a two-dimensional square matrix with the number of columns equal to the number of nodes, initializing all elements to 0, and inserting one's where links exist. Figure 3.14 shows how this is done. Note the data list is input in pairs. Each pair means that the first node links to the second.

3.4.2 Traversing

Determining if a link exists between two nodes is extraordinarily simple. A link exists and is directed from node A to B if a one is found at the intersection of row A and column B; a 0 means that no link exists. This procedure, when iterated, determines if there is a continuous path between a sequence of nodes. For a sequence $x_1, x_2, x_3, \ldots, x_n$, test first for a link between x_1 and x_2, then x_2 and x_3, and so on until x_n is reached or a link is not found. If x_n is reached, the sequence is connected; otherwise, it is not. Figure 3.15 give general subprograms for any n.

```
1000 REM BASIC SUBPROGRAM, BUILDS ADJACENCY MATRIX
1010 REM DATA INPUT AS A NUMERICAL VECTOR (DAT(I) ENDING WITH -1
1020 REM ZERO ADMAT
1030  FOR I=1 TO N:FOR K=1 TO N:ADMAT(I,K)=0:NEXT K,I
1040    REM PLACE 1'S IN APPROPRIATE ELEMENTS
1050      FOR I = 1 TO N STEP 2
1060        IF DAT(I+1)=-1 THEN RETURN ELSE ADMAT(DAT(I),DAT(I+1))=1
1070      NEXT
1080 RETURN
```

(a)

```
PROCEDURE Badmat; {BUILDS ADJACENCY MATRIX}
BEGIN
  {FILL ADMAT WITH ZEROES}
  FOR I:=1 TO N DO FOR J:=1 TO N DO Admat[I,J]:=0;
     I:=1;
     WHILE Dat[I] > 0 DO BEGIN Admat[DAT[I],DAT[I+1]]:=1;
     I:=I+2;END; {PLACES 1'S IN APPROPRIATE  ELEMENTS}
END;
```

(b)

Figure 3.14 Programs for building adjacency matrices: (a) BASIC; (b) Pascal.

```
1100 REM SUBPROGRAM A-PATH-B, TESTS FOR LINK BETWEEN A AND B
1110 REM INPUT IS ADMAT(I,K), NODE X AND NODE Y
1120 REM OUTPUTS 1 IF LINKS EXISTS ELSE 0
1130    REM CHECKS PATH
1140       IF ADMAT(X,Y)=1 THEN R=1 ELSE R = 0
1150 RETURN
```

(a)

```
FUNCTION ApathB(X,Y:INTEGER):INTEGER; {TESTS FOR LINKS
   BETWEEN A AND B}
   BEGIN {SEARCHES FOR 1'S IN ADJACENCY MATRIX}
     IF Admat[X,Y] = 1 THEN ApathB:=1 ELSE ApathB := 0;
   END;
```

(b)

Figure 3.15 Traversing between nodes: (a) BASIC; (b) Pascal.

3.4.3 Path Matrix

Determining if a path of any length exists between two nodes is a useful digraph function. This is accomplished by finding the path matrix and checking for a direct link between nodes by looking for a one or zero at the row-column intersection. The path matrix can be set up using repeated self-multiplication and addition, but a faster algorithm is available. This algorithm, the Roy Warshall algorithm, establishes the path matrix by tracing paths from each node to every other node. Figure 3.16 displays this algorithm in BASIC and Pascal.

3.4.4 Other Operations

The other operations mentioned previously are easily implemented. To display all nodes that a given node connects to, read out the entire row identified by the node. To find all nodes that connect to a given node, display the entire column identified by the node. To perform these operations for paths of length n, multiply (inner multiplication) the adjacency matrix by itself n times and repeat the preceding procedures. A sequence of nodes can be tested for compatibility with a given structure by checking for one's between successive members of the sequence.

```
1200 REM PATH-MAT, USES ROY WARSHALL ALGORITHM,GIVES PATH MATRIX
1210 REM  INPUT ADMAT, OUTPUT PATHMAT
1220   REM SET UP AUXILLIARY MATRIX
1230    FOR I= 1 TO N
1240     FOR K=1 TO N
1250     PATHMAT(I,K)=ADMAT(I,K)
1260     NEXT K
1270    NEXT I
1280   REM CHECK PATHS THROUGH ADMAT
1290   FOR J= 1 TO N
1300    FOR I=1 TO N
1320    IF PATHMAT(I,J)=1 THEN FOR K=1 TO N:
        PATHMAT(I,K)=PATHMAT(I,K) OR PATHMAT(J,K):NEXT K
1330 NEXT I
1335 NEXT J
1340 RETURN
```

(a)

```
PROCEDURE Path;{finds path matrix}
  BEGIN
    FOR I := 1 TO N DO FOR K:=1 TO N DO Pathmat[I,K]:=Admat[I,K];
    {SETS UP NEW MATRIX}
    FOR J:= 1 TO N DO FOR I:= 1 TO N DO
      BEGIN
       IF Pathmat[I,J] = 1 THEN FOR K:=1 TO N DO Pathmat[I,K] :=
                                    Pathmat[I,K] OR Pathmat[J,K];
      END;
  END;
```

(b)

Figure 3.16 Path matrix: (a) BASIC; (b) Pascal.

3.5 SPECIFIC APPLICATIONS

3.5.1 Number Filter

An automated telephone exchange can work efficiently only if unrecognizable numbers are prevented from entering the system. The numbers contain seven digits and are coded by restricting the numbers that can follow any given number. For example, two can only be followed by three, five, or seven, five can only be followed by one, four, two, or five, and so on. The task is to compose a program that will block unauthorized numbers from the system.

At first, a program consisting of conditions might be thought to serve—for example, "IF NUMBERIN = NUMBEROUT(I) THEN GET NUMBERIN," where NUMBERIN is the received number and NUMBEROUT(I) varies over the entire authorized number list. The size of the authorized number list makes this impracticable. A seven-digit number can generate ten million numbers with a maximum of 24 bits per number. Suppose the authorized list contained about half of these numbers. Obviously, this is too much for the core memory of most machines, would require a hard disk, and would be much too slow anyway.

The *structure* of the data must first be examined. It is of the form $2\,r\,3$, $2\,r\,5$, $2\,r\,7$, or $2\,r\,\{3, 5, 7\}$, where r means "can be followed by." This is a *connection* structure and therefore suggests the digraph as the appropriate data structure. The digraph structure is indeed appropriate here, for it immediately suggests an efficient algorithm:

> Set up a digraph with nodes 0 to 9. Transfer the data to this digraph by linking each node to the nodes that can follow it. Given a seven-digit number, see if a link exists between the first and second number using the digraph. If not, reject the number (or note error). If so, continue this test for the second and third, third and fourth, etc. If the seventh digit is reached without error, the number is passed onto the telephone system.

This is a straightforward, concise, and efficient algorithm. It requires core storage of only *one hundred* one or zero elements of an array. It promises to be fast since there is a maximum of six comparisons per seven-digit number. This is the kind of algorithm that we expect to arise from a well-chosen data structure.

This justification of the chosen data structure, together with the informal statement of the algorithm, constitutes the top level of our top-down program planning procedure. At the next level we implement the digraph as an adjacency matrix and modularize (segment) the program on the basis of the required digraph operations.

Figure 3.17 shows a sample succession digraph and its adjacency matrix representation. The required operations are:

1. Build adjacency matrix from succession data.
2. Compare n and $n + 1$ digits of the number under test (n varies from 1 to 6).
3. If n reaches 6 without error, pass number, or else reject.

Where appropriate, each operation can now be composed as a subprogram (or delegated to a programmer). The subprograms will then be called by the main program. Figure 3.18 shows the BASIC program and Figure 3.19, the Pascal equivalent.

Both programs demonstrate the advantages of structured programming and modularization. They are both strongly segmented. The subprograms in the BASIC version have been merged out of a disk library. Only lines 10, 20, 30, and the main program have been written. The version of Pascal used here makes matters even simpler. The {$I B:BUADMAT.PAS) and {$I B:APATHB.PAS} copy these subprograms from disk into core memory as needed. Only declarations and the main program need to be composed.

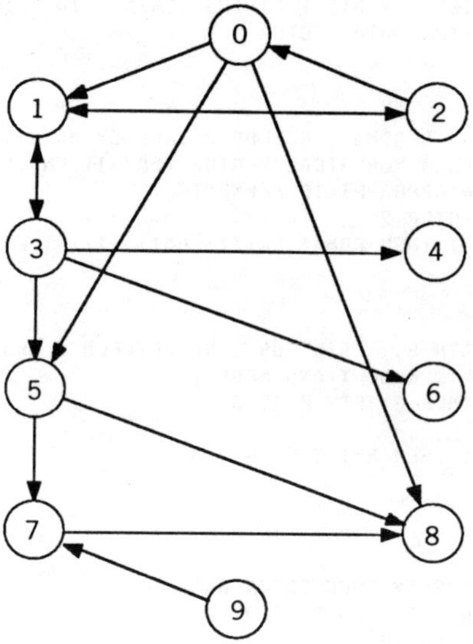

	0	1	2	3	4	5	6	7	8	9
0	0	1	0	0	0	1	0	0	1	0
1	0	0	1	1	0	0	0	0	0	0
2	1	1	0	0	0	0	0	0	0	0
3	0	1	0	0	1	1	1	0	0	0
4	0	0	0	0	0	0	0	0	0	0
5	0	0	0	0	0	0	0	1	1	0
6	0	0	0	0	0	0	0	0	0	0
7	0	0	0	0	0	0	0	0	1	0
8	0	0	0	0	0	0	0	0	0	0
9	0	0	0	0	0	0	0	1	0	0

Figure 3.17 Sample succession matrix.

Figure 3.20 displays a sample result. The succession matrix shows the acceptable digit pairs. (The rows and column both range from 0 to 9.) The results of testing a seven-digit number are also shown. In operation, the first "NG" encountered in the test would block the number and the test cycle would end.

The Number Filter program has wide general application. If the elements within the succession matrix represent algebraic symbols, the program can

```
10 REM  NUMBER FILTER, TESTS 7 DIGIT STRING AGAINST 10 X 10 DIGRAPH
20 DIM DAT(100) 'SUCCESSION DATA VECTOR
30 GOTO 1900

900 REM  SUBROUTINES
1000 REM BASIC SUBPROGRAM B-ADMAT, BUILDS ADJACENCY MATRIX
1010 REM DATA IS INPUT AS A NUMERICAL VECTOR (DAT(I) ENDING WITH -1
1020    REM PLACE 1'S IN APPROPRIATE ELEMENTS
1030    FOR I = 0 TO 99 STEP 2
1040       IF DAT(I)<> -1 THEN ADMAT(DAT(I),DAT(I+1))=1 ELSE RETURN
1050      NEXT
1060 RETURN

1100 REM SUBPROGRAM A-PATH-B, TESTS FOR LINK BETWEEN A AND B
1110 REM INPUT ADMAT(I,K), NODE X AND NODE Y
1120 REM OUTPUTS 1 IF LINKS EXISTS ELSE 0
1130   REM CHECKS PATH
1140     IF ADMAT(X,Y)=1 THEN R=1 ELSE R = 0
1150 RETURN

1900   REM  MAIN PROGRAM
2000  I=0
2010   READ DAT(I) ' READS IN SUCCESSION DATA
2020   IF DAT(I)>=0 THEN I=I+1:GOTO 2010
2030    DATA 1,1,1,0,1,0,1,0,0,1
2040    DATA 0,1,0,0,0,2,0,4,0,6,0,9
2050    DATA 1,1,1,3,1,4,1,5,1,7,1,8
2060    DATA 3,1,3,2,3,4,3,8,3,9
2070    DATA 4,0,4,2,4,5,4,8
2080    DATA 5,1,5,2,5,4,5,7,5,8
2090    DATA 6,0,6,1,6,2,6,5
2100    DATA 7,1,7,2,7,3,7,5,7,6,7,8
2110    DATA 8,3,8,5,9,1,9,4,9,8,9,9,-1
2120  N = 9 ' ADMAT GOES FROM 0..9,0..9
2130   GOSUB 1000 'CALLS B-ADMAT TO BUILD ADJACENCY MATRIX
2140    PRINT "SUCCESSION MATRIX":PRINT:PRINT
2150    FOR I=0 TO N:FOR K=0 TO N 'DISPLAYS SUCCESSION MATRIX
2160      PRINT ADMAT(I,K);
2170      NEXT K:PRINT:NEXT I
2180  INPUT "ENTER NO. AS STRING";N$ 'ACCEPTS TEST NO.
2190   FOR I=1 TO 7: T(I)=VAL(MID$(N$,I,1)):NEXT 'CONVERTS STRING TO NUMBER
2200   FOR PP=1 TO 6  'PREPARES VARIABLES FOR SUBROUTINE CALL
2210      X=T(PP): Y=T(PP+1)
2220      GOSUB 1100  'CALL A-PATH-B
2230      IF R=0 THEN PRINT T(PP);T(PP+1);" NG" 'DISPLAYS ERRORS
2240   NEXT 'END OF MAIN PROGRAM
```

Figure 3.18 Number filter in BASIC.

check literal equations. If the elements of the succession matrix are the *words* of a computer language, the program becomes a syntax checker. There is only a logistical limit on the number of elements tested. Indeed, the succession matrix can represent any structure of connections or relations, physical or abstract where the relation between two elements depends only on the two elements concerned. The generalized program can then determine if a test sequence of any size conforms to the parent structure.

```
PROGRAM NUMBERFILT(INPUT,OUTPUT);
TYPE
  DTA =  RECORD BIT: INTEGER;END;

  VAR I,J,K,N:INTEGER;
      Admat :ARRAY[0..9,0..9] OF INTEGER;
      DD:DTA;NN:ARRAY[1..7] OF INTEGER;
      Dat:ARRAY[0..100] OF INTEGER;
      DTT:FILE OF DTA;

      {$I B:BUADMAT.PAS}    {LINKS PROCEDURES ON DISKS}
      {$I B:APATHB.PAS}

  {MAIN PROGRAM}
     BEGIN
      ASSIGN(DTT,'B:DITE');   {ACCESSES FILES}
      RESET(DTT); J:=1; DD.BIT:=0;

      {FILLS DAT ARRAY FROM FILE DITE}
      WHILE DD.BIT<>-1 DO
      BEGIN READ(DTT,DD);DAT[J]:=DD.BIT;J:=J+1;END;
      FOR K:=1 TO 10 DO WRITE(DAT[K]);WRITELN;WRITELN;

      {BUILDS ADMAT}
      BADMAT;FOR I:=0 TO 9 DO BEGIN FOR K:=0 TO 9
      DO WRITE(Admat[I,K]);WRITELN;END; {DISPLAYS ADMAT}

      {PERFORMS TEST ON TEST NUMBER}
      WRITELN('ENTER TEST NO.');
      FOR K:=1 TO 7 DO READ(NN[K]);WRITELN;   {RECEIVES TEST NO.}
      {TESTS FOR LINKS}
      FOR I:=1 TO 6 DO BEGIN IF  APATHB(NN[I],NN[I+1])<>1
      THEN WRITELN(NN[I],' ',NN[I+1],' NG');END;{DISPLAYS RESULTS}
    END.
```

Figure 3.19 Number filter in Pascal.

3.5.2 Linkage Evaluation

A large, complex transportation system is considering a merger with one of several other large systems. It seeks to determine which other system will give it the largest increment in connections between destination points. These new linkages need not be direct but could include stops along the route. The new linkages must also be enumerated. The requirement is to automate this task.

The structure of the data of the task involves connections and is similar to the Number Filter input. Therefore, the digraph data structure is appropriate here. As noted, digraph operations include traversing, *pathing* (forming the path matrix), and the matrix operations of addition, subtraction, and outer and inner multiplication. All these operations suggest the following algorithm:

> From the raw data, form the adjacency matrix of the parent firm and the candidate. From this, form the path matrices. Subtract the path matrix of the parent firm from the candidate's. The positions of the remaining one's enumerate the new paths.

SUCCESSION MATRIX

1	1	1	0	1	0	1	0	0	1
1	1	0	1	1	1	0	1	1	0
0	0	0	0	0	0	0	0	0	0
0	1	1	0	1	0	0	0	1	1
1	0	1	0	0	1	0	0	1	0
0	1	1	0	1	0	0	1	1	0
1	1	1	0	0	1	0	0	0	0
0	1	1	1	0	1	1	0	1	0
0	0	0	1	0	1	0	0	0	0
0	1	0	0	1	0	0	0	1	1

TEST NUMBER IS 1324250

2	4	NG
2	5	NG
5	0	NG

Figure 3.20 Output of number filter.

```
3000 REM SUBROUTINE ENUM1S 'ENUMERATES LINKS
3010  FOR I= 0 TO 9
3020    A(I)=I 'ASSIGNS VALUES TO EACH NODE
3030  NEXT
3040 FOR I=0 TO N-1 'SEARCHES FOR 1'S AND DISPLAYS POSITION
3050  FOR K=0 TO N-1
3060    IF Z(I,K)=1 THEN PRINT Z(I,K)" AT ROW "A(I)" COLUMN "A(K)
3070  NEXT K,I
3080  RETURN
```

(a)

```
PROCEDURE ENUM1S; {ENUMERATES LINKS}
  BEGIN
    FOR I:=0 TO 9 DO A[I]:=I; {NAMES NODES}
    {SEARCHES FOR 1'S AND GIVES LOCATIONS}
    FOR I:=0 TO N-1 DO FOR K:=0 TO N-1 DO IF Xmat[I,K]=1 THEN
      WRITELN(Xmat[I,K],' AT ROW ',A[I],' AND COLUMN ',A[k]);
  END;
```

(b)

Figure 3.21 Subprograms to enumerate links: (a) BASIC; (b) Pascal.

The algorithm is required to (1) build adjacency matrices, (2) transform the adjacency matrices to path matrices, (3) subtract one matrix from the other, and (4) display the positions of the one's. We already have functions 1, 2, and 3. Function 4 is shown in Figure 3.21. The complete program is displayed in Figures 3.22 (BASIC) and 3.23 (Pascal).

Although both programs make use of previously composed and tested subprograms, some small changes were made in the subprograms for the sake of efficiency. XMAT was changed to PATHMAT in the subtraction and ENUM1S BASIC subprograms. In the subtracting program, X, Y, and Z were replaced by the variables PATHMAT, PATHMAT1, and PATHMAT, respectively. Other-

Figure 3.22 Link evaluation program (BASIC).

```
10 REM PROGRAM EVALUATES LINKS FOR COMBINED MATRICES
20 DIM DAT(900),A(20),ADMAT(30,30),PATHMAT(30,30),PATHMAT1(30,30)
30 GOTO 470
40 REM SUBPROGRAMS
50 REM PATH-MAT, USES ROY WARSHALL ALGORITHM,GIVES PATH MATRIX
60 REM  INPUT ADMAT, OUTPUT PATHMAT
70   REM SET UP AUXILLIARY MATRIX
80    FOR I= 1 TO N
90     FOR K=1 TO N
100      PATHMAT(I,K)=ADMAT(I,K)
110     NEXT K
120    NEXT I
130    REM CHECK PATHS THROUGH ADMAT
140    FOR J= 1 TO N
150     FOR I=1 TO N
160      IF PATHMAT(I,J)=1 THEN FOR K=1 TO N:PATHMAT(I,K)=PATHMAT(I,K) OR PATHMAT(J,K):
         NEXT K
170 NEXT I,J
180 RETURN
190 FOR I = 1 TO N
200    FOR K = 1 TO N
210  SUM = SUM + XMAT(I,K)
220 NEXT K,I
230 RETURN
240 REM BASIC SUBPROGRAM, BUILDS ADJACENCY MATRIX
250 REM DATA INPUT AS A NUMERICAL VECTOR (DAT(I) ENDING WITH -1
260    REM PLACE 1'S IN APPROPRIATE ELEMENTS
265   FOR I=1 TO N :FOR K=1 TO N :ADMAT(I,K)=0:NEXT K,I
270      FOR I = 1 TO NN STEP 2
280      IF DAT(I)<>-1 THEN ADMAT(DAT(I),DAT(I+1))=1 ELSE RETURN
290      NEXT
300 RETURN
310 REM SUBROUTINE SUBTRACTS PATHMATS
320  FOR I=1 TO N
330    FOR J=1 TO N
340    PATHMAT(I,J)=PATHMAT(I,J)-PATHMAT1(I,J)
350  NEXT J,I
360 RETURN
370 REM SUBROUTINE ENUM1S
380 FOR I=1 TO N
390   A(I)=I
400  NEXT
410 FOR I=1 TO N
420  FOR K=1 TO N
430    IF PATHMAT(I,K)=1 THEN  PRINT PATHMAT(I,K)" AT ROW "A(I)" COLUMN "A(K)
440  NEXT K,I
450  RETURN
```

Figure 3.22 *(Continued)*

```
460 REM MAIN PROGRAM
470 A=0:N=10:NN=100
480 REM FORM PATHMAT1
490 A=A+1: READ DAT(A):IF DAT(A)<>-1 THEN GOTO 490
500 GOSUB 240:GOSUB 50 'FORMS ADMAT THEN PATHMAT
510 REM PLACES PATHMAT IN PATHMAT1
520 FOR I=1 TO N:FOR K = 1 TO N:PATHMAT1(I,K)=PATHMAT(I,K):NEXT K,I
530 REM FORM PATHMAT2
540 A=0
550 A=A+1:READ DAT(A):IF DAT(A)<>-1 THEN GOTO 550
560 GOSUB 240:GOSUB 50
570 REM LET PATHMAT BE CANDIDATE MATRIX
580 REM DATA SECTION
590 DATA 1,2,1,4,2,3,2,5,3,1,3,7,5,6,5,9,7,1,7,8,10,1,10,9,-1
600 DATA 1,2,1,4,1,5,2,3,2,6,3,1,3,7,5,6,5,8,5,5,7,1,7,6,10,1,-1
610 REM DISPLAYS PATHMATS
620 FOR I=1 TO N:FOR K=1 TO N:PRINT PATHMAT1(I,K);:NEXT:PRINT:NEXT
640 PRINT:PRINT:PRINT
650 FOR I=1 TO N: FOR K=1 TO N:PRINT PATHMAT(I,K);:NEXT:PRINT:NEXT I
660 FOR I=1 TO 5:PRINT:NEXT
680 REM SUBTRACTS PARENT PATH MATRIX FROM CANDIDATE
700 GOSUB 310:GOSUB 370
710 END
```

wise, subprograms were called from the library (disk). The superiority of Pascal over BASIC for structured programming is revealed by the shorter length of the Pascal program. This is due to the efficient way procedures can be linked to main programs in Pascal.

Figure 3.24 displays the printout. The parent and candidate path matrices are shown followed by an enumeration of the differences. This lists the additional paths provided by a merger of the parent and candidate systems.

The link evaluation procedure can be generalized. The analysis can be deepened by comparing parent and candidate matrices n-times removed ($n = 1, 2, \ldots$). A summation of the increments can be made by counting one's at each stage. Link evaluation is basically structure comparison. These structures may be either concrete or abstract. Concrete examples include comparison of the interconnection of elements in physical systems (tables of organization, salespersons routes, mazes, machine assemblies, mapping, and etc.). Abstract examples may involve comparisons of syntactical, semantic, or other linguistic relations. Comparison of mathematical, logical, and other analytic relations is another important application area.

3.6 SUMMARY AND DISCUSSION

We have discussed the applications of the digraph data structure to programming. Tasks involving connection or relations have been simplified by organizing the data into digraphs. The subsequent ease with which the algorithm is established, and the resulting simplification of the program, have been remarkable. This demonstrates again how crucial the role of data structure is in programming.

```
PROGRAM EVALLINKS(INPUT,OUTPUT);
TYPE
DTA= RECORD BIT:INTEGER;END;
MAT = ARRAY[1..10,1..10] OF INTEGER;
VAR PATHMAT1,Admat,Pathmat:MAT;
Dat:array[1..100] of INTEGER;A:ARRAY[1..10] OF INTEGER;
I,J,K,N,NN:INTEGER; DTT:FILE OF DTA;DD:DTA;
{LINK SUBPROGRAMS}
{$I B:BUADMAT.PAS}{LINKS BUILD-ADMAT}
{$I B:FIG3-16B.PAS}{LINKS PATHMAT}
{$I B:FIG3-20B.PAS} {LINKS ENUM1S}
{$I B:MATSUB.PAS} {LINKS MATSUB}

BEGIN {MAIN PROGRAM}
N:=10;NN:=100; {SETS LIMITS}
{INPUT DATA FOR PARENT MATRIX}
ASSIGN(DTT,'B:DITE'); {OPENS FILE OF RAW DATA}
RESET(DTT);
J:=1;DD.BIT:=0;
WHILE DD.BIT<>-1 DO
BEGIN
READ(DTT,DD);DAT[J]:=DD.BIT;J:=J+1;
END;

{BUILDS  AND DISPLAYS PARENT PATHMAT}
BADMAT; PATH;WRITELN(' PARENT');WRITELN;WRITELN;
FOR I:=1 TO N DO BEGIN FOR K:=1 TO N DO WRITE(PATHMAT[I,K],'   ');
WRITELN;END;WRITELN;
{PLACE PATHMAT INTO PATHMAT1, PARENT MATRIX}
FOR I:=1 TO N DO FOR K:=1 TO N DO PATHMAT1[I,K]:=PATHMAT[I,K];
J:=1;DD.BIT:=0;
WHILE DD.BIT<>-1 DO
BEGIN
READ(DTT,DD);DAT[J]:=DD.BIT;J:=J+1;
END;

{BUILDS  AND DISPLAYS CANDIDATE PATHMAT}
BADMAT; PATH;WRITELN(' CANDIDATE');WRITELN;WRITELN;
FOR I:=1 TO N DO BEGIN FOR K:=1 TO N DO WRITE(PATHMAT[I,K],'   ');
WRITELN;END;{PATHMAT IS NOW CANDIDATE MAT

{SUBTRACT PARENT FROM CANDIDATE AND OUTPUT RESULTS}
FOR I:=1 TO 5 DO WRITELN;
MATSUB;ENUM1S;

END.
```

Figure 3.23 Link evaluation program (Pascal).

We have provided a mere glimpse. Digraph applications can be very sophisticated. For example, succession restrictions can be established for elements n-times removed or for combinations of n-times. These combinations can support some very complex coding. The highly developed applications of signal flow graphs can be accessed by digraph representation. Weighted digraphs open a wide range of further application, including solutions of symbolic equations, syntax analysis, word generation, and more. Many of these applications appear to be abstract and of interest only to theoreticians. However, the alert program-

```
                     PARENT

1    1    1    0    1    1    1    1    1    0
1    1    1    0    1    1    1    1    1    0
1    1    1    0    1    1    1    1    1    0
0    0    0    0    0    0    0    0    0    0
0    0    0    0    0    1    0    0    1    0
0    0    0    0    0    0    0    0    0    0
1    1    1    0    1    1    1    1    1    0
0    0    0    0    0    0    0    0    0    0
0    0    0    0    0    0    0    0    0    0
0    0    0    0    0    0    0    0    1    0

                    CANDIDATE

1    1    1    1    1    1    1    1    0    0
1    1    1    1    1    1    1    1    0    0
1    1    1    1    1    1    1    1    0    0
0    0    0    0    0    0    0    0    0    0
0    0    0    0    1    1    0    1    0    0
0    0    0    0    0    0    0    0    0    0
1    1    1    1    1    1    1    1    0    0
0    0    0    0    0    0    0    0    0    0
0    0    0    0    0    0    0    0    0    0
1    1    1    1    1    1    1    1    0    0

      1  AT  ROW  1  AND  COLUMN  4
      1  AT  ROW  2  AND  COLUMN  4
      1  AT  ROW  3  AND  COLUMN  4
      1  AT  ROW  5  AND  COLUMN  5
      1  AT  ROW  5  AND  COLUMN  8
      1  AT  ROW  7  AND  COLUMN  4
```

Figure 3.24 Output of link evaluation program.

mer will find that almost all of these theoretical studies have important, practical use in the prosaic world.

PROGRAMMING PROJECTS

3.1 Compose a program to pass all acceptable permutations of a given literal equation. Errors should be indicated.

3.2 A large number of transportation links between parties is to be installed in a nationwide business. Although it is not possible to provide direct links between each branch, it is necessary that all branches be connected, if only indirectly. Compose a program to test proposed linkage plans.

3.3 An railroad information program is required to answer the following questions:

(a) Is there a direct connection (not passing through any other station) between any two points?
(b) Can I go from point X to point Y, passing through a designated sequence of intermediate stops?
(c) What stations lie within n stops? (n is any number.)
(d) What are the least number of stops that I must pass through to go from point X to point Y?

3.4 Modify the Number Filter so that it can handle a succession matrix too large for core memory.

3.5 Modify the Link Evaluation program to determine the increment in n-times removed connections, where n is any appropriate number. For example, find the increase in connections of path length 2, 3, 4, 5, etc.

4 Linked Lists

4.1 CONCEPTS

Suppose you are a busy executive or a homemaker. Each morning brings a load of chores you must personally attend to. To organize your efforts, you first make a list of what must be done so that you may carry out each task in order. Unfortunately, your work day is filled with interruptions and new tasks suddenly arise, so the list must be continually altered. Some tasks must be postponed, interchanged with others, moved to different positions, and new tasks must be entered. The neat list composed in the morning is now an illegible mess. Lines are crossed out, new entries scrawled in, and arrows indicating changes in priorities crisscross the paper. Obviously, a static list of tasks is not the appropriate data structure for organizing your day's work.

What you need is a dynamic list. A list that will facilitate moving existing items, deleting unwanted items, and inserting new items. You need a list composed of readily movable items as contrasted to a list of fixed items.

The linked list is just such a dynamic sequence of items. Think of it as a chain of flat plates, each plate having a hole at top and a projecting hook at the bottom. The chain is formed by hanging each plate on the hook of its predecessor. Each plate constitutes an item. To delete an item, we simply unhook it from the item it is hooked to and from the item hooked to it. Then, we hook the lower chain to the upper plate, and the deletion is completed. To add a new item after a specified existing item, we unhook the chain below the specified item, hook the new item to the specified item, and hook the rest of the chain to the new item. To move an item to a new position, we just delete it and insert it at the new position.

The linked list has some useful characteristics. Its length depends solely on the number of items contained in it. It grows and shrinks as items are added and deleted. Items can be added, deleted, or transposed—either singly or in groups—with remarkable ease. Entire sections can be removed by a single unhooking. Unlike the digraph, it usually has a beginning and an end and can be joined to other linked lists by a single hooking.

In the real world our chain of plates is best kept hooked together. However, this is not a necessity. If the first plate contains the address of (points to) the second plate, the second plate could be kept anywhere. The whole chain could be poked into little nooks and crannies around our home or office so that every bit of space could be efficiently used. Although this disjoint storage may not be useful in your office or home, it is very useful within the core memory of a computer. The computer can access any area of its core memory with equal speed. Therefore, disjoint storage has no effect upon access time. However, the ability to use isolated memory areas is a plus and results in significant gains in storage space.

Linked lists can be represented as linked nodes. The linked node representation resembles the digraph except that a starting *(head)* node and an ending *(terminal)* node are required. Figure 4.1 shows the linked node representation of a singly-linked and doubly-linked list. The directed links indicate permissible movement through the list. Only one-way, left-to-right movement is permitted in the singly-linked list. Its nodes can only be accessed by starting at the head node and progressing to the terminal node. The doubly-linked list, however, permits two-way movement. The letter or number within each node is its address, or *key*.

Linked lists can also be represented as disparate *records*. Figure 4.2 shows the singly- and doubly-linked lists represented in this way. A typical record contains a name field (key), some content fields, and *pointers* to nodes it connects to. A record in the singly-linked list contains a single pointer field directed toward its succeeding node; the doubly-linked record contains two pointer fields in addition to its key and content fields. The left field points to the preceding node, and the right field, to the following one. Note that the position of the record is irrelevant. The disparate record representation is not as congenial to human thought processes as the linked node form, but it is a truer computer-oriented representation.

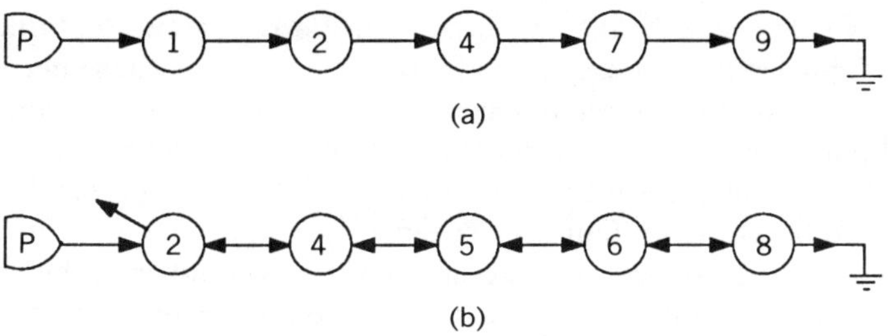

Figure 4.1 Linked lists: (a) singly-linked; (b) doubly-linked.

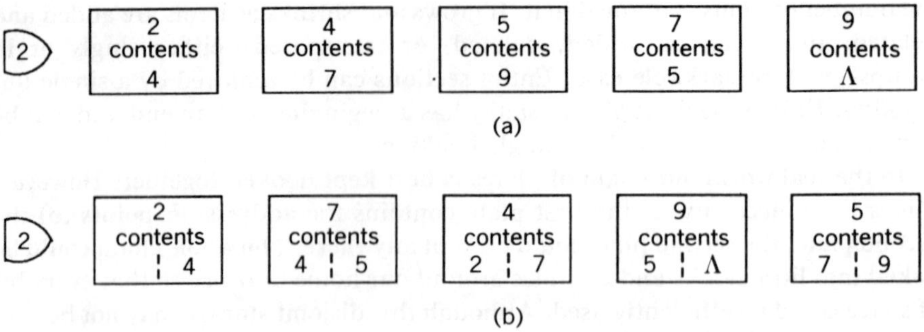

Figure 4.2 Record representation: (a) singly-linked list; (b) doubly-linked list.

4.2 SINGLY-LINKED LIST

The singly-linked list is an efficient, dynamic storage structure. It occupies minimum space in memory and is the structure of choice when items are to be, inserted, deleted, or transposed. In one particular form called a *stack* (items are only added or deleted from the front), it is widely used in compilers. Operations on the singly-linked list consist of building, traversing, adding, and deleting.

4.2.1 Building a Singly-Linked List

Singly-linked lists are built to contain data. This data is placed into the content fields of the records. An identifying key, usually related in some way to the content is placed into the single-key field and a pointer to the next record is placed in the single-pointer field. Some languages like Pascal directly support pointers; other languages like BASIC do not. However, it is a simple matter to simulate pointers in languages that do not directly support them.

Before a linked list can be built, a source of appropriately structured nodes must be established. Pascal does this automatically, retaining these nodes in an unstructured *heap,* but BASIC requires us to establish this source of nodes explicitly. It is convenient in BASIC to contain the supply of empty nodes in a linked list. This list is then easy to maintain and service because needed nodes can be deleted from this list and unused, or deleted nodes, can be returned to it.

First, the structure of the node must be established. In BASIC a node can be represented by a single row of a two-dimensional matrix. Column 1 is the key field, followed by as many columns as needed to contain the contents. The last column contains the *pointer.* This pointer is the row number of the next node. This next node need not be the next row in the matrix but is free to appear anywhere. Figure 4.3 shows a collection of source (empty) nodes stored in a matrix for BASIC and its linked list representation. Since the list is only accessed

Row	Column 1	2	3	4	5
1	1	0	0	0	2
2	2	0	0	0	3
3	3	0	0	0	4
4	4	0	0	0	5
.	.	.	.	.	.
.	.	.	.	.	.
.	.	.	.	.	.
100	100	0	0	0	0

(a)

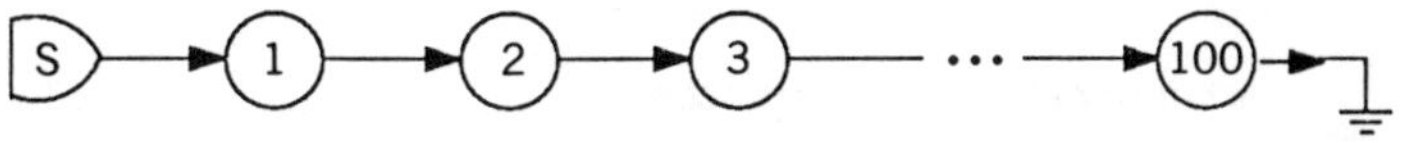

(b)

Figure 4.3 Source nodes used to build singly-linked lists (BASIC): (a) matrix form; (b) linked list form.

through its pointer, nodes are most conveniently removed from or returned to its head end.

Figure 4.4 illustrates the construction of a singly-linked list. (Throughout this discussion remember that a node can only be reached via its pointer.) A head node (P) is established connecting to the termination (NIL) symbol (⏚). This constitutes an *empty list.* A temporary pointer (T) to the first node in the source node list is established. This is necessary to prevent the loss of this node once the source pointer (S) is detached. This first node is now pointed to by two pointers, the temporary pointer and S. Before detaching this node, let S point to whatever this first node pointed to. S now points to the second node in the source node list, and the first node is partially detached. Detach this node completely by letting its pointer field point to whatever P points to. In this case, the detached node will point to NIL. Now, let P point to whatever the temporary pointer does—in this case, the detached node. Place a key in the key field, contents in the content fields, and the P list now contains one node. The procedure is repeated for each node transferred from the source node list to the linked list P.

At first, this procedure appears somewhat complicated. It really isn't. The key task is to ensure that there is always a pointer path to your destination. For that reason, the temporary pointer to the new node was established before the node was detached from S. For the same reason, S was directed to the second node in the source node list, before the new node was completely detached. The

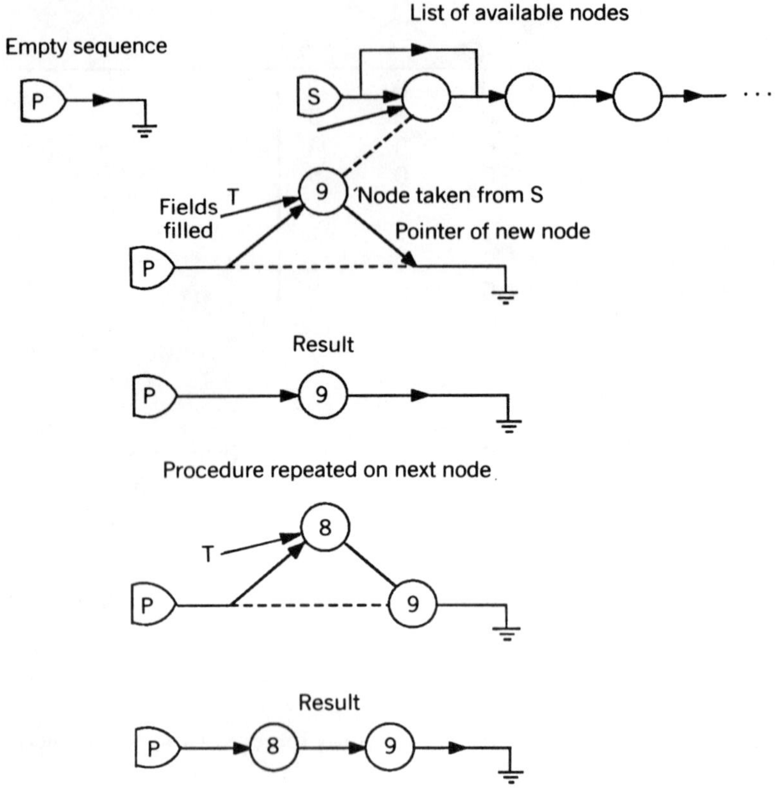

Figure 4.4 Construction of the singly-linked list (BASIC).

task is similar to traversing a gym ladder rung by rung. The trick is always to grasp the ladder by at least one hand.

Building the Singly-Linked List in BASIC

Figure 4.5 translates this schematic procedure into a BASIC program. The record key is placed in the first column of the source node list (AVAIL). The contents field is left alone since we do not care what is in it. The pointer to the next record (next row) is placed in the third column and column 3 of row 100 is set to NIL (zero in this case). We have created a linked list of source nodes containing 100 nodes each one containing a key, content, and pointer field. The pointer to each node is given by its key or row number; the pointer to the next node is given by the number in column 3.

Figure 4.6 displays a BASIC subroutine that constructs a singly-linked list using AVAIL. We assume that the input data is a list of nodes in any desired order paired with their contents. The contents occupy *n* fields, and there is no

```
100 REM SUBROUTINE SOURCE-NODES, BUILDS SOURCE-NODE LIST
110 DIM AVAIL(100,3) '100 SOURCE NODES, 3 FIELDS
120 REM ESTABLISHES STRUCTURE OF EACH NODE
130    FOR I=1 TO 100
140       AVAIL(I,1)= I 'SETS KEYS
150       AVAIL(I,3)=I+1 'SETS POINTERS
160    NEXT
170       AVAIL(100,3)=0  'TERMINATES LIST
180 RETURN
```

Figure 4.5 BASIC subroutine: builds list of source nodes.

```
200 REM SUBROUTINE BUILSL, CONSTRUCTS LINKED LIST
210 REM KEY AND CONTENTS ENTERED EXTERNALLY
220    TEMP = AVPNT  ' SETS TEMPORARY POINTER
230    AVPNT=AVAIL(AVPNT,N+1) 'SETS SOURCE POINTER TO NEXT NODE
240    AVAIL(TEMP,N+1) = P' SETS POINTER FIELD OF NEW NODE TO P
250    FOR I= 2 TO N
260     AVAIL(TEMP,I)= C(I) 'FILLS CONTENT FIELD
270    NEXT
280    AVAIL(TEMP,1) = C(1)  'SETS KEY FIELD
290    P = TEMP ' SETS POINTER TO ROW POSITION OF NODE
300 RETURN
```

Figure 4.6 BASIC subroutine BUILSL: builds singly-linked list.

restriction on the value or order of the keys. The pointer field occupies the $n + 1$ position in the node.

The subroutine implements the procedure illustrated in Figure 4.4. Line 220 points a temporary pointer to the source node pointed to by the source node pointer (AVPNT). AVPNT (S in Figure 4.4) is directed to the next empty node in the source list (line 230). Line 240 sets the pointer field of the node to be inserted to the same target as P (the listpointer). Lines 250, 260, and 270 fill the content fields. Line 280 inserts the key into the key field, and line 290 points the list-pointer (P) to the newly inserted node. This subroutine is called each time a node is to be inserted.

The new list actually resides in the AVAIL matrix. The first list built would occupy the first n rows (n = number of nodes), with P pointing to the last node inserted and AVPNT pointing to the start of the empty source nodes. However, with subsequent construction of other lists and additions and deletions, the nodes of a single list will not remain contiguous and may reside anywhere in the AVAIL matrix. The positions of the nodes in a list are of no concern to the user. Each list is accessed through its listpointer and (as we shall see) traversed by moving from node to node without regard to the node positions.

Building the Linked List in Pascal

Linked lists are directly supported by Pascal. Source nodes are contained in an internally managed *heap*. The user need only structure the node using the REC-

ORD format. Subsequently, a single statement will supply as many nodes as available. For example, a node containing a key, content, and pointer field is declared by

```
TYPE
   RECPOINTER = ↑Node;
   Node = RECORD
            KEY: INTEGER;
            CONT: INTEGER;
            RIGHT: RECPOINTER;
          END;
VAR Avpnt,Listpointer,Q:Recpointer;
```

Subsequently, a node pointed to by Q and with the structure Node is retrieved from the heap by the statement

```
NEW(Q);
```

Figure 4.7 displays a Pascal procedure for constructing lists. This procedure also closely follows Figure 4.4. NEW(Q) retrieves a source node. Q∧.Right:=P points the pointer field to the same target as P. The next two lines fill the content and key fields, and P:= Q points the listpointer to the inserted node. Each call to this procedure inserts one node. (Note "∧" and "↑" are identical symbols to the computer.)

4.2.2 Traversing the Singly-Linked List

Traversing the singly-linked list (moving from node to node in search of a key) is readily accomplished. Indeed, this easy traversal is one of the good reasons for using the structure. Traversal always begins at the node that points to the start of the list—the head node. Since this points to the first node, the key field in the first node can be inspected. If the node does not contain the target of the search, the pointer field is used to access the next node in the list, and so on. Traversal is stopped at the last node, using the fact that its pointer field contains the termination symbol.

```
PROCEDURE BUILSL(VAR P:Recpointer;N:INTEGER);
   VAR I:INTEGER;Q:Recpointer;
    BEGIN
       NEW(Q); {retrieves source node from heap}
       Q^.Right := P; {sets pointer field to P}
       FOR I:= 1 TO N DO Q^.Cont[I]:=C; {fills contents fields};
       Q^.Key= Key {sets key}
       P:= Q;  {points P to inserted node}
    END;
```

Figure 4.7 Pascal procedure BUILSL: builds singly-linked list.

A caution must be observed in traversing. After a traversal search, the list-pointer points to either the target or the termination symbol. Unless the pointer to the start of the list has been preserved, it will be lost, and the list will no longer be accessible. To prevent this calamity, a temporary listpointer is created and used in the traversal. Figure 4.8 displays a BASIC and Pascal subprogram for carrying out these operations.

4.2.3 Inserting and Deleting

Inserting a node in a list after a specified node is similar to building a list. In building a list, each node is inserted after the head pointer. To insert a node in a list, just replace the head pointer with the pointer field of the specified node and follow the same procedure. The pointer field of the specified node is found using TRAVERSE. Figure 4.9 displays BASIC and Pascal subprograms for this purpose.

Inserting a node before a given node is not a natural operation for the singly-linked list. Because of the unidirectional right-directed links, moving to the left is awkward. However, it can be done using a stratagem. The new node is inserted after a given node, and all fields of the two nodes are interchanged. This inappropriate use of a structure is not recommended, and sooner or later it breaks down. For example, try to insert a new node several nodes before a given node. If movement to the right as well as the left is required, a doubly-linked list should be used.

Deleting a node from a list after a given node is quickly accomplished. Call the node to be removed node Y, the one prior to it, node X, and the one after it,

```
400 REM SUBROUTINE TRAVERSE SEARCHES SINGLY-LINKED LIST
410 REM RETURNS P POINTER TO NODE, P= 0 IF TARGET ABSENT
420  IF AVAIL(P,K)=TARGET THEN RETURN
430  IF AVAIL(P,N+1)= 0 THEN P=0:RETURN
440  P=AVAIL(P,N+1): GOTO 420
450 REM  RETURN
```

(a)

```
PROCEDURE TRAVERSE(Q:Recpointer;Target:INTEGER);
      BEGIN
        WHILE (Q^.KEY <> Target AND (Q <>NIL) DO {SEARCHES FOR TARGET}
          Q:= Q^.RIGHT;
      END;
```

(b)

Figure 4.8 Subprogram to traverse a singly-tuned list: (a) BASIC; (b) Pascal.

```
500 REM SUBROUTINE INSERT, INSERTS NODE AFTER GIVEN NODE
510    GOSUB 400 ' FINDS GIVEN NODE
520    TEMP = AVPNT 'SETS TEMPORARY POINTER TO SOURCE NODE LIST
530    AVPNT= AVAIL(AVPNT, N+1))'SETS SOURCE POINTER TO NEXT NODE
540    AVAIL(TEMP,N+1)=AVAIL(P,N+1) 'POINTS NEW NODE TO NODE AFTER GIVEN NODE
550    AVAIL(TEMP,1) = C(1)   'SETS KEY IN NEW NODE
560    FOR I=2 TO N
570       AVAIL(TEMP,I)=C(I) 'FILLS CONTENTS FIELD
580    NEXT I
590    AVAIL(P,N+1)=TEMP 'POINTS TARGET NODE TO NEW NODE
595 RETURN
```

(a)

```
PROCEDURE INSERT (TARGET,NKEY:INTEGER;P:RECPOINTER);
(INSERTS NEW NODE AFTER GIVEN NODE)
VAR Q,PP:RECPOINTER;I:INTEGER
 BEGIN
   PP:=P;TRAVERSE(PP,TARGET); (FINDS TARGET NODE)
   NEW(Q); (SELECTS NEW NODE FROM HEAP)
   Q^.RIGHT:=PP^.RIGHT; (POINTS NEW NODE TO WHERE TARGET NODE POINTED)
   Q^.KEY := NKEY;FOR I:=1 TO N DO Q^.CONT[I] := C[I];
   (SETS KEY AND CONTENTS IN NEW NODE)
   PP^.RIGHT := Q;  (POINTS TARGET NODE TO NEW NODE)
 END;
```

(b)

Figure 4.9 Inserting a node after a given node: (a) BASIC; (b) Pascal.

node Z. The pointer field of node X is targeted to the node pointed to by the pointer field of node Y (node Z). The pointer field of node Y is then detached from node Z. In Pascal the detached node becomes inaccessible *(garbage)* and is subsequently returned to the heap by a *garbage disposal* routine. In BASIC the programmer must insert the detached node at the beginning of the source node list. Figure 4.10 displays the BASIC and Pascal subprograms for node deletion.

The procedures for inserting and deleting single nodes also work for groups of nodes. Think of the group of nodes as a single node. The pointer to the group corresponds to the pointer to the single node. The pointer field of the last node in the group corresponds to the pointer field of the single node. Otherwise, the procedures are the same.

4.3 THE DOUBLY-LINKED LIST

Adding a left pointer field to the nodes of the singly-linked list transforms it into a doubly-linked list and extends its capabilities. For BASIC, this is done by add-

```
600 REM SUBROUTINE DELETE, DELETES NODE AFTER GIVEN NODE
610 GOSUB 400 'GOES TO TRAVERSE TO FIND GIVEN NODE
620 TEMP = AVAIL(TARGET,N+1)) ' TEMPORARY POINTER TO NODE TO BE DELETED
625 REM CONTENTS OF NODE SHOULD BE READ HERE IF DESIRED
630 AVAIL(TARGET,N+1)= AVAIL(TEMP,N+1) ' GIVEN NODE POINTS TO NODE AFTER DELETED NODE
640 AVAIL(TEMP,N+1)=AVPNT 'DELETED NODE POINTS TO FIRST SOURCE NODE
650 AVPNT = TEMP 'DELETED NODE PLACED BACK IN SOURCE NODE LIST
660 RETURN
```

(a)

```
PROCEDURE DELETE(TARGET:INTEGER;P:RECPOINTER);
  VAR PP,Q:RECPOINTER;I:INTEGER;
  BEGIN
    PP:=P;TRAVERSE(PP,TARGET);{FINDS GIVEN NODE X}
    Q:=PP^.RIGHT; {TEMPORARY POINTER TO NODE TO BE DELETED Y}
    PP^.RIGHT:=Q^.RIGHT;  {GIVEN NODE POINTED TO NODE AFTER Y, NODE Z}
    Q^.RIGHT := NIL;  {NODE Y DETACHED FROM NODE Z}
    FOR I:=1 TO N DO INFO[I] :=Q^.CONT[I]; {TO READ CONTENTS OF NODE IF DESIRED}
  END;
```

(b)

Figure 4.10 Deleting a node after a given node: (a) BASIC; (b) Pascal.

ing another column (N + 2) to the AVAIL matrix. For Pascal this is done within the RECORD declaration by

```
TYPE
  RECPOINTER = ↑Node;
  Node = RECORD
           KEY: INTEGER;
           CONT: INTEGER;
           RIGHT: RECPOINTER;
           LEFT: RECPOINTER;
         END;
```

The doubly-linked list permits moving through the list either left or right. Insertion is easily performed either before or after given nodes. Deletion is readily performed before, after, or on given nodes. Algorithms that require these operations on nodes that are several nodes before or after a given node, should always use doubly-linked lists instead of struggling with singly-tuned lists and complicated stratagems.

The left link of the first node in the list is often undirected (Figure 4.1*b*). This can cause trouble when traversing leftward since the statement

```
P:= P∧.LEFT;
```

will look for a target that does not exist and abort the program. It is therefore good practice to NIL this pointer field or to insert a dummy node between it and the head pointer.

4.4 A SCHEDULING PROGRAM

Figures 4.11 and 4.12 show programs for scheduling appointments at a medical clinic. Both programs handle 20 physicians but can easily handle more. The

Figure 4.11 Scheduling program (BASIC).

```
10 REM APPOINTMENT SCHEDULING PROGRAM FOR A MEDICAL CLINIC
20 REM SCHEDULES 100 APPOINTMENTS FOR ANY NUMBER OF DOCTORS
25    DIM AVAIL$(100,3),D$(21),P(20):    P=0:N=2
30    GOTO 2000    'TO MAIN PROGRAM

100 REM SUBROUTINE SOURCE-NODES, BUILDS SOURCE-NODE LIST
120  REM ESTABLISH STRUCTURE OF EACH NODE
130   FOR I=1 TO 100
140      AVAIL$(I,1)= STR$(I): AVAIL$(I,3)=STR$(I+1)'SETS KEYS AND POINTERS
160   NEXT
170      AVAIL$(100,3)=STR$(0)   'TERMINATES LIST
180  RETURN

400 REM SUBROUTINE TRAVERSE$, SEARCHES SINGLY-LINKED LIST
410 REM RETURNS P POINTER TO NODE
420   IF VAL(AVAIL$(P,1)) = TARGET THEN RETURN 'SEARCHES FOR TARGET NODE
430   IF VAL(AVAIL$(P,N+1))=0 THEN RETURN 'RETURNS AT END OF LIST
440   P=VAL(AVAIL$(P,N+1)): GOTO 420 'ADVANCES POINTER
450 RETURN

500 REM SUBROUTINE INSERT$, INSERTS NODE AFTER GIVEN NODE
510   GOSUB 400 ' FINDS GIVEN NODE
520   TEMP = AVPNT 'FINDS NEXT SOURCE NODE
530   AVPNT= VAL(AVAIL$(AVPNT, N+1))'SETS SOURCE POINTER TO NEXT NODE
540   AVAIL$(TEMP,N+1)=AVAIL$(P,N+1) 'POINTS NEW NODE TO NODE AFTER GIVEN NODE
550   AVAIL$(TEMP,1) = C$(1)  'SETS KEY IN NEW NODE
560   FOR I=2 TO N
570     AVAIL$(TEMP,I)=C$(I) 'FILLS CONTENTS FIELD
580   NEXT I
590   AVAIL$(P,N+1)=STR$(TEMP) 'POINTS TARGET NODE TO NEW NODE
592   D$(21)=STR$(AVPNT) 'RECORDS AVPNT
595 RETURN

600 REM SUBROUTINE DELETE$, DELETES NODE AFTER GIVEN NODE
610 GOSUB 400 'CALLS TRAVERSE$ TO FIND TARGET NODE
620 TEMP=VAL(AVAIL$(P, N+1)) ' TEMPORARY POINTER TO NODE TO BE DELETED
630 AVAIL$(P,N+1)=AVAIL$(TEMP,N+1) 'GIVEN NODE POINTS TO NODE AFTER DELETED NODE
640 AVAIL$(TEMP,N+1)=STR$(AVPNT) 'DELETED NODE POINTS TO FIRST SOURCE NODE
650 AVPNT = TEMP ' DELETED NODE REPLACED IN SOURCE NODE LIST
660 RETURN

700 REM SUBROUTINE DISPLAY$,DISPLAYS AND SETS DOCTORS LISTPOINTER
720 REM DISPLAYS ACTIVE DOCTORS LIST SO 1 CAN BE CHOSEN OR NEW ONE ADDED
740   FOR   DD=1  TO   20:PRINT   D$(DD),DD:NEXT 'DISPLAYS DOCTORS LIST
750   INPUT "CHOOSE DOCTOR ENTER NAME AND NO.";A$,NN
770   D$(NN)=A$ 'RECORDS DOCTORS NAME IN DOCTORS MATRIX
795 RETURN
```

```
800 REM SUBROUTINE INITIAL$,INITIALIZES ALL LISTS WITH A DUMMY NODE
810  GOSUB 100  'REBUILDS SOURCE NODE MATRIX
820  AVPNT =1  'SETS POINTER TO SOURCE NODES
830  FOR L=1 TO 20: C$(1)=STR$(L):C$(2)=D$(L):P=0:GOSUB 200:NEXT
     'ENTERS FIELDS INTO DUMMY NODES
840  AVPNT=21:D$(21)=STR$(21) 'SETS POINTER TO SOURCE NODE AND ENTERS IT INTO ARRAY
850 RETURN

900 REM SUBROUTINE INSERT-APPT$, INSERTS APPOINTMENTS IN DOCTORS LIST
910   FOR L=1 TO 20:PRINT D$(L),L:NEXT  'DISPLAYS DOCTORS AND LIST NUMBERS
920   INPUT "DOCTORS NO.";P:LP=P:PRINT
922   PRINT AVAIL$(LP,2):PRINT 'DISPLAYS DOCTOR'S NAMES
925   PRINT AVAIL$(LP,1);"   ";:IF VAL(AVAIL$(LP,3))<>0 THEN LP=VAL(AVAIL$(LP,3)):
      GOTO 925 'PRINTS APPOINTMENT TIMES
930   PRINT: INPUT "PRECEDING APPOINTMENT, NEW APPOINTMENT AND PATIENTS NAME";
      TARGET,C$(1),C$(2)
940   GOSUB 500  'INSERTS NEW NODE
950 RETURN

1100 REM SUBROUTINE ADD/DELETE$, ADDS OR DELETES DOCTORS
1110   GOSUB 700:GOSUB 1300: RETURN 'FIRST DISPLAYS DOCTORS THEN ADDS NEW DOCTOR
(TO DELETE ADD "EMPTY")

1200  REM SUBROUTINE DISPLAY$, DISPLAYS APPOINTMENTS
1205   FOR LL=1 TO 20:PRINT D$(LL),LL:NEXT 'DISPLAYS DOCTORS
1207   INPUT "DOCTORS NO.";I:PRINT:PRINT
1210   PRINT "DOCTOR ";AVAIL$(I,2);"--APPOINTMENTS"
1220   IF VAL(AVAIL$(I,3))<>0 THEN I=VAL(AVAIL$(I,3)):PRINT AVAIL$(I,1);" ";
       AVAIL$(I,2);"   ";:GOTO 1220 'APPOINTMENTS
1230   PRINT:PRINT:RETURN

1300 REM SUBROUTINE  CHANGES DOCTORS NAME ON LIST
1310 T1 = NN 'SAVE POINTER TO LIST
1320 IF VAL(AVAIL$(T1,3))<>0 THEN T1= VAL(AVAIL$(T1,3)):GOTO 1320 'FINDS END OF LIST
1330 AVAIL$(T1,3)=STR$(AVPNT)  'CONNECTS END OF LIST TO SOURCE NODE LIST
1340 T2 = VAL(AVAIL$(NN,3)) 'T2 POINTS TO SECOND NODE
1350 AVPNT = T2  'SOURCE NODE CONTAINS STRING
1360 AVAIL$(NN,3)= STR$(0)  'SEPARATES LIST FROM AVAIL$
1365 AVAIL$(NN,2)=A$ 'ENTERS DOCTORS NAME IN AVAIL$
1370 RETURN

1400 REM SUBROUTINE DELETE-ORG$, ORGANIZES NODE DELETION
1410 GOSUB 1200 'DISPLAYS APPOINTMENTS
1420 INPUT "ENTER DR'S NO. AND PRECEDING APPOINTMENT";P,TARGET
1430 GOSUB 600 'CALLS DELETE$
1440 RETURN
2000 REM MAIN PROGRAM
2010  OPEN  "I",#2,"B:APPTS":OPEN  "I",#1,"B:DOCTORS"  OPENS  ALL FILES
2015 FOR I=1 TO 100:FOR K=1 TO 3:INPUT#2,AVAIL$(I,K):NEXT K,I:
CLOSE#2 'READS INFO FROM LAST SESSION
2017 FOR I=1 TO 21:INPUT#1,D$(I):NEXT:CLOSE#1:AVPNT=VAL(D$(21))
'READS DOCTORS LIST PLUS AVPNT POSTION
2020 PRINT"1-ZERO (INITIALIZE) ALL LISTS. 2-ADD OR DELETE DOCTORS" "BEGIN SELECTION MENU
2030 PRINT"3-INSERT APPOINTMENTS. 4-DISPLAY APPOINTMENTS
2035 PRINT"5-DELETE APPOINTMENT. 0-END" 'END SELECTION MENU
2050 INPUT C:IF C=1 THEN INPUT "ARE YOU SURE,Y/N";R$:IF R$<>"Y" THEN GOTO 2020
2055 ON C GOSUB 800,1100,900,1200,1400
2060 IF C <>0 GOTO 2020
3000 OPEN"O",#2,"B:APPTS":OPEN"O",#1,"B:DOCTORS" 'OPEN FILES FOR OUTPUT
3010 FOR I=1 TO 100:FOR K=1 TO 3:PRINT#2,AVAIL$(I,K):NEXT K,I:
CLOSE#2 'FILL APPOINTMENT FILE
3020 FOR I=1 TO 21:PRINT#1,D$(I):NEXT:CLOSE#1 'FILL DOCTORS FILE
3030 END  'END OF PROGRAM
```

Figure 4.12 Scheduling program (Pascal).

```
PROGRAM SCHEDULE(INPUT, OUTPUT);
TYPE    RECPOINTER=^NODE;
        DATUM = STRING[15];
        NODE = RECORD
                KEY:REAL ;
                CONT:DATUM;
                RIGHT:RECPOINTER ;
            END;                (SETS UP NODE STRUCTURE)

        APPT = RECORD
                KEYNUM:REAL;
                NAME:DATUM;
            END;            (SETS UP FILE STRUCTURE)

  VAR  APPTFILE:FILE OF APPT;APPTREC:APPT;DOCARRAY:ARRAY[1..100]OF DATUM;
   APPTARRAY:ARRAY[1..100] OF REAL;ST,C,DOCTORS:DATUM;PP,TT:ARRAY[1..20] OF RECPOINTER;
   SELECT,J,K,I,A,N:INTEGER;Q,LISTPOINTER:RECPOINTER;
   FFILE:ARRAY[1..20] OF DATUM;TARGET,NKEY:REAL;
  LABEL SEL,RR,FIN;

PROCEDURE BUILSL(VAR P:RECPOINTER); (BUILDS LIST OF NODES)
   VAR I:INTEGER;Q:RECPOINTER;
    BEGIN
       NEW(Q); (retrieves source node from heap)
       Q^.RIGHT := P; (sets pointer field to P)
       Q^.Cont:=C; (fills contents fields);
       Q^.KEY:= NKEY;
       P:= Q;  (points P to inserted node)
    END;

PROCEDURE INIT;
   BEGIN
     FOR I:=1 TO 20 DO WRITELN(PP[I]^.CONT,'   ',I);WRITELN;
     WRITELN('DOCTORS NO., NEW/OLD NAME'); READLN(I,C);
     PP[I]^.RIGHT:= NIL;PP[I]^.CONT:=C;
   END;

PROCEDURE DISPLAY;  (DISPLAYS ALL LISTS)
 VAR N,M:INTEGER;
   BEGIN
    WRITELN('0-ALL OR DRS NO.D');READLN(K);
    IF K=0 THEN BEGIN N:=1;M:=20;END ELSE BEGIN N:=K;M:=K;
     FOR K:=N TO M DO BEGIN TT[K]:=PP[K];
       WHILE TT[K]<>NIL DO BEGIN WRITE(TT[K]^.KEY:8:0,'   ',TT[K]^.CONT,'   ');
       TT[K]:=TT[K]^.RIGHT;END; WRITELN ;END;
   END;

PROCEDURE TRAVERSE(VAR Q:RECPOINTER;TARGET:REAL); (FINDS TARGET NODE)
      BEGIN WHILE (Q^.KEY <> TARGET) AND (Q <>NIL) DO (SEARCHES FOR TARGET)
           Q:= Q^.RIGHT;
      END;

PROCEDURE INSERT (TARGET,NKEY:REAL;P:RECPOINTER);
(INSERTS A NEW NODE AFTER A GIVEN NODE)
VAR Q,PP:RECPOINTER;
      BEGIN
        PP:=P;TRAVERSE(PP,TARGET); (FINDS TARGET NODE)
        NEW(Q); (SELECTS NEW NODE FROM HEAP)
        Q^.RIGHT:=PP^.RIGHT; (POINTS NEW NODE TO WHERE TARGET NODE POINTED)
        Q^.KEY := NKEY; Q^.CONT := C; (SETS KEY AND CONTENTS IN NEW NODE)
        PP^.RIGHT := Q;  (POINTS TARGET NODE TO NEW NODE)
      END;
```

```
PROCEDURE DELETE(TARGET:REAL;P:RECPOINTER); {DELETES THE NODE AFTER GIVEN NODE}
    VAR PP,Q:RECPOINTER;I:INTEGER;
      BEGIN
        PP:=P;TRAVERSE(PP,TARGET);{FINDS GIVEN NODE X}
        Q:=PP^.RIGHT; {TEMPORARY POINTER TO NODE TO BE DELETED Y}
        PP^.RIGHT:=Q^.RIGHT;  {GIVEN NODE POINTED TO NODE AFTER Y, NODE Z}
        Q^.RIGHT := NIL;  {NODE Y DETACHED FROM NODE Z}
       END;

{MAIN PROGRAM}
 BEGIN
   FOR I:=1 TO 20 DO BEGIN STR(I:1,ST);FFILE[I]:='B:DUUTE'+ST; END;{SETS UP 20 FILES}
   FOR I:=1 TO 20 DO PP[I]:= NIL; {SETS UP 20 EMPTY LISTS}
   FOR K:=1 TO 20 DO BEGIN {READS 20 FILES AND ENTERS VALUES INTO ARRAYS}
     ASSIGN(APPTFILE,FFILE[K]);N:=1;
     RESET(APPTFILE);A:=FILESIZE(APPTFILE);
        WHILE NOT EOF(APPTFILE) DO
          BEGIN
            READ(APPTFILE,APPTREC);
            DOCARRAY[A]:=APPTREC.NAME;
            APPTARRAY[A]:=APPTREC.KEYNUM;A:=A-1;
          END;CLOSE(APPTFILE);
        FOR J:=1 TO FILESIZE(APPTFILE) DO BEGIN
          C:=DOCARRAY[J];NKEY:=APPTARRAY[J];BUILSL(PP[K]);END;
  END;
SEL:   WRITELN('SELECT: 1-INITIALIZE. 2-DISPLAY. 3-INSERT. 4-DELETE. 5-END');
   READ(SELECT);WRITELN;
   CASE SELECT OF {SELECTS DESIRED PROCEDURE}
      1:INIT;
      2:DISPLAY;
      3:BEGIN
         DISPLAY;WRITELN('DOCTORS NO.,PREVIOUS APPT, APPT, PATIENT');
         READLN(K,TARGET,NKEY,C);INSERT(TARGET,NKEY,PP[K]);
        END;
      4:BEGIN DISPLAY;WRITELN('DOCTORS NO. PREC. APPT');
        READLN(K,TARGET);DELETE(TARGET,PP[K]);END;
      5:GOTO FIN;
   END;GOTO SEL;
FIN:WRITELN;
   FOR K:=1 TO 20 DO BEGIN {WRITES DATA BACK INTO FILES}
       ASSIGN(APPTFILE,FFILE[K]);REWRITE(APPTFILE);
      WHILE PP[K]<>NIL DO BEGIN
        APPTREC.KEYNUM:=PP[K]^.KEY;APPTRECT.NAME:=PP[K]^.CONT; {SETS UP RECORD FOR FILE}
        WRITE(APPTFILE,APPTREC); {WRITES RECORD INTO FILE}
        PP[K]:=PP[K]^.RIGHT;END;CLOSE(APPTFILE);
   END;
END.
```

BASIC program holds a total of 100 entries (also easily increased), and the Pascal program is limited only by available memory. The programs have the following features:

1. Physicians' names can be entered or changed individually.
2. Entire appointment lists for individual doctors can be displayed.
3. Appointments can be inserted or deleted for individual physicians as required.
4. An entire appointment list for a physician can be cleared by a single command.
5. The appointment lists occupy minimum memory.

To emphasize the efficacy of the linked list structure in this application, let us try to handle this task with a different structure—the two-dimensional array.

What are the memory requirements for the array? Suppose that the 20 doctors in this clinic work irregular hours. Some may see many patients in some weeks and few patients in other weeks. Not knowing how long an appointment list is required for each doctor, we must provide maximum room for each one. This maximum occurs when one physician sees 100 patients in one week and none of the other physicians are working. Each member of the clinic then requires an array with 100 rows for a total of 2000 rows. Each row might typically require about 20 bytes. Therefore, 40 kilobytes of memory are required to hold this matrix in core memory. This requirement applies to both the BASIC and Pascal programs. Clever overhead management schemes could be devised to reduce this number, but they would certainly complicate the program.

By contrast, the BASIC program using the singly-linked list structure, requires a matrix of only 100 rows (2000 bytes). A single physician working alone could use the entire matrix. Several physicians working together would share the matrix, each using only what was required. The Pascal linked list program does not use a matrix. The nodes are stored in memory without regard to contiguity. This increases available storage. In addition, memory is used only as required. Heap management procedures also permit unused nodes to be returned to the heap.

Data management would be cumbersome for the matrix structure. If appointments had to be entered contiguously into each matrix, insertion of a new appointment between two existing ones would require that all later appointments be advanced one row. To retain maximum space, deletion would require that all later appointments be reduced one row.

The linked list structure eliminates these inefficiencies. Nodes can be inserted or deleted easily with a minimum of overhead. A node is inserted or deleted simply by changing pointer destinations. Only the preceding and following node pointers are affected. These operations are implemented by simple, concise algorithms, easily formulated and debugged (see Figures 4.11 and 4.12).

Both programs illustrate the advantages of segmenting large programs. Both have about 100 statements. If they had been written as monolithic blocks, debugging and verification would have been difficult and time-consuming. Instead, the programs were highly segmented. Each subprocedure was tested as it was written. (Most subprocedures were already on disk and were simply merged with the programs.)

The segmentation also simplifies adding or changing features of the program. New features can be composed as additional subprograms and placed anywhere in the program. They can then be accessed by a few statements in the main program. Readers who attempt the assigned projects will appreciate this. These programs are interesting and instructive. We suggest that the reader take the time to check them out.

4.4.1 The BASIC Program

The BASIC program consists of 11 subroutines and a main program. The subroutines are all short, the longest having ten lines of code (ignoring REM statements). Consequently, each subroutine can be quickly and easily debugged. The main program does little more than request and collect input data and assemble the necessary subroutines.

All lists, source nodes or appointment, are contained in the string matrix, AVAIL$. A string matrix has been used so that it can contain doctors' and patients' names. Doctors' numbers and appointments are also stored as strings but are converted to numerical values as needed. Therefore, subroutines shown previously have been transformed to handle strings.

Most of the subroutines are self-explanatory. SOURCE-NODES builds the source nodes list, ADD/DELETE$ adds or deletes doctors' names, TRAVERSE$ finds a target node, and so on.

Some of the subroutines are called from within other subroutines. INSERT$ (inserts node after a given node) is called from within INSERT-APPT$. INSERT-APPT$ displays the list of active doctors and their assigned numbers so that the user can select a desired doctor. It queries the user for preceding appointment, new appointment, and patient's name. Then, it calls INSERT$ to insert the new appointment after the preceding one. Note that the INSERT$ calls TRAVERSE$ to find the given node. This kind of *piggybacking* simplifies and accelerates programming. Subroutines DELETE-ORG$, INITIAL$, AND ADD/DELETE$ use piggybacking.

The main program begins by reading AVAIL$ from a sequential disk file. AVAIL$ contains the appointment list as updated by the last session. A list of doctor's names in numerical, order is also read into the program. (Note initially both lists are empty and are set up by selecting "1" from the main menu.) Subsequently, the disk file is not read from. All operations are performed on the AVAIL$ matrix. At sign-off, the updated AVAIL$ is returned to the disk file.

This BASIC program is a good example of how an exotic data structure can be implemented in a language not designed to handle it directly. Pointers and linked lists are used in this program with only slightly more fuss than in the Pascal program. Moreover, the lack of built-in heap management forces the BASIC programmer to account for every aspect of the exotic data structure. This leads to a more thorough understanding.

4.4.2 The Pascal Program

The Pascal program contains only six procedures and a main program. This smaller number (five less than in BASIC) is due largely to the use of the CASE statement to accept commands and to assemble and call the required procedures. Also there is no need to set up a list of source nodes. Other than that, the procedures are similar to and only slightly shorter than the BASIC ones.

The main program begins by reading in the updated data from the last session. This data is used to build 20 separate lists. We found it convenient to store this data in 20 separate disk files, although they could be stored in one file if desired. All files must be initialized with a header node containing the doctor's name and number before the program can be used for the first time. This is done by selecting "1" from the main menu. Subsequently, this is not necessary. All operations within the program are conducted on the lists. At sign-off, updated data is reentered into the disk files.

Except for the INIT procedure, the Pascal procedures are similar to the BASIC subroutines. The BASIC program clears all appointments (initializes) by rebuilding the AVAIL$ matrix. This leaves 20 header nodes containing the doctor's name and number and returns all other nodes to the source node list. The Pascal program clears the lists by pointing the header nodes to NIL. This can leave a large number of inaccessible nodes (called *garbage*). Most Pascal implementations have a procedure that returns these nodes to the heap. Although the program makes no provision for using this procedure, it might be necessary to do so.

4.5 MULTIPLY-LINKED LIST

An ordered list can always be more efficiently searched than an unordered one. For example, the presence or absence of a key in a numerically ordered list can be determined by searching for keys immediately below and above it. If the target key is not found between these two keys, it is absent. This procedure applies to lexically ordered lists as well. Lists can be ordered and searched in respect to content fields as well as keys so that keys are not always necessary.

Sometimes it may be desirable to effect several different orderings within a single list. For example, suppose we have a list of nodes, each containing three content fields (a policy number, a name, and the year of birth). We wish to order this list in terms of these three items, concurrently, without forming separate lists for each ordering.

The multiply-linked list is the appropriate structure for this task. Figure 4.13 shows two representations of this structure: linked nodes and disparate records. In these representations the policy number (PN) is used to identify the node.

The linked node representation resembles a digraph except that it contains three header nodes and one termination. This makes it a list with entry restricted to the header nodes. The path taken through the list depends on the header node selected. The three paths in the figure are separately represented as dotted, dashed, and solid lines. It is seen that each header node provides a path that is independent of all other header nodes.

The disparate record representation reveals the structure required of the nodes. Each path requires a head pointer pointing to the first node in the path (starting node). Each node must contain at least one content field for each path and a pointer field for each path through the structure. Sometimes a key field is

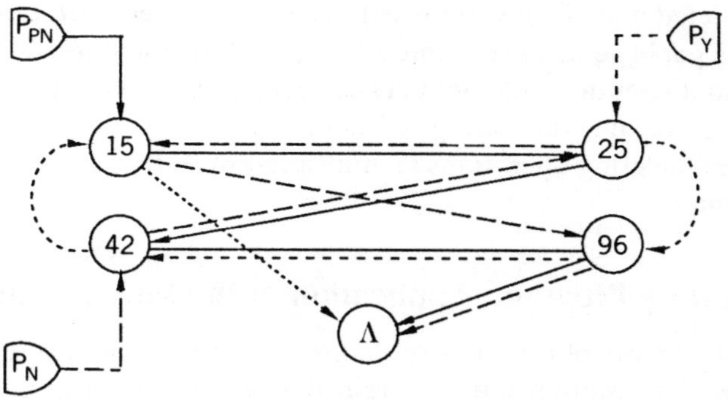

(a)

P_{PN}	P_N	P_Y
15	42	25

PN	Name	Year	P'_N	P'_Y	P'_{PN}
15	SMITH, J	82	96	Λ	25
25	HODGES, P	21	15	96	42
42	DOAKES, K	75	25	15	96
96	THOMAS, P	45	Λ	42	Λ

(b)

Figure 4.13 The multiply-linked list: (a) node representation; (b) record representation.

also required, although a numeric content field may often be used in its place. For a structure with three paths and one content field per path (Figure 4.13b), we need nodes with three content fields and three pointer fields. This arrangement can be used to support any number of paths (orderings) in a single list.

Building the multiply-linked list is similar to building the singly-linked list except that there are more choices. Inserting a node into a singly-linked list requires one choice—the node it is to follow (target node). Three choices are required (in our example) when a node is inserted. We must choose the target node for the key field (policy number), a different one for the name field, and another one for the year field. In effect, the new node is inserted in three different places, although actually only pointers in the three-pointer fields are manipulated.

Deletion of a node is also similar to the singly-linked operation except for the number of target choices. Three target nodes that precede the node to be deleted must be selected. The three pointers pointing to the deleted node must be made to point to the node following the deleted node in accordance with their own paths. The deleted node is then returned to a singly-linked source node list (BASIC) or left as garbage until reclaimed (Pascal). Multiply-linked lists may also incorporate double-ended linkages between each appropriate fields. This structure supports direct deletion of a given node.

Building and deleting operations on multiply-linked lists are illustrated in the following example.

4.5.1 Inventory Program: Application of the Multiply-Linked List

A warehouse inventory of products-on-hand is to be maintained on a microcomputer. Product information must contain item number, price, product name, number-in-stock, and manufacturer. The inventory listing must be capable of being displayed in numeric order by item number, price, and number-on-hand and in lexical order by product name. We must be able to add items at any desired location to maintain order. We must be able to delete items on the basis of item number.

Easy addition, deletion, and multiple-display paths call for and highlight the virtuosity of the multiply-linked list. No other data structure would permit us to contain the data in single nodes without repetition. No other structure would permit us to insert or delete nodes easily, while maintaining the order and continuity of the paths.

To permit deletion of a specific node, the list must also be doubly-linked. The singly-linked version facilitates removal of the node following the target but not the target. To remove the target, it is necessary to connect the preceding node to the one after the target. Therefore, it is necessary to back up to the preceding node, hence the need for a doubly-linked version.

To contain the required data and pointers, the node must contain five content fields, four left-pointer fields and four right-pointer fields. The content fields are respectively identified as Item No., Product Name, Price, and Number-on-Hand fields. The fifth field, Manufacturer, is not included in a path. Each of the first four content fields has two associated pointer fields, left and right.

Figure 4.14 shows a three-node list. Node 1 is a dummy node containing the titles and providing an anchor for the left pointers of the starting nodes. The pointer pairs are associated with their respective content fields; RPT1 and LPT1 refer to the Item No. field, and so on. Paths through the list are given by Item No.-10-20, Prod Name-AWL-DRILL, Price-25.50-30.00, and On-Hand-50-100. These paths are easily traced by following the RPTs.

BASIC Program

The BASIC program is shown in Figure 4.15. This is a complete program, lacking only the safeguards and graphics ornamentation found in most commercial programs. It is weak in only one respect: all inventory items must be held in core when the program is used. This serious limitation, however, is not hard to over-

DUMMY NODE 1

Item No.	Prod Name	Price	On Hand	Mfr	RPT1	RPT2	RPT3	RPT4	LPT1	LPT2	LPT3	LPT4
					2	3	2	3	NIL	NIL	NIL	NIL

NODE 2

					RPT1	RPT2	RPT3	RPT4	LPT1	LPT2	LPT3	LPT4
10	DRILL	25.50	100	GM	3	NIL	3	NIL	1	3	1	3

NODE 3

					RPT1	RPT2	RPT3	RPT4	LPT1	LPT2	LPT3	LPT4
20	AWL	30.00	50	GE	NIL	2	NIL	2	2	1	2	1

Figure 4.14 Node structure for inventory program (Pascal).

Figure 4.15 Inventory program (BASIC).

```
10    REM MULTIPLY-LINKED LIST INVENTORY PROGRAM
20    DIM AVAIL$(100,13),C$(5),I$(5),P(8),N$(9)
30    GOTO 2000 'TO MAIN PROGRAM

100   REM SUBROUTINE SOURCE-NODES, BUILDS DOUBLY-LINKED SOURCE-NODE LIST
120   REM ESTABLISH STRUCTURE OF EACH NODE
130   FOR I=1 TO 100
140      AVAIL$(I,0)= STR$(I) 'SETS KEYS
145      FOR K=1 TO 5:AVAIL$(I,K)="0":NEXT 'CLEARS CONTENTS
150      AVAIL$(I,9)=STR$(I+1) 'SETS POINTER TO NEXT NODE
160   NEXT
170     AVAIL$(100,9)=STR$(0)   'TERMINATES LIST
175     GOSUB 200 'SETS UP DUMMY NODE
180   RETURN

200   REM SUBROUTINE INITIALIZE-BUILDS DUMMY HEAD NODE
205    AVAIL$(1,1)="ITEM NO.":AVAIL$(1,2)="PROD. NAME":AVAIL$(1,3)="PRICE"
210    AVAIL$(1,4)="NO.-ON-HAND":AVAIL$(1,5)="MFR" 'FILLS DUMMY NODE
230    FOR I=6 TO 9:AVAIL$(1,I)="0":NEXT 'ZEROES ALL POINTER FIELDS
240    AVPNT = 2 'SETS POINTER TO SOURCE NODE LIST
250   RETURN

300   REM SUBROUTINE INSERT$, INSERTS NODES IN MULTIPLY LINKED LIST
310    TEMP = AVPNT 'TEMPORARY POINTER TO SOURCE NODE LIST
320    AVPNT=VAL(AVAIL$(AVPNT,9)) 'SETS SOURCE NODE POINTER TO NEXT SOURCE NODE
325    I$(1)="ITEM NO.":I$(2)="PROD-NAME":I$(3)="PRICE":I$(4)="NO.-ON-HAND"
       'FILLS PROMPT VARIABLE
330    FOR I=1 TO 4 'STEPS THROUGH FOUR FIELDS
335      GOSUB 500 'DISPLAYS NODES IN NUMERICAL OR LEXICAL ORDER
340      PRINT"PREC. "I$(I);" NEW "I$(I):INPUT TARGET$,C$(I) 'PROMPT
345      K=I 'K IS USED IN TRAVERSE$ SUBROUTINE
350      GOSUB 405 'CALLS TRAVERSE$ TO FIND TARGET NODE
370      AVAIL$(TEMP,I+5)=AVAIL$(P(I),I+5) 'POINTS NEW NODE TO WHATEVER TARGET
         NODE POINTED TO
375      AVAIL$(P(I),I+5)=STR$(TEMP) 'POINTS TARGET NODE TO NEW NODE
377      AVAIL$(TEMP,I+9)=STR$(P(I)) 'SETS LEFT POINTER
380      AVAIL$(TEMP,I)= C$(I) 'FILLS KEY AND CONTENTS FIELDS
385      P(I)=1 'RESTORES POINTER TO BEGINNING OF LIST
390    NEXT
395      INPUT "MFR";G$:AVAIL$(TEMP,5)=G$ 'INFO FOR MFR FIELD
402   RETURN

405   REM SUBROUTINE M-TRAVERSE$--FINDS TARGET NODE
410   REM RETURNS P(K), POINTER TO TARGET NODE
420    IF AVAIL$(P(K),K) = TARGET$ THEN RETURN 'RETURNS IF TARGET NODE IS FOUND
430    IF VAL(AVAIL$(P(K),K+5))=0 THEN PRINT"CANT FIND":RETURN
'RETURNS IF TARGET IS NOT FOUND
440     P(K)=VAL(AVAIL$(P(K),K+5)): GOTO 420 'ADVANCES POINTER AND CONTINUES SEARCH
450   RETURN

500   REM SUBROUTINE DISPLAY$, DISPLAYS  IN DESIRED ORDER
520    C=0 'INITIALIZES COUNTER
530    FOR II=1 TO 5:  PRINT AVAIL$(P(I),II), :NEXT: C=C+1
'DISPLAYS AVAIL$ & INCREMENTS COUNTER
540    IF C MOD 15 = 0 THEN INPUT "RETURN TO CONTINUE";X 'PAUSES AFTER 15 LINE DISPLAY
550    P(I) = VAL(AVAIL$(P(I),I+5)) 'ADVANCES POINTER
560    IF P(I)<>0 GOTO 530 'STOPS AT END OF LIST
565    FOR IJ=1 TO 5:P(IJ)=1:NEXT 'RESETS POINTERS
570   RETURN

600   REM SUBROUTINE S-DISPLAY, SEPARATE DISPLAY
610    INPUT"1-ITEM-NO.,2-PROD-NAME, 3-PRICE, 4-NO.-ON-HAND";I
       'SELECTS FIELD TO BE DISPLAYED IN ORDER
620    GOSUB 500 'DISPLAYS NODES IN SELECTED ORDER
630   RETURN
```

```
700    REM SUBROUTINE DELETE$, DELETES TARGET NODE
710     PRINT"SELECT ITEM NO. FOR DISPLAY"
720     GOSUB 600 'DISPLAYS NODES
730     INPUT "ITEM NO. FOR DELETION";TARGET$:K=1 'SELECT ITEM NO. TO BE DELETED
740     GOSUB 405 'FIND TARGET NODE
760     TEMP=P(K) :PRINT TEMP'TEMPORARY POINTER TO NODE TO BE DELETED
765     FOR I=1 TO 4 'STEPS THROUGH 4 FIELDS
770       PP= VAL(AVAIL$(TEMP,I+9)) 'SETS POINTER TO PREVIOUS NODES
780       FF = VAL(AVAIL$(TEMP,I+5)) 'SETS POINTER TO FOLLOWING NODE
790       IF FF<>0 THEN AVAIL$(FF,I+9)=STR$(PP) 'LEFT POINTER OF FOLLOWING NODE SET
800       AVAIL$(PP,I+5) = AVAIL$(TEMP,I+5) 'PREC. NODE SET TO POINT TO FOLL. NODE
802       AVAIL$(TEMP,I+9)="0" 'DISCONNECTS LEFT POINTERS OF DELETED NODE
805     NEXT
807     P(K)=1 'INITALIZES LIST POINTER
810     AVAIL$(TEMP,9)=STR$(AVPNT) 'POINTS NODE TO SOURCE LIST
820     AVPNT =TEMP 'SETS AVPNT TO DELETED NODE
840    RETURN

2000 REM MAIN PROGRAM
2010 FOR I=1 TO 5:P(I)=1:NEXT 'INITIALIZES LIST POINTERS TO START OF LIST
2020 OPEN "I", #1,"B:INVTRY" 'OPENS DISK FILE FOR INPUT
2025 INPUT#1,AVPNT 'READS PREVIOUS SETTING OF SOURCE NODE POINTER
2030  FOR I=1 TO 100:FOR K=0 TO 13:INPUT#1,AVAIL$(I,K):NEXT K,I :CLOSE #1
      'INPUTS FILE INTO AVAIL$
2040 INPUT "1-INITIALIZE,2-INSERT,3-DISPLAY, 4-DELETE, 0-END";S 'SELECTS OPERATION
2050 ON S GOSUB 100,300,600, 700 'ROUTES TO SELECTED SUBROUTINE
2060 IF S=0 GOTO 2080 'ROUTE TO END
2070 GOTO 2040 'RESELECT OPERATION
2080 OPEN "O",#1,"B:INVTRY" 'OPEN FILES FOR OUTPUT
2085 PRINT#1,AVPNT 'OUTPUTS UPDATED POSITION OF SOURCE NODE POINTER
2090 FOR I=1 TO 100:FOR K=0 TO 13:PRINT#1,AVAIL$(I,K):NEXT K,I:CLOSE #1'OUTPUTS AVAIL$
2100 END
```

come and makes a nice project for the ambitious reader. Between sessions, all items are stored on disk.

In this program the inventory is stored in the 100 by 13 matrix, AVAIL$. All entries are stored as strings. Each row of the program constitutes a node. Column 0 contains the row (node) number. This column is used as the key field, but it could have been eliminated. Columns 1 through 5 contain the contents, columns 6 through 9, the right pointers, and columns 10 through 13, the left pointers. The pointers are integers that refer to the row number of a targeted node.

The subroutine SOURCE-NODES builds the empty source node list by placing 1, 2, 3, etc., in column 0, placing the row number of the next contiguous row in column 9, and placing 0's in the remaining columns. A 0 is placed in column 9 of the last row to indicate the end of the list (NIL).

Subroutine INITIALIZE constructs the dummy head node of the inventory list. Titles are placed in the content fields, and all pointer fields are zeroed. The source-node pointer AVPNT is advanced to the second node. INITIALIZE can also be used to discard an inventory.

Subroutine INSERT$ builds the inventory list. First, the subroutine DISPLAY$ is called to display the existing list. Since this list may be large, it is displayed a screenful at a time. Entries are made into one content field at a time by responding to prompts. All rows are displayed with the particular content

```
1-INITIALIZE. 2-DISPLAY. 3-INSERT. 4-DELETE. 5-END
3
      ITEMNO    PRODNAME        PRICE      ON-HAND        MFR
          10       DRILL        25.50         1000         GM
          20         AWL        35.50          500         GE

PREC.ITEMNO NEW ITEMNO
10 15
HIT
      ITEMNO    PRODNAME        PRICE      ON-HAND        MFR
          20         AWL        35.50          500         GE
          10       DRILL        25.50         1000         GM

PREC.PRODNAME NEW PRODNAME
DRILL FILE
HIT
      ITEMNO    PRODNAME        PRICE      ON-HAND        MFR
          10       DRILL        25.50         1000         GM
          20         AWL        35.50          500         GE

PREC.PRICE NEW PRICE
25.50 32.00
HIT
      ITEMNO    PRODNAME        PRICE      ON-HAND        MFR
          20         AWL        35.50          500         GE
          10       DRILL        25.50         1000         GM
```

```
PREC.ON-HAND NEW ON-HAND
1000 2000
HIT
MFR
GG

1-INITIALIZE. 2-DISPLAY. 3-INSERT. 4-DELETE. 5-END
2
1-ITEM-NO, 2-PROD NAME, 3-PRICE, 4-ON-HAND
1
      ITEMNO    PRODNAME        PRICE     ON-HAND        MFR
          10       DRILL        25.50        1000         GM
          15        FILE        32.00        2000         GG
          20         AWL        35.50         500         GE

1-INITIALIZE. 2-DISPLAY. 3-INSERT. 4-DELETE. 5-END
2
1-ITEM-NO, 2-PROD NAME, 3-PRICE, 4-ON-HAND
2
      ITEMNO    PRODNAME        PRICE     ON-HAND        MFR
          20         AWL        35.50         500         GE
          10       DRILL        25.50        1000         GM
          15        FILE        32.00        2000         GG
```

Figure 4.16 Sample screen of inventory program.

field (column) in lexical or alphabetical order, as appropriate. The user enters the preceding item followed by the item to be inserted. Then, the next content field is similarly displayed, and the user makes the same choice. This permits the user to enter items in order. Figure 4.16 shows a sample screen for the INSERT$ and DISPLAY$ operation. (Titles are slightly different than for the BASIC program.)

In the example illustrated by Figure 4.16, the row (node) 15, FILE, 32.00, 2000, and GG, under ITEMNO, PRODNAME, PRICE, ON-HAND, and MFR respectively, is to be added with all items in numerical or lexical order. First INSERT is requested and the existing list showing two items, a drill and an awl, is displayed. The program then requests the preceding item-number and the new one. On entry, the program reports a HIT, meaning that the item-number cell is in place. This procedure is repeated for the product-name, price, and quantities on hand. Then in response to the prompt, MFR, the manufacturer's name is entered. This completes the entry of the new node. To check this entry, a request for DISPLAY is made. The program asks which cell of the node is to be ordered and responds appropriately.

INSERT$ uses the subroutine TRAVERSE$ to find the node preceding the node to be inserted. TRAVERSE$ is similar to that used in the scheduling program except that it operates on any one of four right-pointer fields. TRAVERSE$ will be confused if two identical entries exist in the same column in different nodes. This can be prevented by adding an additional distinguishing character that will not change the meaning of the entry—for example, 2000 and 2000.1 or DRILL and DRILL.1.

Subroutine DELETE$ deletes an entire row. The row to be deleted is indicated by Item No. Nodes are displayed as they are for INSERT$. The user is prompted to enter the item number of the node to be deleted. The node is deleted and returned to the source-node list.

The short main program first reads previously stored data from a disk file, and then presents the selection menu and directs the program accordingly. At the end of session, the updated AVAIL$ is output to the disk file.

Figure 4.17 shows the first 15 rows of the AVAIL$ matrix after several insertions and deletions. A path can be traced as follows. Item No. (RT1=2) — 10, (RPT1=3) — 20, (RPT1=9) — 25, (RPT1=4) — 30, (RPT1=7) — 37, (RPT1=6) — 40, (RPT1=8) — 55, (RPT1=10) — 57, (RPT1=5) — 60, (RPT1=0). (The reader should trace all other paths.)

Pascal Program

Figure 4.18 shows the Pascal inventory program. The program is not as complete as the BASIC program. We have not bothered to divide the display into screen-sized modules (the reader can easily do this), nor have we included disk storage at the end of a session. Disk storage of a pointer driven list is tricky in Pascal and beyond the scope of this text. Therefore, it has been omitted. Otherwise, the two programs are similar.

1	ITEM NO.	PROD. NAME	PRICE	NO. ON HAND	MFR	2	9	9	2				
2	10	DRILL	25.50	1000	GM	3	4	3	9	1	1	4	1
3	20	HAMMER	35.50	2000	GM	9	6	7	10	2	4	2	2
4	30	FILE	10.00	3000	SEARS	7	7	2	6	3	2	1	3
5	60	LIGHT	2.50	1700	GE	0	8	10	8	8	6	9	7
6	40	KNIFE	11.00	4200	DELTA	8	5	5	0	4	3	4	4
7	37	GRILL	55.99	1500	ORTHO	6	3	8	5	4	4	3	2
8	55	MALLET	10.50	1700	DELTA	10	10	0	3	6	6	7	7
9	25	AWL	2.00	1200	SEARS	4	2	5	7	3	1	1	2
10	57	PICK	3.50	2500	SORS	5	0	4	4	8	8	5	3
11	0	0	0	0	0	12							
12	0	0	0	0	0	13							
13	0	0	0	0	0	14							
14	0	0	0	0	0	15							
15	0	0	0	0	0	16							

Figure 4.17 Sample inventory matrix.

The node structure is established by the type declaration. As required it contains five content fields structured as an array of strings, four right-pointer fields structured as an array of pointers, and four left-pointer fields similarly structured. The declaration section also includes the necessary variable and label declarations.

Procedure INITIALIZE establishes the dummy head node, placing titles into the content fields and NILs into the pointer fields.

Procedures DISPLAY and TRAVERSE are similar to the BASIC versions. To use DISPLAY, the user responding to a prompt selects the item he or she wishes to see displayed in order. The procedure then starts at the dummy head node and advances through the list following the designated path. TRAVERSE acts in the same way except that instead of displaying the results, it looks for the designated target node, returning the target pointer when it is found.

INSERT and DELETE are also similar to the BASIC program. The Pascal versions give particularly clear illustrations of the insertion and deletion processes. DELETE also illustrates the need for doubly-linking the fields. They are both completely annotated and should be studied closely.

Figure 4.18 Inventory program (Pascal).

```
PROGRAM INVENTORY(INPUT,OUTPUT);
 TYPE
   PT=^NODE;DATUM=STRING[10]; CT=ARRAY[1..5] OF DATUM;
   PP=ARRAY[1..4] OF PT;
   NODE = RECORD
           CONT:CT;
           RIGHT:PP;
           LEFT:PP;
         END;
  VAR PO,Q,P,QQ:PT;N:CT;I,OFFSET,K,II,S,KK:INTEGER;C:CT;D,X,TARGET:DATUM;
  LABEL FIN,SEL;

PROCEDURE INITIALIZE; {SETS UP DUMMY NODE}
 BEGIN
   NEW(Q);{SELECTS NEW NODE}
   FOR I:=1 TO 5 DO Q^.CONT[I]:=N[I]; {FILLS CONTENT FIELDS OF DUMMY NODE}
   FOR I:=1 TO 4 DO Q^.RIGHT[I]:=NIL; {NILS RIGHT POINTER FIELDS}
   FOR I:=1 TO 4 DO Q^.LEFT[I]:=NIL; {NILS LEFT POINTER FIELDS}
 END;

PROCEDURE DISPLAY(LL:PT;K:INTEGER); {DISPLAYS LIST}
 BEGIN
  WHILE LL<>NIL DO BEGIN
     FOR II:=1 TO 5 DO WRITE(LL^.CONT[II]:12); {DISPLAYS CONTENT FIELDS}
     WRITELN;LL:=LL^.RIGHT[K];   END;
  END;

PROCEDURE TRAVERSE(VAR P:PT); {FINDS TARGET NODE}
 BEGIN
   WHILE (P^.CONT[I]<>TARGET) AND (P<>NIL) DO P:=P^.RIGHT[I];{FINDS TARGET NODE} END;

PROCEDURE INSERT; {INSERTS NODE}
  BEGIN
      P:=Q; {P IS POINTER TO DUMMY NODE}
      TRAVERSE(P); {FINDS TARGET NODE}
      IF P^.CONT[I]=TARGET THEN WRITELN('HIT');{VERIFIES TARGET FOUND}
      QQ^.RIGHT[I]:=P^.RIGHT[I]; {NEW NODE POINTS RIGHT TO SAME NODE AS TARGET NODE}
      QQ^.LEFT[I]:=P; {NEW NODE POINTS LEFT TO TARGET NODE}
      QQ^.CONT[I]:=D; {FILLS DATA FIELDS}
      P^.RIGHT[I]:=QQ; {TARGET NODE POINTED TO NEW NODE}
      IF QQ^.RIGHT[I]<>NIL THEN BEGIN PO:=QQ^.RIGHT[I];PO^.LEFT[I]:=QQ;END;
{FOLLOWING NODE POINTS TO NEXT NODE}
  END;

PROCEDURE DELNODE;{DELETES NODE}
  VAR PL,PR:PT;
  BEGIN
    P:=Q; I:=1;
     TRAVERSE(P); IF P^.CONT[1]=TARGET THEN WRITELN('HIT');{FINDS NODE}
     FOR I:=1 TO 4 DO
       BEGIN
        PL:=P^.LEFT[I]; {FINDS PRECEDING NODE}
        PR:=P^.RIGHT[I]; {FINDS SUCCEEDING NODE}
        PL^.RIGHT[I]:=PR; {LINKS PRECEDING TO SUCCEEDING NODE}
        PR^.LEFT[I]:=PL;  {LINKS SUCCEEDING TO PRECEDING NODE}
        P^.LEFT[I]:=NIL;P^.RIGHT[I]:=NIL; {DISCONNECTS NODE}
       END;
  END;

BEGIN
    N[1]:='ITEMNO';N[2]:='PRODNAME';N[3]:='PRICE';
    N[4]:='ON-HAND';N[5]:='MFR'; {CONTENTS}
SEL:WRITELN('1-INITIALIZE. 2-DISPLAY. 3-INSERT. 4-DELETE. 5-END');
       READLN(S); {SELECTS OPERATION}
```

```
        CASE S OF {ROUTES TO SELECTED OPERATION}
         1:INITIALIZE;
         2: BEGIN {DISPLAY}
               WRITELN('1-ITEM-NO, 2-PROD NAME, 3-PRICE, 4-ON-HAND');
               READLN(K);
               DISPLAY(Q,K);
            END;
         3: BEGIN {INSERT}
               NEW(QQ);
               FOR I:=1 TO 4 DO BEGIN   {BEGINS ITERATION}
               DISPLAY(Q,I); {DISPLAYS NODE IN APPROPRIATE ORDER}
               WRITELN('PREC.',N[I],' NEW ',N[I],' ');{REQUESTS DATA}
               READ(TARGET);WRITE(' ');READLN(D); {INPUTS TARGET NODE}
               INSERT;END;
               WRITELN('MFR');READLN(D);QQ^.CONT[5]:=D;
            END;
          4: BEGIN {DELETE NODE BY ITEM NO.}
               WRITELN('ITEM NO.');READLN(TARGET);DELNODE;
            END;
          5:GOTO FIN;
        END;
      GOTO SEL;
 FIN:
END.
```

The main program sets up an array of *titles* and outputs the selection menu. Note how efficiently the CASE statement supports the menu.

4.6 SUMMARY AND DISCUSSION

The linked list is the appropriate data structure for tasks involving addition and deletion of nodes. This is an important class and covers a wide area of application. We have given an example of its application to a specific scheduling task, but scheduling itself has important applications beyond our simple example. For example, consider an *artificial intelligence* task in which an attempt is made to reach a conclusion based on a database of information. One approach might call for the construction of a linked list of nodes containing the atomic bits of information. This list is then subjected to one or more logical tests. Frequent additions and deletions are made until the logical test is satisfied. Clearly, the linked list will facilitate this procedure.

The multiply-linked list is a particularly fascinating example of a data structure that simplifies an otherwise difficult task. At first, devising an algorithm that will provide multiple paths through a lengthy list of items is intimidating. However, once the multiply-linked list is selected, the algorithm starts to become obvious. The inventory program is a good illustration of this process.

PROGRAMMING PROJECTS

4.1 Modify the scheduling program so that an appointment can be directly removed without specifying a preceding appointment.

4.2 Extend the capacity of the scheduling program by making it disk-based.

4.3 Create a personal appointment calendar to cover a calendar month. Display options should include (a) appointments for any specified date, (b) all appointments at a specified time for the entire month, (c) all appointments for a given day of the week for the entire month, and (d) all appointments in alphabetical order based on names.

4.4 Modify the inventory program so that all items supplied from a particular manufacturer can be displayed in item order. Assume a maximum of five manufacturers.

5 Recursion

5.1 FLOW STRUCTURE

Flow structure, another important parameter in programming, defines the potential paths that may be taken by data structures as they move through a program. Flow structures have not been as extensively developed as data structures, but they are equally decisive in shaping the resulting program. An ill-considered choice of flow structure will lengthen and complicate the program in much the same way as a poor data structure choice.

There are many types of flow structures. Data may follow a linear path through a program with only a few jumps ahead or behind (production line flow). Data may pursue a binary treelike branching flow based on a yes/no decision for each statement (tree flow). The program may perform a single operation and then wait for a decision by the user (tool box flow). The potential flow structures are analogous to and as numerous as data structures.

This chapter is restricted to the study of *recursion.* Recursion is one of the more important flow structures, one that has been most thoroughly investigated. We need to be conversant with recursion in order to continue our study of data structures.

5.2 CONCEPTS AND REQUIREMENTS

A programming language has recursive capability when it supports functions and subprograms that can call themselves. For this to be possible, the language must first of all support free-standing (independent) functions and subprograms. (The Pascal procedure is an example of a free-standing subprogram.) Second, when a subprogram calls itself with a new set of parameters, the preceding set must be saved for use on exit from the newly called subprogram. Also to meet practical needs, the language must permit very deep nesting (subprograms must be able to call themselves many times).

Not all programming languages support recursion. Pascal, APL, LISP, and PL1 support recursion, but only some versions of BASIC do. Microsoft BASIC allows subroutines to call themselves but does not actually support recursion. Recursion is supported in full by SBASIC on microcomputers, BASIC-PLUS on mainframes, and by several new compiler BASICS. All BASICS can be extended to support recursion, but this leads to impractical complications. Therefore, we will use SBASIC and Pascal from here on. We advise programmers who want to use recursion to choose a language that directly supports it.

Recursion can be approached by comparing it with its cousin, *iteration.* Although some tasks can be handled with equal *efficiency* by either recursion or iteration, the two are fundamentally different flow structures, recursion being the more powerful one.

The basic difference between recursion and iteration lies in the evaluation process. Iteration always generates evaluated variables for each iteration (pass). It produces a stream of evaluated results, starting with the first pass and ending with the last. Iteration is unidirectional. It never backs up, and there is never a need to. Recursion, on the other hand, *must* be bidirectional. It proceeds through recursive calls without generating an evaluated result until it bottoms. Then, it uses the bottom result to move up to the first call, evaluating results as it moves.

Computing the *n*th root of a number provides a good comparison. Suppose we wish to find $2^{1/8}$ by iteration and recursion. Iteration requires a series of realized computations given by

$$W = SQR(2) \quad (2^{1/2})$$

$$W = SQR(W) \quad (2^{1/4})$$

$$W = SQR(W) \quad (2^{1/8})$$

The recursive solution would be realized by

$$W = SQR(SQR(SQR(2)))$$

The leftmost SQR can not be computed because it requires a solution of the next SQR to the right. This in turn awaits the solution of the next SQR to the right. This term can be computed because it calls for the square root of 2. Once this is found, the previous SQR can be computed. This result permits the leftmost SQR to be finally evaluated.

This example is not intended to demonstrate the superiority of recursion over iteration for this operation, nor does it do so. However, it does expose a fundamental difference in flow structures. By now the reader must realize the value of such a discovery. A new structure, be it data or flow, is potentially valuable. It holds out the promise that this structure may match a task and simplify an otherwise intimidating undertaking. We shall see that this is indeed true of recursion.

Finding factorials provides another demonstration of the difference in flow structure between iteration and recursion. Figure 5.1 shows pseudocode programs for finding factorial n ($n!$) by iteration and recursion, along with sample outputs.

```
FACT(N) /ASSUMES THE VALUE OF N FACTORIAL
BEGIN
     SET FACT = 1
     SET I = 1
       WHILE I =< N DO
         BEGIN
           SET FACT = FACT *I
         END
END
```

I	FACT	FACT*I
1	1	1
2	2	1*2
3	3	1*2*3
4	4	1*2*3*4

(a)

```
FACT(N) /ASSUMES THE VALUE OF N FACTORIAL
 BEGIN
     SET FACT = 1
     IF N<>1 THEN DO
          SET FACT = N*FACT(N-1)
 END
```

CALL	N	RESULT
1	4	$FACT_4$=4*FACT(3)
2	3	$FACT_3$=3*FACT(2)
3	2	$FACT_2$=2*FACT(1)
4	1	$FACT_1$=1
	(FACT(1) EVALUATED)	
3	2	$FACT_2$=2*1
2	3	$FACT_3$=3*2*1
1	4	$FACT_4$=4*3*2*1

(b)

Figure 5.1 Comparison of iteration and recursion: (a) $n!$ by iteration; (b) $n!$ by recursion.

Figure 5.1*a* gives the iterative solution and sample output for $n = 4$. The program is straightforward. The first pass ($I = 1$), computes 1×1 and places a 1 in FACT. I increments to 2 in the second pass, and FACT is updated to $1 \times 2 = 2$. By the final pass, we get the definition for 4! equal to $1 \times 2 \times 3 \times 4$.

Figure 5.1*b* gives the recursive solution plus sample output. The first call to Fact(4) proceeds to SET FACT = 4 * FACT(3). The program cannot process past this point until it evaluates FACT(3). Call 1 is therefore held *pendant* (i.e., hanging or suspended). On call 2, the same thing happens at SET FACT=3*FACT(2). The sample output shows that all calls are held pendant until call 4. There, FACT(1) is evaluated. This permits FACT(2) to be evaluated, then FACT(3), and finally at the top call level, FACT(4). This final evaluation gives 4*3*2*1, the definition of 4!.

The Figure 5.1 subprogram contains the basic elements of an efficient recursive function: an identifying name that makes it possible to call the function, and an argument list that facilitates changing the function values. Also evident is the terminating condition contained in the IF statement. Without this statement, the function would continue calling itself until the system stacks are full.

Not so evident is the fact that when the function emerges from a lower-level call into the next higher level, the original values of the higher-level variables are restored. Note how N increases from 2 to 4 as the call level increases from 3 to 1. This action is required by recursion. It is described as parameter passing by value instead of address and is usually accomplished by placing higher-level calls in a stack before entering a lower level and removing these same values when emerging. It is the capacity of this stack that limits recursive nesting.

5.3 APPLICATION CRITERIA

Tasks exhibit flow structures as well as data structures. Tasks appropriate to recursive programs can be identified by abstracting their most characteristic flow structure. If the flow structure can be efficiently described by a recursive definition, the task is a likely candidate for recursion. The rationale for this test is demonstrated next.

Let us apply this test to the task of building a singly-linked list headfirst (nodes inserted at the beginning of the list). We attempt to define this task recursively. Let L_E = an empty list, L_S, the list, $n+$, node insertion, and the slash (/) signify *or*. Then, the task can be defined by

$$L_S = L_E/n + L_S \tag{5.1}$$

This definition is both concise and efficient. We show next that it can generate lists of any length.

$$L_{S1} = L_E \quad \text{(empty list)} \tag{5.2}$$

$$L_{S2} = n + L_{S1} \quad \text{(list with one node)} \tag{5.3}$$

$$L_{S3} = n + L_{S2} \quad \text{(list with two nodes)} \tag{5.4}$$

and so on.

Next apply this test to traversing an existing list (singly- or doubly-linked). This task can be defined recursively by

$$L_P = L_P \backslash L_P + n \tag{5.5}$$

where $L_P =$ node location and $+n$ advances L_P to the next node. This definition permits us to move through every node in the list starting from the head node. For example,

$$L_{P1} = L_P \quad \text{(first node)} \tag{5.6}$$

$$L_{P2} = L_{P1} + n \quad \text{(second node)} \tag{5.7}$$

$$L_{P3} = L_{P2} + n \quad \text{(third node)} \tag{5.8}$$

We now try to define adjacency matrix construction recursively. Input consists of pairs of data defining linked nodes. The operation calls for inserting a 1 at an appropriate position in a zeroed matrix. A moment's consideration reveals that each phase of this operation is self-contained. Each data pair completely establishes a link. Succeeding operations do not build upon preceding ones as in the first two examples. Therefore, we conclude that the recursive flow structure is not called for.

The rationale of the test should now be clear. The recursive definition is more than a static definition. It describes an operation and is in itself an algorithm. If the definition is concise and efficient, so is the algorithm.

5.4 EXAMPLES

5.4.1 Singly-Linked List

Figure 5.2 shows recursive SBASIC and Pascal procedures for building and traversing a singly-linked list. The traversing operation is here used to display the keys of the list. These procedures reveal another interesting aspect of recursion. Notice in all cases that if the recursive call were omitted, the operation would have been performed just once. In RBUILD one node would have been inserted, and in RDISPLAY one key would have been displayed. It is the recursive call that causes the operation to repeat. This gives us another valuable way to view recursive programming. The programming procedure can be viewed as a teaching (or learning process). The computer is led through the desired operation once. Then the recursive call directs it to continue repeating the operation with progressively altered parameters.

```
PROCEDURE RBUILD(J=INTEGER) ;BUILDS LINKED LIST
 VAR TEMP=INTEGER
  IF J<>0 THEN  ;TERMINATING CONDITION
   BEGIN
   TEMP= AVPNT  ;TEMPORARY POINTER
   AVPNT=AVAIL(TEMP,2) ;POINTS TO NEXT SOURCE NODE
   AVAIL(TEMP,1)=J ;SET KEY
   AVAIL(TEMP,2)=P ;POINT NEW NODE TO OLD P
   P=TEMP \POINT P TO NEW NODE
   RBUILD J-1 ;RECURSIVE CALL
 END
END

PROCEDURE RDISPLAY(PP=INTEGER) ;DISPLAYS LIST
  VAR JJ=INTEGER
  JJ=PP \PROTECT HEAD POINTER OF LIST
  PRINT AVAIL(JJ,1)   ;DISPLAY KEYS
  IF AVAIL(JJ,2)<>0 THEN ;TERMINATING CONDITION
RDISPLAY AVAIL(JJ,2) ;RECURSIVE CALL
END
```

(a)

```
PROCEDURE RBUILD(NN:INTEGER); {BUILDS LIST}
 BEGIN
  IF NN<>0 THEN
    BEGIN
      NEW(Q);
      Q^.RTPTR:=P; {Q POINTS TO FIRST NODE IN P LIST}
      Q^.KEY := NN; {FILLS KEY FIELD}
      P:= Q; {POINTS LISTPOINTER TO NEW NODE}
      RBUILD(NN-1); {CALLS RBUILD RECURSIVELY WITH DECREMENTED NN}
    END;
 END;


PROCEDURE RDISPLAY(P:LSTPT); {DISPLAYS LIST}
 BEGIN
   IF P<>NIL THEN {TERMINATING CONDITION}
    BEGIN
     WRITE(P^.KEY,' ');
     DISPLAY(P^.RTPTR);   {RECURSIVE CALL}
    END;
  END;
```

(b)

Figure 5.2 Recursive singly-linked list procedures: (a) SBASIC; (b) Pascal.

Figure 5.2 also reveals the similarity of SBASIC to Pascal. The language has the same block structure and the same procedure and function calls as Pascal. Therefore, it supports recursion as readily.

5.4.2 Binary Search

The power of recursive programming is only revealed by procedures containing two or more recursive calls. In these cases, recursion surpasses iteration in providing a simple way to handle otherwise difficult tasks. Iteration is appropriate when the flow of program control is known or perturbed only slightly. However, when the program flow is unknown and potentially highly convoluted, recursion is a must.

The binary search task illustrates the utility of recursion in a program with a convoluted flow structure. It also illustrates the *teaching* approach discussed earlier.

The binary search procedure provides a highly efficient way to search a vector (one-dimensional array) for a specific target. The vector must first be sorted into numeric order (usually increasing order). The value of the most central element is found. If the vector contains an odd number of elements, this is the true median; otherwise, the next higher element is used. If the target equals this value, the search is terminated. If the target is lower, the operation is repeated within the lower section. If the target is higher, operation is repeated within the upper section. Instead of wastefully searching the entire vector, the procedure searches only the section most likely to contain the target. This is clearly a highly efficient process.

Binary searching readily lends itself to recursive programming. There is really a single operation, inspection followed by division performed repeatedly with different parameters. We can program this task by leading the computer through one cycle followed by either a recursive call to the left or the right. Figure 5.3 gives a complete SBASIC program that sets up an array and then performs a binary search. Sample output is also shown.

To understand the BINSCH (binary search) procedure, focus first on the arguments L and M in the SBASIC procedure. On first call, L = the lowest element in the vector (1) and M, the highest (50). The operation

```
K=INT((L+M)/2)                                                    (5.9)
```

finds the midpoint. If the target is less than this midpoint, then K becomes the M for the recursive call and L remains 1. If the target is more than this midpoint, K + 1 becomes the new L, and M remains M. This procedure is then performed recursively, with L and M changing as dictated by the target value. The procedure is not only concise but, when understood, surprisingly straightforward. This is of course a good indication that we have matched the fundamental flow structure of the task.

The sample output (note the label *PATH* has been added for clarity) demonstrates the efficiency of the search pattern. The target 25 is found on the first call. Dividing the array of 50 elements in half gives 25 as the first comparison element. Searches for targets closer to the extremes require only a few more calls. Target 3 is found by five recursive calls to the left and one to the right. Target 46 is also found by five recursive calls. Compare this with the 46 comparisons required to move from the first element to the 46th if a linear search technique had been used.

Figure 5.4 shows the Pascal version of the binary search program. The program is fully annotated and very similar to the SBASIC one.

```
REM BINARY SEARCH
VAR TARGET,I,K=INTEGER
DIM INTEGER A(50)

PROCEDURE BINSCH(L,M=INTEGER) ;BINARY SEARCH
  K=INT((L+M)/2)   ; FINDS MIDPOINT
  PRINT A(K);
  IF A(K)<>TARGET THEN
   IF TARGET <A(K) THEN BINSCH L,K ELSE BINSCH K+1,M ;RECURSIVE CALLS
END

BEGIN
  FOR I=1 TO 50 ;SETS UP TEST VECTOR
  A(I)=I
  NEXT
  INPUT "TARGET";TARGET
  BINSCH 1,50  ;CALLS PROCEDURE
  PRINT
  PRINT"FOUND";A(K)
END
```

(a)

```
COMMAND? B:SEARCH
 TARGET? 25
 PATH (25)
 FOUND 25

COMMAND? B:SEARCH
 TARGET? 3
 PATH (25 13 7 4 2 3)
 FOUND 3

COMMAND? B:SEARCH
 TARGET? 46
 PATH (25 38 44 47 46)
 FOUND 46
```

(b)

***Figure* 5.3** Binary search (SBASIC): (a) program; (b) output.

5.4.3 Median-Ordered List

There are other possible lexical or numerical orderings, besides ascending or descending. One very useful type is median ordering. A median is an element that has an equal number of elements to its right and left (or above and below). For lists with odd numbers of nodes, the median node exists. For lists with even numbers of nodes, the median node does not exist. In this case, we will arbitrarily select the node closest to the head. The median list is formed by repeatedly extracting medians from the resulting divided lists and placing these medians in a new list.

The ordering procedure is illustrated by Figure 5.5. Removing the first median (5) from P_0 leaves two lists, L_2 and R_3. Node 5 is placed in list M, and the

```
PROGRAM BSEARCH(OUTPUT); {BINARY SEARCH}
 TYPE
   VECT=ARRAY[1..10] OF INTEGER;
   VAR I,K,TARGET:INTEGER;A:VECT;

PROCEDURE BINSCH(L,M:INTEGER);
 BEGIN
    K:=(L+M)DIV 2; {DIVIDES LIST}
    IF A[K]<>TARGET THEN {SEARCHES RECURSIVELY}
     BEGIN
      IF TARGET <A[K] THEN BINSCH(L,K) {SEARCHES LOWER HALF}
      ELSE BINSCH(K+1,M); {SEARCHES UPPPER HALF}
     END;
 END;

BEGIN
  FOR I:=1 TO 10 DO A[I]:=I; {SETS UP TEST VECTOR}
  WRITELN('TARGET'); READLN(TARGET); {GETS TARGET KEY}
  BINSCH(1,10); {CALLS PROCEDURE}
  WRITELN;
  WRITELN('FOUND ',A[K]); {OUTPUT}
END.
```

Figure 5.4 Binary search program (Pascal).

procedure is repeated on L_2. The median 1 is removed and placed in M. This leaves the empty lists L_3 and R_1. L_3 being empty, the procedure moves to R_1. Node 3 is extracted and placed in M. The level 1 (call 1) left list is now empty. Therefore, the procedure moves to the level 1 right list and proceeds as before. When P_0 is empty, M is complete.

This admittedly complicated operation can be replaced by a simpler schema that generates the same results. (Note a schema is just an alternate way of achieving a known result. We do not maintain that this is the way the processing occurs.) The schema is illustrated in Figure 5.6 and proceeds as follows: Imagine a parallel processing machine that is capable of partially completing a call, suspending that operation and proceeding to the next. We have met this machine earlier in our introduction to recursion. Using this machine, the first call (MEDIAN P_0) extracts the median 5 and leaves two suspended (pendant) calls, MEDIAN(L) (M(L)) and MEDIAN(R) (M(R)). M(L) operates on the left list 1 through 3, and M(R) operates on the right list, 6 through 10. The next call (pass) extracts the 1 and in turn leaves a new M(L) and M(R) on the left and an 8 and a M(L) and M(R) on the right. Each pass generates the same result, the maximum number of new lists increasing by the factor 2 each time. The procedure is continued until P_0 is exhausted. The median-ordered list is assembled by selecting the nodes from left to right and placing them tail first into M.

The median-ordered list is important. The targeting of medians is closely related to the binary search operation because each computation of K in the binary search routine actually identifies a new median. Therefore, we would suspect that median ordering plays a role in efficient searching. This it does. In the next chapter we show how.

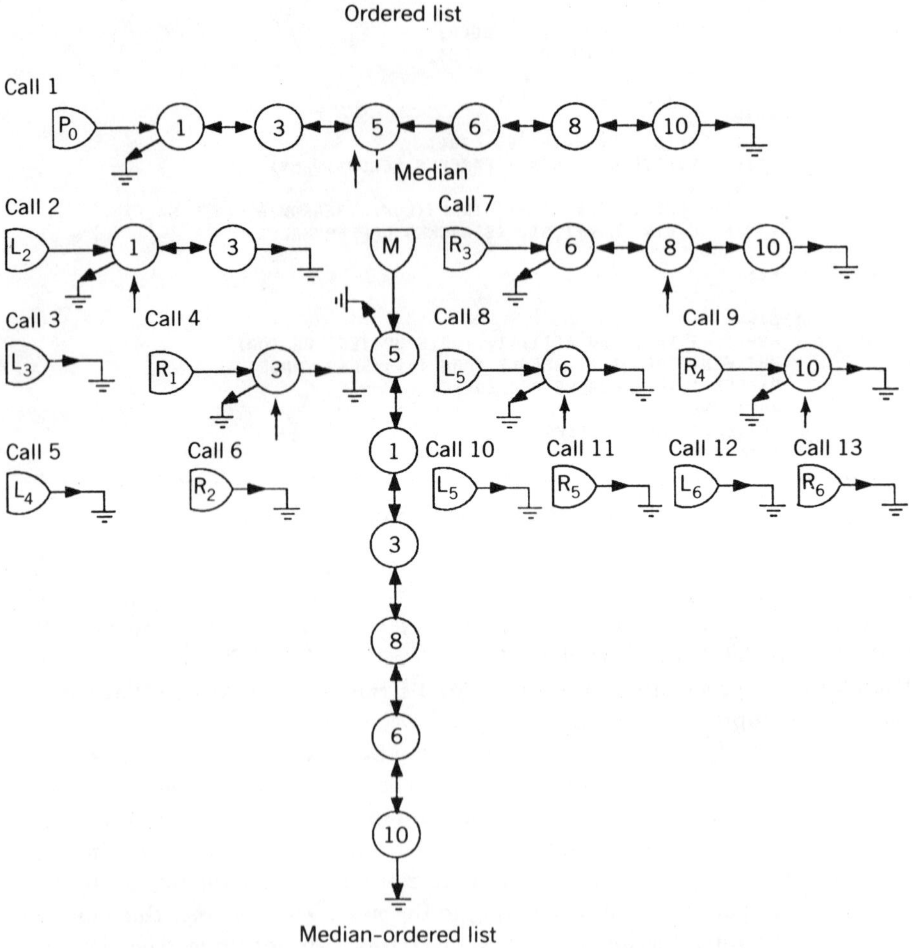

Figure 5.5 Construction of a median-ordered list.

5.4.4 Median-Ordering Programs

Figures 5.7 and 5.9 show SBASIC and Pascal programs that transform numerically ordered lists into median order. Both programs illustrate the ability of recursion to simplify an otherwise difficult task. This of course is what we have learned to expect from appropriate structuring. In both cases, we led the program through the operation for the first time. First we extracted the median from the numerically ordered list. Then, we terminated the left list, set a pointer to the right list, and inserted the median node into the median-ordered list. By

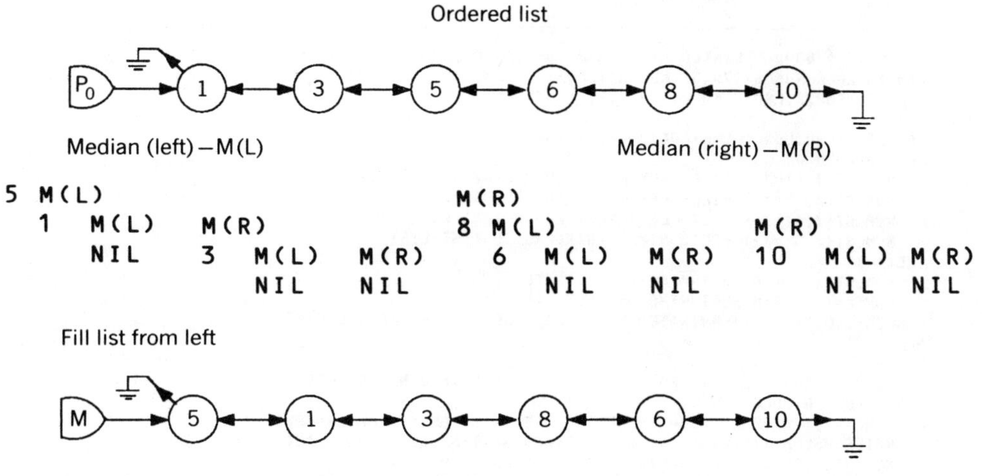

Figure 5.6 Schematic procedure for constructing the median-ordered list.

doing so, we recreated the initial conditions of each list. Then, we simply added recursive calls to the left and right lists, and we were finished. The recursive entries into and exits from the recursively called procedure are tortuous and difficult to predict in advance, but it was unnecessary for us to do so. Try duplicating this program with iteration in place of recursion. You will then appreciate the power of recursion.

Figure 5.7 shows the SBASIC program. Procedure BUILD constructs a doubly-linked test list with nodes in ascending numerical order. BUILD also constructs an empty list to receive the median-ordered nodes. Since SBASIC does not directly support pointers and nodes, we use the matrix simulation technique of Chapter 4. At the start of the run, NUMLST contains the test list, and MEDLST is empty. At the end of the run, NUMLST is empty, and MEDLST contains the median-ordered list.

The doubly-linked structure is necessary. The algorithm requires identification and separation of the median node and reconstitution of the resulting left and right lists. Therefore it must move to the left from the median node, to the last node in the left list so that the left list can be terminated. This action is facilitated by the doubly-linked structure.

Procedure MTRAVERSE is conventional and was composed by modifying an existing traversing function to handle doubly-linked lists. Procedure INSERTAIL is new. Unlike the previous inserting procedures, nodes are inserted tailfirst instead of headfirst. This is accomplished by first finding the last node in the list and then performing a normal insertion after this node.

Figure 5.7 Median-ordered list program (SBASIC).

```
REM SORTS A DOUBLY LINKED LIST INTO  MEDIAN ORDER
 DIM INTEGER NUMLST(25,3) MEDLST(25,3)
 VAR JJ,MPOS,S,LSPTR,MDORDPTR,J,I,K=INTEGER

 PROCEDURE BUILD  ;CONSTRUCTS TEST LIST
  FOR J=0 TO JJ
    MEDLST(J,1)=J  ;FILLS KEY FIELD IN MEDIAN ORDERED LIST
    NUMLST(J,1)=J ; FILLS KEY FIELD IN TEST LIST
    NUMLST(J,2)=J-1 ;SETS LEFT POINTER IN TEST LIST
    NUMLST(J,3)=J+1 ;SETS RIGHT POINTERS IN TEST LIST
  NEXT J
    NUMLST(JJ,3)=0  ;TERMINATES TEST LIST
    LSPTR=1 ; SETS BEGINNING OF TEST LIST
   MEDLST(0,3)=0  ;TERMINATES DUMMY NODE OF MEDIAN ORDERED LIST
END

PROCEDURE INSERTAIL(N=INTEGER) ;INSERTS NODES INTO MEDIAN ORDERED LIST TAIL FIRST
  VAR TEMP=INTEGER
    TEMP=0 ;TEMPORARY POINTER SET TO BEGINNING OF MEDIAN ORDERED LIST
    WHILE MEDLST(TEMP,3) <>0 DO TEMP=MEDLST(TEMP,3) ;FINDS LAST NODE
    MEDLST(N,3)=0  ;NEW MEDIAN NODE POINTED TO 0
    MEDLST(N,2)=TEMP ;LEFT NODE POINTED TO PREVIOUS LAST NODE
    MEDLST(TEMP,3)=N ;PREVIOUS NODE POINTED TO NEW NODE
END

PROCEDURE MTRAVERSE(LSZ,LRP=INTEGER) ;FINDS POINTER TO MEDIAN NODE IN TEST LIST
  VAR KK=INTEGER
   KK=LSZ  ;TEMPORARY VALUE GIVING THE RELATIVE POSITION OF MEDIAN
   MPOS=LRP ;POINTER TO MEDIAN NODE SET AT START OF TEST LIST
   WHILE KK<>1 DO ;POINTS MPOS TO MEDIAN NODE
    BEGIN
     MPOS=NUMLST(MPOS,3)
     REM ADVANCE  MPOS  THROUGH TEST LIST UNTIL MEDIAN  POSITION  IS REACHED
     KK=KK-1
    END
END

PROCEDURE MEDIAN(LSIZE,LLSTPR=INTEGER) ;FINDS MEDIANS AND BUILDS MEDIAN ORDERED LIST
  VAR N,SIZEL,SIZER,RP,LL=INTEGER
    REM FIND LIST SIZES AND MEDIAN POSITION
   LL=LLSTPR
   IF LSIZE <> 0 THEN ;TERMINATING CONDITION OF RECURSIVE CALLS
   BEGIN
    SIZER=FINT(LSIZE/2) ;FINDS SIZE OF RIGHT LIST
    SIZEL=SIZER ;FINDS SIZE OF LEFT LIST FOR ODD LENGTH
    IF FINT(LSIZE/2)=LSIZE/2 THEN SIZEL=SIZER-1 ;FINDS LEFT LIST SIZE FOR EVEN LENGTH
    N=SIZEL+1 ;FINDS RELATIVE POSITION OF MEDIAN FOR ALL LENGTHS
    MTRAVERSE N,LLSTPR  ;FINDS POINTER TO MEDIAN NODE
    REM SPLIT LIST IN TWO
    IF MPOS<>0 THEN NUMLST(MPOS-1,3)=0 ;TERMINATES LEFT LIST
      RP=MPOS+1 ;SETS POINTER TO RIGHT LIST
      NUMLST(RP,2)=0 ;ISOLATES LEFT POINTER OF RIGHT LIST
      IF MPOS<>0 THEN NUMLST(MPOS,3)=0 ;ISOLATES RIGHT SIDE OF MEDIAN NODE
      IF MPOS<>0 THEN NUMLST(MPOS,2)=0 ;ISOLATES LEFT SIDE OF MEDIAN NODE
      INSERTAIL MPOS ;INSERTS MEDIAN NODE IN MEDIAN ORDERED LIST
      MEDIAN SIZEL,LL  ;RECURSIVE CALL TO LEFT LIST
      MEDIAN SIZER,RP  ;RECURSIVE CALL TO RIGHT LIST
     END
  END

  REM MAIN PROGRAM
   BEGIN
      10 INPUT "SIZE";JJ ;SETS SIZE OF TEST LIST
      BUILD ;CALLS BUILD PROCEDURE
      MEDIAN JJ,LSPTR ;CALLS RECURSIVE MEDIAN PROCEDURE
```

```
  PRINT
 REM DISPLAYS ARRAY CONTAINING MEDIAN ORDERED LIST
  PRINT "MEDLIST ARRAY"
  PRINT
  FOR I=0 TO JJ
       FOR K=1 TO 3
        PRINT MEDLST(I,K);
       NEXT K
      PRINT
  NEXT I
END
```

Procedure MEDIAN is the recursive heart of the program. Its input consists of the size of the list and a pointer to the list. Recursive calls access the procedure with the appropriate sizes and list references. In all cases, a zero size causes the call to bottom and emerge at the next highest level. Note that since the left call is first, the program actually burrows left, exhausting all left lists before proceeding to the next right list. After extracting the median from this next right list, it again burrows left in the resulting lists.

The main program sets the size of the test list, calls BUILD, and displays the end result. The end result is an array (N by 3, in this case) containing the median-ordered list. This array is accessed by starting with a pointer to row 0 and using normal list traversal. Column 1 contains the keys, column 2, the left pointers, and column 3, the right pointers. The zero in column three is the NIL symbol. The reader should traverse the arrays shown in Figure 5.8 to see that the contained list is indeed median ordered.

Figure 5.9 shows the Pascal version of the median-ordering program. The type declarations establish a node with a key integer field and a left- and right-pointer field. This structure is used for both test and median-ordered lists. MTRAVERSE is entered with the position of the median node and the pointer to the list. It outputs a pointer to the median node. This pointer is used in MEDIAN to terminate the right side of the left list generated by extracting the median. It is also used to set a pointer to the newly established right list. As previously noted, this action is facilitated by the doubly-linked structure. INSERTTAIL first finds the last node in the median-ordered list and then inserts the median node after this node. Note that both left and right nodes must be targeted.

MEDIAN is the recursive heart of the program. The program terminates when the pointer to the test list segments equal NIL. Until that occurs, the position of the median node is found and extracted, lists divided, and left and right recursive calls made. Note that before nodes to the left or right are terminated, a check must be made to ensure that these nodes exist. Otherwise, the program will be attempting to access pointer fields that do not exist. These checks

```
SIZE? 6

MEDLIST ARRAY
 0 0 3
 1 3 2
 2 1 5
 3 0 1
 4 5 6
 5 2 4
 6 4 0
```

(a)

```
SIZE? 10

MEDLIST ARRAY
 0 0 5
 1 2 3
 2 5 1
 3 1 4
 4 3 8
 5 0 2
 6 8 7
 7 6 9
 8 4 6
 9 7 10
 10 9 0
```

(b)

Figure 5.8 Output arrays of SBASIC median-ordering program: (a) list of size 6; (b) list of size 10.

are seen in the statements beginning IF RIGHTP<>NIL. . . and IF TP<>NIL. . .

The main program establishes an empty test list and builds and displays the test list. It creates a dummy head node for the median-ordered list. This dummy node prevents the accessing error described here. MEDIAN is called, and the median-ordered list is displayed. Figure 5.10 shows some sample outputs.

5.5 SUMMARY

Structures play a crucial role in programming. The concept can be generalized to include more than data structures. Flow structure, the pattern of potential

```
PROGRAM MEDLIST(INPUT, OUTPUT);
  TYPE
    REF=^NODE;
    NODE = RECORD
            KEY:INTEGER;
            LEFT:REF;
            RIGHT:REF;
          END;
     VAR MDPTR,TEMP,LRPTR,MDORDPTR:REF;SIZE,N:INTEGER;

     PROCEDURE MTRAVERSE(POS:INTEGER;X:REF; VAR Y:REF);
     {OUTPUTS POINTER TO MEDIAN NODE}
      VAR K:INTEGER;
      {POS-POSITION OF MEDIAN NODE; X-POINTER TO}
      {ORIGINAL LIST, Y-POINTER TO MEDIAN NODE}
          BEGIN
            K:=POS
            Y:=X; {SETS MEDIAN POINTER TO BEGINNING OF LIST}
              WHILE K<>1 DO
                BEGIN
                  Y:=Y^.RIGHT; {MOVES RIGHT}
                  K:=K-1; {DECREMENTS K}
                 END;
           END;

     PROCEDURE INSERTTAIL(VAR X:REF); {INSERTS MEDIAN NODE TAIL FIRST}
        VAR TEMP:REF;
          BEGIN
            TEMP:=MDORDPTR; {PREVENTS CHANGING MDORDPTR}
            WHILE TEMP^.RIGHT<>NIL DO TEMP:=TEMP^.RIGHT;
            {FINDS LAST NODE IN LIST}
            X^.RIGHT := NIL; {RIGHT POINTER OF NEW NODE SET TO NIL}
            TEMP^.RIGHT:=X; {POINTS LAST NODE OF OLD TAIL NODE TO NEW NODE}
            X^.LEFT:=TEMP; {POINTS LEFT POINTER OF NEW NODE TO OLD TAIL NODE}
          END;

     PROCEDURE MEDIAN(LLRPTR:REF;SIZEE:INTEGER); {CONSTRUCTS MEDIAN ORDER LIST}
     {$A-}  {ENABLES RECURSIVE STACK}
       VAR SIZEL,SIZER:INTEGER;RIGHTP,TP,MMDPTR:REF;
       BEGIN
       IF LLRPTR<>NIL THEN
         BEGIN

            {FINDS POSITION OF MEDIAN NODE}
            IF ODD(SIZEE) THEN BEGIN SIZEE:=SIZEE DIV 2 +1;SIZEL:=SIZEE -1;
                 SIZER:=SIZEL; END
            ELSE BEGIN SIZEE:=SIZEE DIV 2; SIZEL:=SIZEE -1;SIZER:=SIZEE;END;
            MTRAVERSE(SIZEE,LLRPTR,MMDPTR); {FINDS POINTER TO MEDIAN NODE}

            {SPLITS LIST IN TWO}
            RIGHTP:=MMDPTR^.RIGHT;{SETS POINTER TO RIGHT LIST}

     IF RIGHTP<>NIL THEN RIGHTP^.LEFT := NIL;
     {TERMINATES LEFT SIDE OF RIGHT LIST}
     TP:=MMDPTR^.LEFT; {CREATES A TEMPORARY POINTER TO END OF LEFT LIST}
     IF TP<>NIL THEN TP^.RIGHT:= NIL ELSE LLRPTR:=NIL; {ISOLATES MEDIAN NODE}
     {LRPNT --LEFT LIST, RIGHTP--TO RIGHT LIST.}
     {SIZEL IS LSIZE OF LEFT LIST, SIZER IS LSIZE OF RIGHT LIST}

     INSERTTAIL(MMDPTR);{INSERTS MEDIAN NODE INTO MEDIAN ORDERED LIST}
     MEDIAN(LLRPTR,SIZEL); {LEFT RECURSIVE CALL}
     MEDIAN(RIGHTP,SIZER); {RIGHT RECURSIVE CALL}
  END;
 END;
```

Figure 5.9 Median-ordered list program (Pascal).

Figure 5.9 (Continued)

```
   {$I B:BUILD}  {BUILDS TEST LIST}

BEGIN  {MAIN}
   LRPTR:=NIL; N:=37;BDSL(LRPTR,N);{INITIALIZES LIST AND BUILDS TEST LIST}
   {DISPLAYS TEST LIST} WRITELN;WRITELN('TEST LIST');WRITELN;
   TEMP:=LRPTR; WHILE TEMP<>NIL DO BEGIN WRITE(TEMP^.KEY,' ');
   TEMP:=TEMP^.RIGHT;END;
   WRITELN;
   NEW(MDORDPTR); {CREATES DUMMY NODE FOR MEDIAN ORDERED LIST}
   MDORDPTR^.RIGHT:=NIL;
   MDORDPTR^.KEY := 0;
   MEDIAN(LRPTR,N); {CALLS MEDIAN}
   WRITELN;WRITELN('MEDIAN ORDERED LIST');WRITELN;
   MDORDPTR:=MDORDPTR^.RIGHT; WHILE MDORDPTR<>NIL DO
   {DISPLAYS MEDIAN ORDERED LIST}
   BEGIN WRITE(MDORDPTR^.KEY,' ');MDORDPTR:=MDORDPTR^.RIGHT;END;

END.
```

```
Running

   TEST LIST

   1 2 3 4 5

   MEDIAN-ORDERED LIST

   3 1 2 4 5



   TEST LIST

   1 2 3 4 5 6 7 8 9 10

   MEDIAN-ORDERED LIST

   5 2 1 3 4 8 6 7 9 10



   TEST LIST

   1 2 3 4 5 6 7 8 9 10 11 12 13 14 15 16 17 18 19 20 21 22 23 24 25 26 27 28 29 30

   31 32 33 34 35 36 37

   MEDIAN-ORDERED LIST

   19 9 4 2 1 3 6 5 7 8 14 11 10 12 13 16 15 17 18 28 23 21 20 22 25 24 26 27 33 30

   29 31 32 35 34 36 37
```

Figure 5.10 Sample printouts of median-ordered list programs.

paths through which data may move, is at least as important as data structure. Other structures can be found in programs—syntactic and semantic structures, for example. The general study of structures and their role in effective programming is beyond the scope of this text, but as the reader may suspect, structural considerations are crucial to the formulation of sophisticated algorithms.

Recursion is a flow structure that has been studied intensively. We have defined it and shown how it differs from *iteration*. Often, iteration can be substituted for recursion in algorithms containing a single recursive call. When this is true, it usually means that the flow structure of the algorithm is predictable. However, when the flow of data becomes complex and unpredictable, iteration fails or becomes too complicated, and recursion is required. This is the case in algorithms that make multiple recursive calls.

Recursion demonstrates its appropriateness in programs with complex data flows, by simplifying and clarifying the task. This we know is always the effect of an appropriate choice of structure and is indeed a measure of its appropriateness. Recursion passes this test in the applications covered in this chapter. In complex data flow tasks such as binary searching and median ordering, recursion relieves the programmer of the need to know the paths data will actually take. The programmer needs only to lead the computer through one cycle of the task and then to call the procedure recursively the required number of times. Caution and care must of course be taken, to be certain that the task's data flow can be efficiently described using recursion, but after that the simplification is impressive.

In succeeding chapters, we will depend heavily on multiple recursive calls to simplify otherwise *complicated* tasks. The reader's appreciation of the contribution of this particular flow structure will be considerably enhanced. (The reader should now begin to wonder about the potential of other flow structures.)

PROGRAMMING PROJECTS

5.1 The *Fibonnacci sequence* is a sequence of integers such that each element (except for the first two) is the sum of the two preceding ones. For example,

$$0, 1, 1, 2, 3, 5, 8, 13, 21, 34, 55, \ldots$$

Define this sequence recursively, and compose a program to generate any three contiguous terms.

5.2 Pseudorandom numbers can be generated by the Box algorithm. N random numbers are chosen from a random number table. The $N + 1$ number is formed by adding the first random number to the Nth one and applying modulus N. Define this procedure recursively, and compose a program to generate a stream of random numbers.

5.3 Compose a trinary search program. Compare with the binary search program in this chapter.

5.4 Compose a program that will find its way through a maze. Represent the maze as a matrix (later we will find a better data structure), and direct the computer to find its way using trial and error recursively. You will have to deal with the problem of the computer cycling endlessly either because it has found a closed path or is simply repeating a sequence of moves.

5.5 The Tower of Hanoi problem is one that can be solved elegantly by recursion. The task begins with three pegs, one of which has n rings on it. Each higher ring is smaller than the one it sits on. The n rings must be moved from the first peg to the last obeying the following restrictions:

(a) Only the top ring on any peg may be moved.
(b) A larger ring may not rest on a smaller one.
(c) the center peg may be used for intermediate storage.

Define this task recursively, and compose a program that will print out the required moves.

6 The Binary Tree

6.1 BASIC STRUCTURE

The binary tree is a linked node structure that resembles a real tree turned upside down. It contains an entrance node called a *root node* from which branches (links) exit and connect to lower nodes. For the binary tree, no more than two branches can exit from any node and, unless otherwise designated, these branches are assumed to be directed downward. The tree can only be entered from the top via the root node. The tree replicates itself recursively by adding branches and nodes to the existing structure. Figure 6.1 shows some sample binary trees.

The binary tree is a more complex—and therefore more interesting structure—than the data structures we have studied so far. Like the linked list, it is a dynamic structure that occupies only as much space as needed. It is two-dimensional. Therefore, it can match the structures of more complex tasks than can the linked list. (In fact, the linked list can usefully be considered as a simple tree with only left or right links.) Because the tree is a complex structure, some definitions are required before we can proceed with our discussion. These are given next and illustrated in Figure 6.1:

Level Level designates the number of links connecting a node to the root. The root is at level 0; the nodes immediately below it (connected by 1 link) are at level 1. Those two links below, are at level 2, and so on.

Subtree Since each deeper level node replicates the tree, it in turn can be viewed as the root node of all nodes connected to it at deeper levels. In effect, a tree several levels deep can be considered as a concatenation of subtrees.

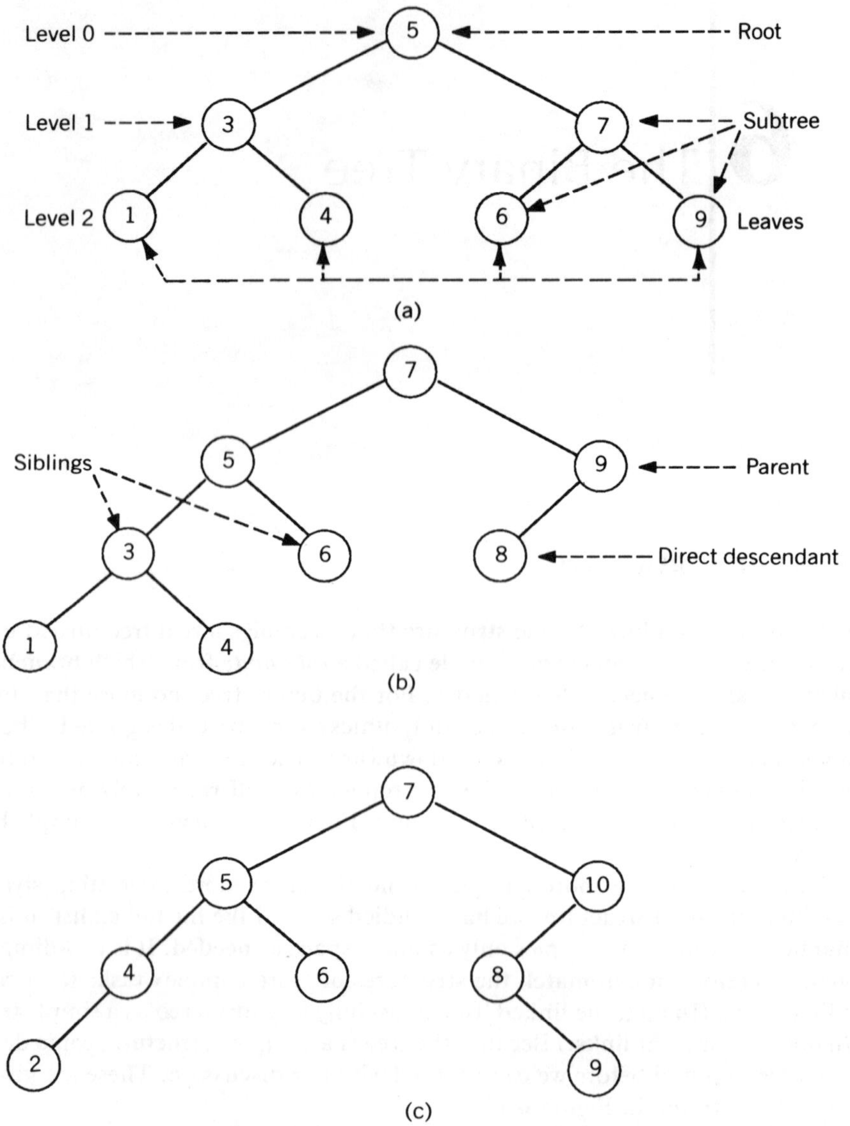

Figure 6.1 Binary trees: (a) complete tree; (b) unbalanced tree; (c) balanced tree.

Leaves As we descend through a tree, nodes will be reached that connect to no deeper level nodes. These are called *leaves.*

Parents, descendants, and siblings A node is the parent of all nodes below it that it directly connects to. Nodes directly connected to their parents are called *direct descendants,* and all direct descendants of the same parent are called *siblings.*

Ordered binary tree Links leaving a binary tree node may be either left or right directed. If specific meanings are assigned to these directions, the tree is ordered; if not, it is unordered.

Complete, unbalanced, and balanced tree The complete tree (Figure 6.1*a*) is symmetrical around the root and subroots; the unbalanced tree (Figure 6.1*b*) is not. The balanced tree (Figure 6.1*c*) may differ in symmetry by one node at any level.

6.1.1 Definition

The binary tree is readily defined recursively. Let T represent any binary tree. Let S represent a subtree consisting of a node with exiting left and right pointers targeted on NILs. Let the operator "+" means that a subtree is added to a pointer previously directed to a NIL. When the subtree is added to a left-directed pointer, it is labeled S_L; when added to a right-directed pointer, it is labeled S_R. These constructs are illustrated in Figure 6.2. The binary tree is then defined recursively by

$$T = S/T + (S_L|S_R) \tag{6.1}$$

where slash means *or* and the vertical bar means *and/or.*

Eq. (6.1) defines binary trees of any depth. For example,

$$T_1 = S \tag{6.2}$$

defines a tree consisting of the root node alone (Figure 6.2*a*). (Note that the links terminating in NILs may be omitted.)

$$T_2 = T_1 + S_L \tag{6.3}$$

defines a root node plus a node connected to its left pointer (Figure 6.2*b*).

$$T_3 = T_1 + (S_L \text{ and } S_R) \tag{6.4}$$

defines the tree shown in Figure 6.2*c*. If linking a subtree to a left pointer is assigned a different meaning than linking it to a right pointer, the binary tree defined by Eq. (6.1) is ordered. If not, it is unordered.

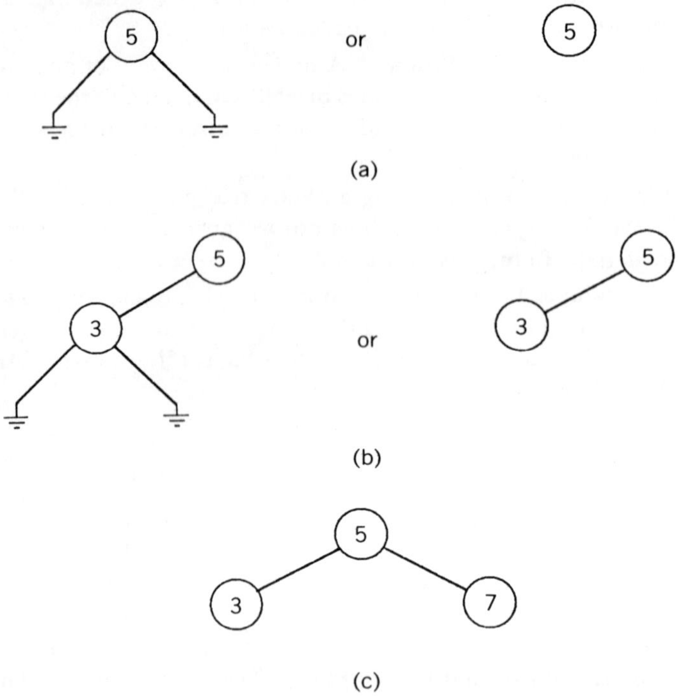

Figure 6.2 Recursive elements of the binary tree: (a) $T_1 = S$; (b) $T_2 = T_1 + (S_L)$; (c) $T_3 = T_1 + (S_L \text{ and } S_R)$.

6.2 GENERAL APPLICATIONS

The ordered binary tree is a complex and interesting structure. It is more versatile and has properties not found in any of the previously studied structures. Remembering that our goal is to match data structure to task, our interest should be aroused by the potential of this structure. Indeed, the ordered binary tree is one of our most useful structures and is widely used in many important applications. Let us consider some of the properties of the ordered binary tree that make it so useful.

6.2.1 Shape

The ordered binary tree possesses *shape.* This is true shape and not the topological shape of the digraph. (Topological shape refers only to connections between nodes and not to their locations.) The shape of the ordered binary tree results from the left and right concatenation of subtrees. Although the ordered binary tree must always look like a tree, appropriate interpretation of left or right links permits it to represent many other physical or abstract shapes.

Figure 6.3 illustrates this property of the binary tree. Figure 6.3*a* shows a string consisting of various sized beads. Suppose that we are concerned not with the sizes of the beads but only with the progression from large to small or small to large. The *shape* of this progression is shown by Figure 6.3*b* in which the left-directed link means *smaller than* the right-directed link, *larger than.* This is an abstract representation that eliminates bead size and simplifies comparisons based on large–small, small–large progressions. For example, we can see at a glance that the string in Figure 6.3*c* does not match (is not isomorphic to) Figure 6.3*a*. We can also quickly see that the substring of Figure 6.3*c* could have come from two locations in the Figure 6.3*a* pattern (subisomorphism). The facility with which these comparisons can be made by eye also applies to the computer.

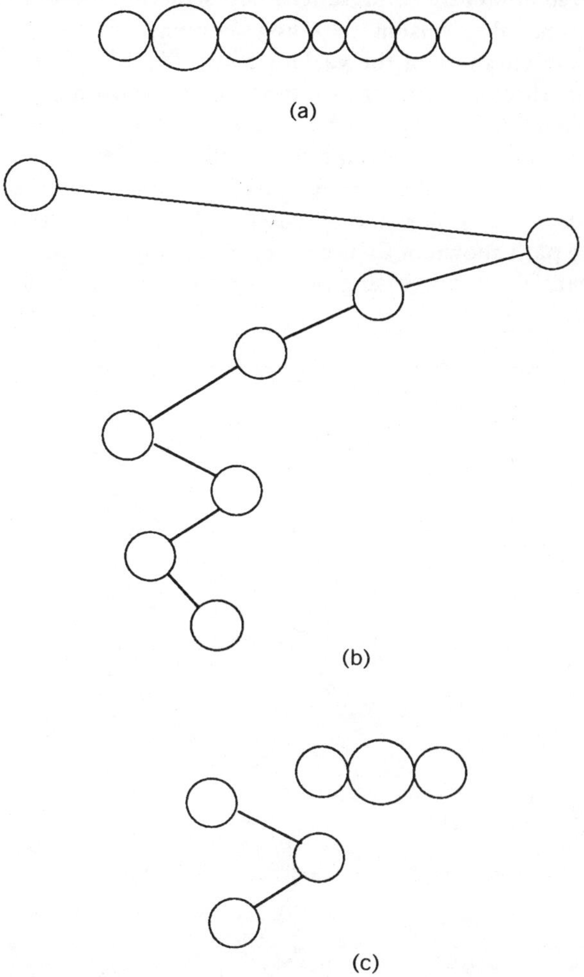

Figure 6.3 Binary tree representations of bead strings.

Figure 6.4 extends this application. Figure 6.4*a* represents all the bead string large–small, small–large configurations produced by a manufacturer. Individual configurations are found by starting at the root and following any path through the tree terminating in a leaf. Tracing out every path would give the entire ensemble. This representation could answer the question; does a particular bead string come from this manufacturers stock?

Figure 6.4 could also represent the abstract shape of a forked maze that presents either a left or right fork choice to its explorer. The root is the entrance and one or more of the terminal nodes could be designated as the exit. Finding the path or paths through this maze is now a simple matter of starting from an exit node and retracing links to the root.

Figure 6.5 illustrates a business application of the ordered binary tree. In this case, the ordered binary tree represents a flow structure rather than a data structure. This tree (called a decision tree) shows how checks are processed at a bank. Each node represents one of the various tests (T1, T2, . . .) that the check is required to pass through in order to determine its disposition (A1, A2, . . .). For example, the root might represent the question, Is the check originator a depositor? If the check survives the test, it moves to the left; if not, it moves to the right. The terminal nodes reached determine the disposition. The tree shows all possible routes a check may follow and all possible dispositions. An individual check might take the path shown in Figure 6.5*b,* for example. This structure could be used to compare check-processing procedures among banks or to streamline a given procedure.

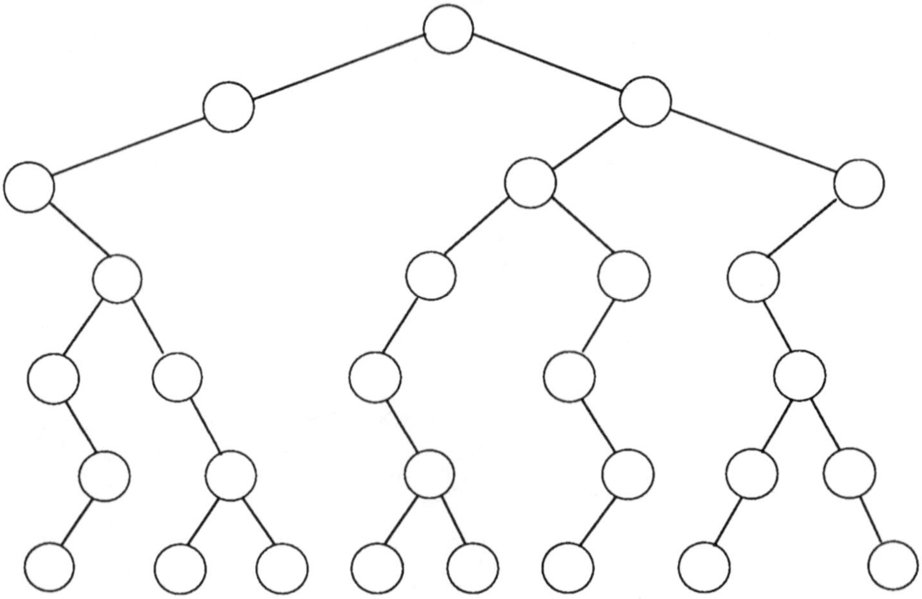

Figure 6.4 Binary tree representation of a manufacturer's stock of bead strings.

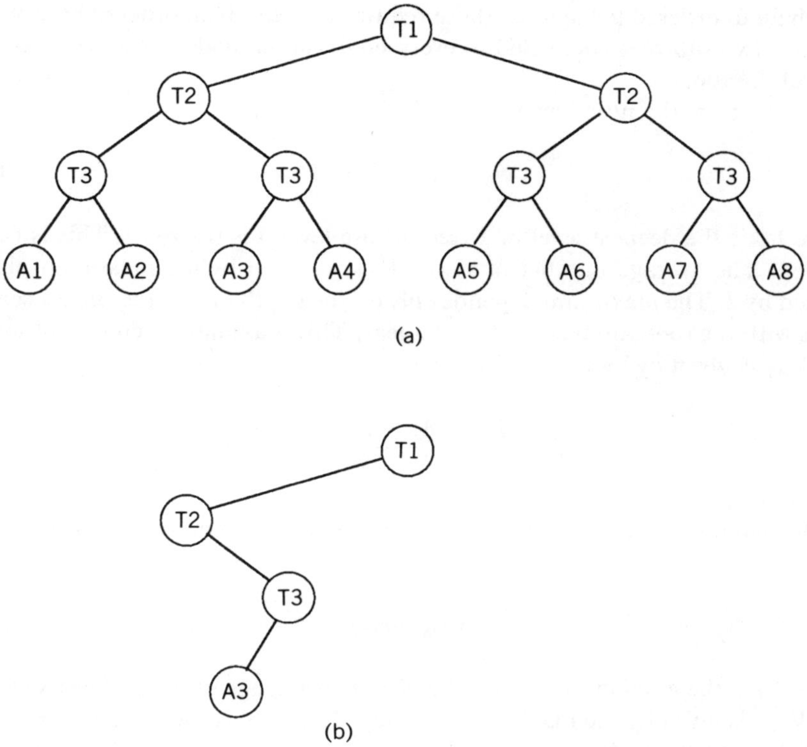

Figure 6.5 Flow structure of a check processing system: (a) decision tree; (b) sample.

All these illustrations are examples of pattern matching, a process with wide application. These include voice, speech, printed material, and visual recognition; structural analysis and comparisons of large systems; and artificial intelligence. Sometimes digraphs are used in attempts to pattern match, but this is an error. The digraph lacks true shape and thus is a poor structure for tasks involving true shape. The ordered binary tree is a better choice.

6.2.2 Searching

The ordered binary tree makes searching for a node simple and fast. The search starts at the root (in a manner analogous to the check-processing routine), proceeds left or right on the basis of some test, and repeats this operation recursively until either the target node is found or a terminal node is reached. This means that the maximum number of comparisons depends on the depth (number of levels) of the tree rather than on the number of nodes. This can make a big difference. This is why most *tables* used in compilers to record symbol parameters are really trees.

As a worst case comparison, consider the number of comparisons required to search an unordered list against those required to search an ordered binary tree that has two subtrees connected to every nonterminal node and is symmetrical around the root.

For the tree, the number of nodes (N_T) is given by

$$N_T = 2^{(L_V+1)} - 1 \tag{6.5}$$

where L_V is the deepest level in a tree (whose level 0 is the root). This is easily verified. The average number of visits (V_{AT}) is given by the maximum plus 1 divided by 2. The maximum depends only on the depth of the tree since a search starts with the root and terminates on a leaf. This maximum is equal to $L_V + 1$ and V_{AT} is given by

$$V_{AT} = \frac{L_V + 1 + 1}{2} = \frac{L_V + 2}{2} \tag{6.6}$$

The maximum number of comparisons (visits, V_{ML}) required by a list is given by

$$V_{ML} = N_L \tag{6.7}$$

where N_L is the number of nodes in the list. The average number of visits for the list, V_{AL}, is given by the maximum number of visits plus the minimum number (1) divided by 2:

$$V_{AL} = \frac{N_L + 1}{2} \tag{6.8}$$

To demonstrate the size of this difference for large lists and trees, let L_V for a tree = 20. Then, for the tree,

$$V_{AT} = \frac{20 + 2}{2} = 11 \text{ visits}$$

Let the number of nodes in the list equal those in the tree. Then,

$$N_L = 2^{(20+1)} - 1 = 2097151 \text{ nodes}$$

and the average number of visits for the list is given by

$$V_{AL} = \frac{2097151 + 1}{2} = 2^L = 1{,}048{,}576 \text{ visits}$$

Remember we obtain these results by matching the best case for the tree—the complete tree—to a search of the worst case for the list—the unordered list. This advantage of the tree over the list diminishes when the list is ordered and disappears entirely when a binary search is used on the list. However, the binary search of an ordered list effectively transforms it into the equivalent of a tree.

6.2.3 Traversing Transformations

Since trees are linked node structures, they can be transformed into linked lists. The nature of the generated list depends on the structure of the tree and the traversing scheme. These traversals lead to interesting and useful applications.

The binary tree can be traversed in three ways. These are shown in Figure 6.6 for a simple tree consisting of a root (2), a left node (1), and right node (3). To

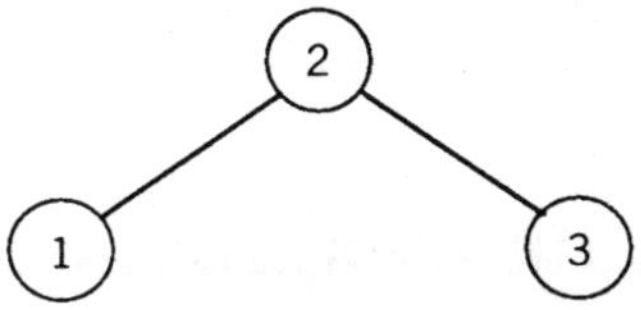

(a)

```
PREORDER
      Visit root of subtree; go left; go right
           2             L               R
                         1  L   R        3  L   R
                            NIL LIL         NIL NIL
           2             1               3

INORDER
      Go left; visit root; go right
            L             2               R
            L   1   R                     L   3   R
            NIL     NIL                   NIL     NIL
            1             2               3

POSTORDER
      Go left; go right; visit
           L              R               2
           L   R  1       L   R  3
           NIL    NIL     NIL NIL
         1                3               2
                         (b)
```

Figure 6.6 Traversing a simple subtree: (a) subtree; (b) traversals.

transform the tree to a list we use the recursive schema developed in Chapter 5 and applied to median ordering. Later, we show how these definitions apply to trees of any depth. (Note *visit* as used here means *display.*)

In the preorder case, the initial pass visits (displays) the root 2 and leaves, pending a left and right call. The next pass visits 1 and then 3, and exhausts the tree. Gathering the results of the visits from left to right generates list 2, 1, 3. This action may be summarized by visit, go left, go right.

In the inorder case, the first pass generates a pending left call, a visit to the root, and a pending right call. The next pass visits 1, then 3, and exhausts the tree. The list 1, 2, 3 results. This may be summarized by go left, visit, go right.

In the postorder case, the first pass generates pending left and right calls followed by a visit to the root. The next pass completes the left and right calls and exhausts the tree. The list 1, 3, 2 results.

These simple examples cannot show how useful traversals are. Later, we shall see that they offer simple solutions to otherwise difficult tasks. These include sorting (ordering) keys, extracting information from trees, transforming from one form of algebraic notation to another, isolating terminal nodes, and balancing trees to improve search efficiency.

6.3 OPERATIONS ON THE ORDERED BINARY TREE

6.3.1 Constructing the Ordered Binary Tree

Tree construction starts with a linked list (or a vector of keys representing a linked list). Since we are constructing an ordered tree, we need first to assign meanings to the left and right links. If the keys are numerical (usually the case), the left link can represent *less than* and the right, *more than.* Equation (6.1) $T = S/T + (S_L|S_R)$ then provides a recursive algorithm for ordered binary tree construction. The + is interpreted to signify that the node is appended when a NIL is encountered. The vertical bar, to mean that the traversal is either left (go-left) or right (go-right), depending on the relative magnitude of the key of the node being tested. Then, the construction procedure can be described as follows: The first node of the list is detached and established as the root. Subsequently, the new first node of the list is detached and its key is compared against the root. If less than the root, the process goes left; if more, it goes right. This action is repeated on every subtree encountered until a NIL is met. Then, the node is appended to the tree.

Figure 6.7 illustrates this operation. A linked list and an empty tree are shown in Figure 6.7*a*. The first node (5) is detached and established as the root of T (Figure 6.7*b*). The next node (2) is detached from the list, and its key is compared with the nodes of the tree starting from the root. It is smaller than 5; therefore, the process goes left. Since the left pointer from 5 terminates in a NIL, node 2 is added to the tree (Figure 6.7*c*). Node 7 is detached from the list, compared against 5 in the tree, moved right, and connected (Figure 6.7*d*). Node 4 is

Figure 6.7 Constructing a binary tree from a list.

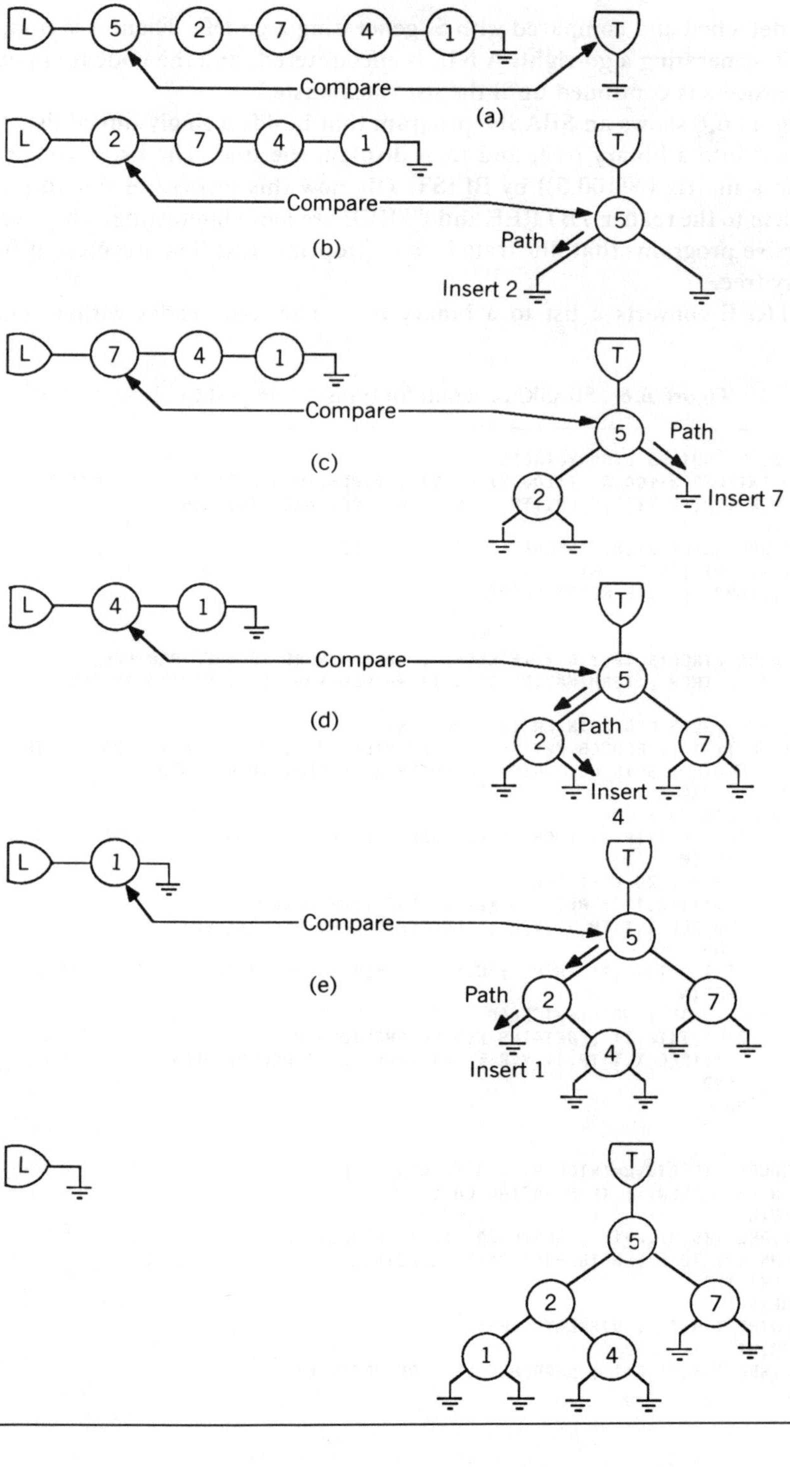

then detached and compared with 5, generating a go-left. Then, it is compared with 2, generating a go-right. A NIL is encountered, and the node is appended. This process is continued until the list is exhausted.

Figure 6.8 shows an SBASIC program that builds a singly-linked list, transforms it into a binary tree, and then displays the tree. The list is constructed within a matrix (N(100,3)) by BLIST. (By now this procedure should pose no problem to the reader.) BTREE and PTREE are more interesting. They are both recursive programs that illustrate how appropriate this flow structure is for the binary tree.

BTREE converts a list to a binary tree. The tree resides within a matrix

Figure 6.8 SBASIC program for transforming list to binary tree.

```
REM  BTREE BUILDS BINARY TREES
 DIM  INTEGER N(100,3) T(100,3) A(15) ; DIMENSIONS LIST AND TREE MATRIX
 VAR N,KEY,P,RR,YY,I,K,LP,TTP = INTEGER ; DECLARES INTEGERS

PROCEDURE BLIST(R1,R2=INTEGER) ; CREATES LIST
 N(R1,1)= R1 ; SETS KEY
 N(R1,3)=R2  ; SETS RIGHT POINTER
END

PROCEDURE BTREE(X,TP,Y,R = INTEGER) ; ADDS 1 NODE TO TREE PER CALL
  IF TP =0 THEN ; TERMINATING CONDITION--NEW NODE IS INSERTED IN TREE
   BEGIN
    TP=X  ;SETS ROW POINTER TO INPUT KEY
    T(TP,1)=X  ; PLACES KEY IN NODE POINTED TO BY TP (INSERTS NODE IN TREE)
    T(Y,R)=TP ; SETS LEFT/RIGHT POINTER OF PARENT TO NEW NODE
   END
  ELSE BEGIN
        IF X < T(TP,1) THEN  ; COMPARES KEY OF NEW NODE TO SUBTREE ROOT
         BEGIN
          R=2 ; GO LEFT FLAG
          Y=T(TP,1) ; RETAINS KEY OF PREVIOUS NODE
          BTREE X,T(TP,2),Y,R ;  SEARCHES LEFT RECURSIVELY
         END
        IF X > T(TP,1) THEN  ; COMPARES KEY OF NEW NODE TO SUBTREE NODE
         BEGIN
           R=3  ; GO RIGHT FLAG
           Y=T(TP,1) ; RETAINS KEY OF PREVIOUS NODE
           BTREE X,T(TP,3),Y,R ; SEARCHES RIGHT RECURSIVELY
         END
       END
END

PROCEDURE PTREE(W,L=INTEGER) ; DISPLAYS TREE
  IF W <> 0 THEN  ; TERMINATING CONDITION
   BEGIN
    PTREE T(W,3),L+1  ; SEARCHES RIGHT RECURSIVELY
    FOR I=1 TO L ; SETS HORIZONTAL SPACINGS
     PRINT "          ";
    NEXT
    PRINT T(W,1  ; DISPLAYS KEY)
    PRINT
    PTREE T(W,2),L+1 ; SEARCHES LEFT RECURSIVELY
  END
END
```

```
REM MAIN PROGRAM
INPUT "NO. OF KEYS THEN KEYS ";N  ; ESTABLISHES SIZE OF LIST
FOR I=1 TO N ; BUILDS ARRAY OF KEYS IN CORRECT ORDER
  INPUT A(I)
NEXT I
FOR I=1 TO N  ; CALLS LIST AS NEEDED

 BLIST A(I),A(I+1)
NEXT

LP=A(1)  ; SETS LIST POINTER TO BEGINNING OF LIST
TTP=N(LP,1)  ; SETS TREE POINTER TO ROOT
WHILE N(LP,3) <> 0 DO ; BEGINS TREE BUILDING
 BEGIN
  YY=0  ; INITIALIZES PREVIOUS NODE VARIABLE
  RR=0  ; INITIALIZES GO LEFT/GO RIGHT FLAG
  T(TTP,1)=TTP  ; SETS KEY IN ROOT
  LP=N(LP,3) ; SETS LIST POINTER TO NEXT NODE
  BTREE N(LP,1),TTP,YY,RR  ; CALLS TREE BUILDING PROCEDURE
 END
FOR I=1 TO N ; DISPLAYS RESULTING TREE MATRIX
 FOR K=1 TO 3
  PRINT T(I,K);
  NEXT K
 PRINT
NEXT I
PTREE TTP,1 ;DISPLAYS TREE--SIDE ORIENTED
```

(T(100,3) containing three fields: key, left pointer, and right pointer, in that order. A root is established; then nodes are peeled off the list compared against the root and subsequent subtrees, as explained earlier, and appended when a NIL is encountered. Appending takes place when the procedure reaches a NIL (TP = 0) and consists of placing the key (X) in field 1 of the appended node (T(TP,1)=X). If the node is appended after a go-left call, then the left pointer field of its parent node must be made to point to it; otherwise, the parent's right-pointer field must be appropriately targeted. The flag R permits this determination to be made. The row number of the parent node must be retained to permit this action. This information is contained in Y. Until the terminating condition is met, the procedure compares the key of the new node against the nodes in its path going left or right recursively. BTREE X,T(TP,2),Y,R is the go-left call; BTREE X,T(TP,3),Y,R, is the go-right call.

PTREE displays the tree, necessarily sidewise with the first node of the list as the root. The procedure is called with W set equal to the root and L set at some value greater than 1 (L controls the location of the root). Since the terminating condition is not met at the start, the procedure burrows right until it encounters the W = 0 termination. Then, it moves to the right under the control of L and displays the node key. This action is repeated recursively until the entire tree is displayed.

Both procedures are excellent examples of the power of recursion when applied to the binary tree. In both cases, the procedures were composed by performing the basic operation once, and then, depending on the recursive left and right calls to lead the program flow through essentially unpredictable paths. Both procedures are relatively succinct compared to the tasks they accomplish.

Figure 6.9 shows input and output of the program. The keys of the list (Figure 6.9*a*) are entered in root first order as shown. The tree matrix is shown in Figure 6.9*b*. Figure 6.9*c* shows the side-oriented tree, the leftmost node being the root. The reader should check that the tree matrix and tree contain identical information.

Figure 6.10 gives the Pascal version of the tree construction and display program. The list-building procedure BUISL is by now entirely familiar. Therefore, let us focus on BTREE, the tree construction procedure, and OUTPUT, the tree display procedure.

The Pascal BTREE procedure uses less memory than the SBASIC one. Two matrices, list and tree, coexist in the SBASIC program. After the tree matrix is filled, the list matrix remains intact. This is characteristic of a static data structure such as the matrix. The Pascal BTREE procedure uses dynamic data structures, the linked list and the tree. Tree construction begins with a full list and an empty tree and ends with just the opposite. Memory requirements depends only on the number of nodes (plus overhead). Since the BTREE procedure strips nodes from a list and appends them to a tree, there is no need to reconstruct each node. Instead, a target node is detached from the list, the tree is searched to

Figure 6.9 Input and output of SBASIC tree construction program: (a) input; (b) output tree matrix; (c) output of PTREE.

```
            COMMAND? B:BTREE

NO. OF KEYS THEN KEYS ? 7

? 4

? 2

? 7

? 1

? 5

? 3

? 6

                  (a)
```

```
              TREE MATRIX

            1 0 0

            2 1 3

            3 0 0

  ROOT  →   4 2 7

            5 0 6

            6 0 0

            7 5 0

              (b)
```

```
                7

                                        6

                            5

    4

                            3

                2

                            1

              (c)
```

locate the correct position of the target node in the tree, and the appropriate pointer field (left or right) of the parent node is pointed to the target node. The target node is inserted whenever the terminating condition, PQ = NIL, is encountered. Until then, the procedure continues to search left or right, depending on the relative magnitude of the target key.

The Pascal OUTPUT is almost identical to the SBASIC PTREE, except for the fact that we are using real pointers. Therefore, the terminating condition is W = NIL. Also, go-left and go-right operations are simplified. Since the right recursive call is encountered first, the procedure burrows right until the rightmost node is found. The number of recursive calls resides in KK. This is used to

```
PROGRAM BTREE(INPUT,OUTPUT);  {CONSTRUCTS BINARY TREE}
 TYPE
  RP=^NODE;
  NODE = RECORD                 {ESTABLISHES NODE }
           KEY:INTEGER ;
           RIGHT:RP ;
           LEFT:RP;
         END;
  VAR ROOT,PW,PP,PR:RP;A:ARRAY[1..30] OF INTEGER;I,N:INTEGER;

PROCEDURE BUILSL(VAR P:RP;NKEY:INTEGER);  {BUILDS LIST}
   VAR I:INTEGER;Q:RP;
    BEGIN
       NEW(Q); {RETRIEVES SOURCE NODE  FROM HEAP}
       Q^.RIGHT := P;  {SETS POINTER FIELD TO PREVIOUS FIRST NODE ON LIST}
       Q^.KEY:= NKEY;  {SETS KEY}
       P:= Q;  {POINTS P (LIST POINTER) TO NEW NODE}
    END;

PROCEDURE BTREE(X:INTEGER; VAR PQ:RP); {BUILDS TREE}
 {$A-}  {ENABLES RECURSION}
       BEGIN
        IF PQ=NIL THEN PQ:=PW {TERINATION--INSERTS NODE IN TREE}
        ELSE
           BEGIN
            IF X < PQ^.KEY THEN  BTREE(X,PQ^.LEFT); {SEARCHES LEFT}
            IF X > PQ^.KEY THEN BTREE(X,PQ^.RIGHT); {SEARCHES RIGHT}
           END;
        END;


PROCEDURE OUTPUT(W:RP;KK:INTEGER); {DISPLAYS TREE}
  VAR II:INTEGER;
    BEGIN IF W <> NIL THEN  {TERMINATING CONDITION}
      WITH W^ DO
        BEGIN OUTPUT(RIGHT,KK+1); {SEARCHES RIGHT UNTIL W=NIL}
              FOR II:=1 TO KK DO WRITE('          '); {SPACES RIGHT}
              WRITELN(KEY); {DISPLAYS KEY}
              OUTPUT(LEFT,KK+1); {SEARCHES LEFT UNTIL W=NIL}
        END;
   END;

{MAIN}
  BEGIN
    WRITELN('NO. OF KEYS');READLN(N); {PROMPTS FOR LIST SIZE}
    PP:=NIL; WRITELN('ENTER KEYS IN REVERSE ORDER'); {PROMPTS FOR KEYS}
    FOR I:=1 TO N DO BEGIN READ(A[I]);WRITE(' ');BUILSL(PP,A[I]);END;{BUILDS LIST}
    PW:=PP;WRITELN;
  ROOT:=NIL; {ESTABLISH ROOT OF TREE}
 WHILE PP<> NIL DO
  BEGIN
   PW:=PP; {TEMPORARY POINTER TO FIRST NODE IN LIST}
   PP:= PP^.RIGHT; {PP POINTS TO SECOND NODE IN LIST}
   PW^.LEFT:=NIL; PW^.RIGHT:=NIL; {NODE TERMINATED IN NILS}
   BTREE(PW^.KEY,ROOT); {CALL BTREE TO INSERT NEW NODE}
  END;
 WRITELN; OUTPUT(ROOT,0); {DISPLAY TREE}
 END.
```

Figure 6.10 Pascal program for transforming list to binary tree.

position the rightmost key. This action continues as the procedure traces its way through the tree. Figure 6.11 shows input and output for a seven-key tree.

6.3.2 Searching the Tree

Tree search is very similar to tree construction. Tree construction is also a search procedure. We construct a tree by searching for a NIL, and upon finding one, we

```
NO. OF KEYS

7


ENTER KEYS IN REVERSE ORDER

3 5 1 2 7 6 4

                  (a)


            7

       6

            5

4

            3

       2

            1


                  (b)
```

Figure 6.11 Input and output of Pascal tree construction program: (a) input; (b) side-oriented tree—output of OUTPUT.

insert a node. In searching a tree, we are seeking a specific node identified by a key. The procedure terminates when that node is found or when the only path in which the node can be, is completely traversed without finding the node. This means that the node is not in the tree.

Tree search is a very efficient operation. The go-left, go-right strategy on which the tree is built guides the search for the node through the most direct path. In the following discussion, we search only for keys. However, it should be clear that it is the content of the node that is of interest, not the keys. Key search is meaningful when the key can be related to the contents of the node, though this is not a necessity. When the tree is built on the basis of a contents strategy, the search can be content controlled.

We have demonstrated that the tree can be searched more efficiently than the list, but how about the matrix? Obviously, if content can be related to the indexes of the matrix, it can be located without a search. However, the matrix is a static structure. It occupies a fixed amount of memory. It must initially be made large enough to hold the maximum anticipated data. Also, if indexes-related contents are spread sparsely throughout the matrix, space will be unused and wasted. In most applications these reasons militate against the matrix in favor of the tree. Therefore, the large symbol *tables* used in compilers are usually trees.

Figure 6.12 shows search procedures for both SBASIC and Pascal. The two

```
PROCEDURE SEARCH(X,TP = INTEGER) ;FINDS TARGET KEY
  PRINT T(TP,1);"---"; ;DISPLAYS SEARCH PATH
  IF TP =0 THEN PRINT X;"NOT FOUND" ELSE ;TERMINATION,PRINTS RESULTS OF SEARCH
  IF T(TP,1) = X THEN PRINT X;" FOUND"
  ELSE BEGIN  ;CONTINUES SEARCH
        IF X < T(TP,1) THEN
          SEARCH X,T(TP,2)   ;RECURSIVE CALL GO LEFT
        IF X > T(TP,1) THEN
           SEARCH X,T(TP,3) ;RECURSIVE CALL GO RIGHT
       END
END
```

(a)

```
PROCEDURE SEARCH(X:INTEGER; VAR PQ:RP); {FINDS TARGET KEY}
 {$A-}  {ENABLES RECURSION}
       BEGIN
        WRITE(PQ^.KEY,'---');   {DISPLAYS PATH}
        IF PQ^.KEY = X THEN WRITELN(X:3, ' FOUND') ELSE  {DISPLAYS RESULTS OF SEARCH}
        IF PQ=NIL THEN WRITE('NOT FOUND')
        ELSE
      BEGIN  {CONTINUES SEARCH}
            IF X < PQ^.KEY THEN  SEARCH(X,PQ^.LEFT); {RECURSIVE CALL GO LEFT}
            IF X > PQ^.KEY THEN SEARCH(X,PQ^.RIGHT); {RECURSIVE CALL GO RIGHT}
          END;
      END;
```

(b)

Figure 6.12 SEARCH procedures: (a) SBASIC; (b) Pascal.

procedures are similar. Both terminate when the target key is found or when the end of the path is reached. The end of a path is indicated by 0's in the pointer fields for SBASIC and by NILs for Pascal. On termination, the appropriate message is displayed. After each unsuccessful comparison, the procedure goes left or right as indicated. The effectiveness of recursion in this application is evidenced by the brevity of the procedures.

Figure 6.13 displays the results of some sample searches. Notice how directly the search moves to the target when it exists. Notice also that the maximum number of comparisons equals the depth plus 1 of the tree. This number would have been larger for the same number of nodes if the tree had been more lopsided.

The symmetry of a tree around its root is defined by its *completeness* or *balance.* A *complete* tree is one that is perfectly *symmetrical* around the root, each node having two links connecting either to two other nodes, two Nils or a node and a NIL. In a *balanced* binary tree, the number of nodes in the left or right subtree of each node differ by 1 at most. Consequently the balanced tree would have leaves that differ in depth by 1 at most. All other trees are unbalanced. Figure 6.14 shows these three types of trees.

The condition of balance determines the maximum length (depth) of the search path, so there is a definite relationship between balance and search efficiency. It is clear that maximum search efficiency is achieved in a complete tree. However, the loss of efficiency in using a balanced tree over a complete tree is usually too slight to justify the extra effort involved in completing a tree.

Figure 6.13 Output of SEARCH: (a) binary tree; (b) sample searches.

```
                                    8

                          7

                6

                          5

      4

                          3

                2

                          1

                   (a)
```

Figure 6.13 *(Continued)*

```
TARGET

8


4---6---7---8---  8 FOUND


TARGET

3


4---2---3---  3 FOUND


TARGET

5


4---6---5---  5 FOUND


TARGET

10


4---6---7---8---0---NOT FOUND
```

(b)

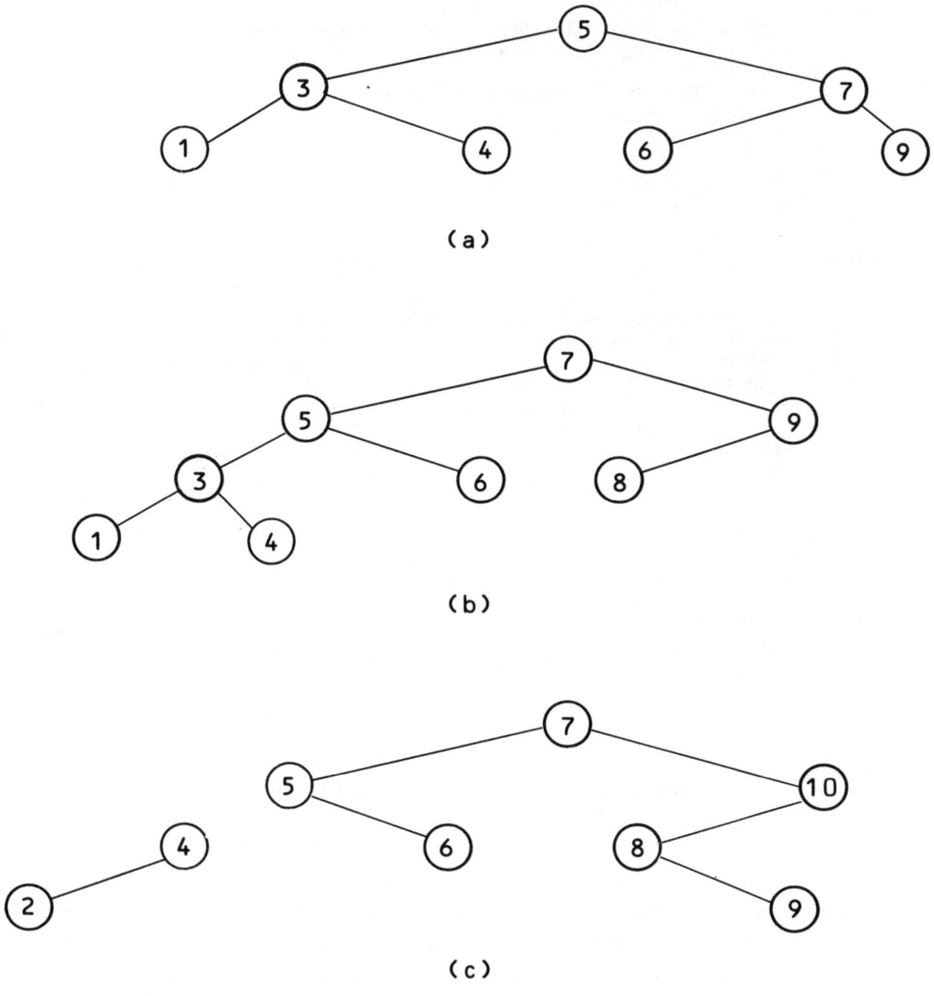

Figure 6.14 Balance in binary trees: (a) complete tree; (b) unbalanced tree; (c) balanced tree.

6.3.3 Traversing the Binary Tree

Traversing transforms trees to linked lists. The structure of the resulting list depends on the structure of the tree and the transformation scheme. The transformation has at least two purposes. One is to exploit the easy deletion and insertion capability of the linked list structure. The other is to exploit the interesting results of the transformations themselves. Often, both properties act in concert to simplify the execution of otherwise difficult tasks.

```
PROCEDURE PREORD(TP=INTEGER) ; PREORDER TRAVERSAL
  IF TP <> 0 THEN  ; TERMINATION
  BEGIN
   PRINT T(TP,1) ; DISPLAY KEY (VISIT)
   PREORD T(TP,2) ; GO LEFT
   PREORD T(TP,3) ; GO RIGHT

  END
END



PROCEDURE INORD(TP=INTEGER)  ; INORDER TRAVERSAL
  IF TP <> 0 THEN ; TERMINATION
  BEGIN
   INORD T(TP,2)  ; GO LEFT
   PRINT T(TP,1)  ; DISPLAY KEY (VISIT)
   INORD T(TP,3)  ; GO RIGHT
  END
END



PROCEDURE POSTORD(TP=INTEGER)  ; POSTORDER TRAVERSAL
  IF TP <> 0 THEN  ; TERMINATION
  BEGIN
   POSTORD T(TP,2) ; GO LEFT
   POSTORD T(TP,3) ; GO RIGHT
   PRINT T(TP,1)   ; DISPLAY KEY (VISIT)
  END
END
```

Figure 6.15 SBASIC traversal procedures.

The elementary traversals of Section 6.2.3 can be extended by recursion to handle trees of any size or configuration. The pending go-left, go-right operations are replaced by recursive calls. The basic operation is thus repeated for each elementary subtree in the structure. Figures 6.15 and 6.16 show SBASIC and Pascal procedures for traversing. For both the SBASIC and the Pascal procedures, the node contains only a key field and left and right pointer fields, but content fields would be added in practice.

Since all three traversing procedures have a go-left as the first recursive call, they are all *left-burrowing* processes. This means that each new call exhausts its left paths before proceeding to a right path. On encountering the first NIL in its right path, the procedure again burrows left. The actual action is complicated and difficult to manage by hand. However, a simpler schema is available. This schema involves the parallel processing fiction used in Section 6.2.3 (and in Chapter 4). Figure 6.17 illustrates this method for preorder traversal. However, parallel processing is applicable to all traversing modes.

The schema assumes that we have a machine capable of holding operations pendant during a pass and completing them in the next pass (or we might as-

```
PROCEDURE PREORD(T:RP);  { PREORDER TRAVERSAL}
{$A-}  {ENABLE RECURSION}
  VAR III:INTEGER;
  BEGIN
     IF T <> NIL THEN  {TERMINATION}
      BEGIN
        WRITE(T^.KEY:3);   {DISPLAY KEY (VISIT)}
        PREORD(T^.LEFT);   {GO LEFT}
        PREORD(T^.RIGHT);  {GO RIGHT}
      END;
  END;


PROCEDURE INORD(T:RP); {INORDER TRAVERSAL}
{$A-}  {ENABLE RECURSION}
  VAR III:INTEGER;
  BEGIN
     IF T <> NIL THEN  {TERMINATION}
      BEGIN
        INORD(T^.LEFT);   {GO LEFT}
        WRITE(T^.KEY:3);  {DISPLAY KEY (VISIT)}
        INORD(T^.RIGHT);  {GO RIGHT }
      END;
  END;


PROCEDURE POSTORD(T:RP);   {POSTORDER TRAVERSAL}
{$A-} {ENABLE RECURSION}
  VAR III:INTEGER;
  BEGIN
     IF T <> NIL THEN  {TERMINATION}
      BEGIN
        POSTORD(T^.LEFT);   {GO LEFT}
        POSTORD(T^.RIGHT);  {GO RIGHT}
        WRITE(T^.KEY:3);    {DISPLAY KEY (VISIT}
      END;
  END;
```

Figure 6.16 Pascal traversal procedures.

sume that we have a large number of machines that can be made to wait for each other before continuing processing). On the first pass (Figure 6.17*b*), the root is visited (displayed), and a left (L) and right (R) call are held pendent. On the next pass, L leads to node 2 which is visited, and left and right pendent calls are generated. This same action is repeated on the right, giving 6 and its L and R calls. This process continues until a pass results entirely in NILs. Then, the results are assembled from left to right (Figure 6.17*b*).

Figure 6.18 shows the results of the three traversals. (The reader should hand-check these results.) Some interesting properties of these results are revealed when the lists generated by the traversals are rebuilt as trees (Figure 6.19).

The preordered list rebuilt as a tree reproduces the original tree (Figure

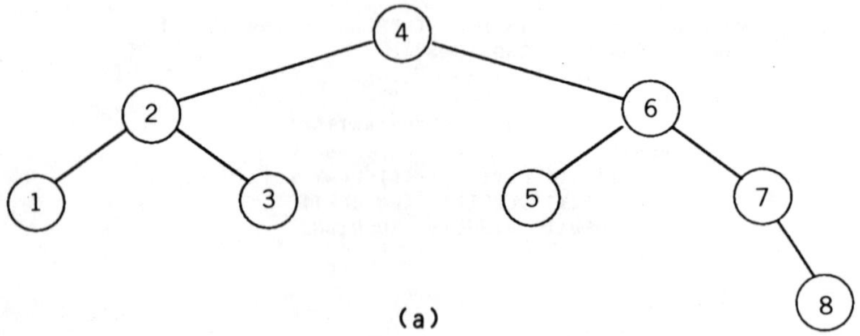

(a)

```
4   L                               R

    2  L        R                   6  L           R

       1 L   R   3 L   R               5  L   R    7  L    R

         NIL NIL   NIL NIL               NIL NIL      NIL  8  L   R

                                                              NIL NIL

4   2  1         3                  6  5           7       8
```

(b)

Figure 6.17 Schema for hand-checking traversals

Figure 6.18 Examples of traversals: (a) input list; (b) binary tree; (c) lists generated by traversals.

```
LIST

4  2  1  3  6  5  7  8
```

(a)

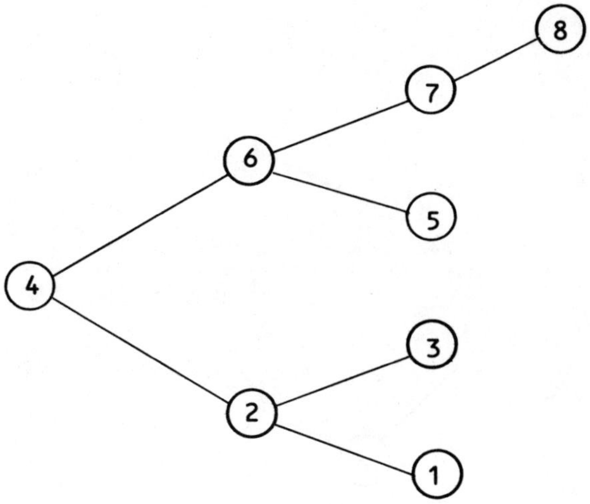

(b)

PREORDER

4 2 1 3 6 5 7 8

INORDER

1 2 3 4 5 6 7 8

POSTORDER

1 3 2 5 8 7 6 4

(c)

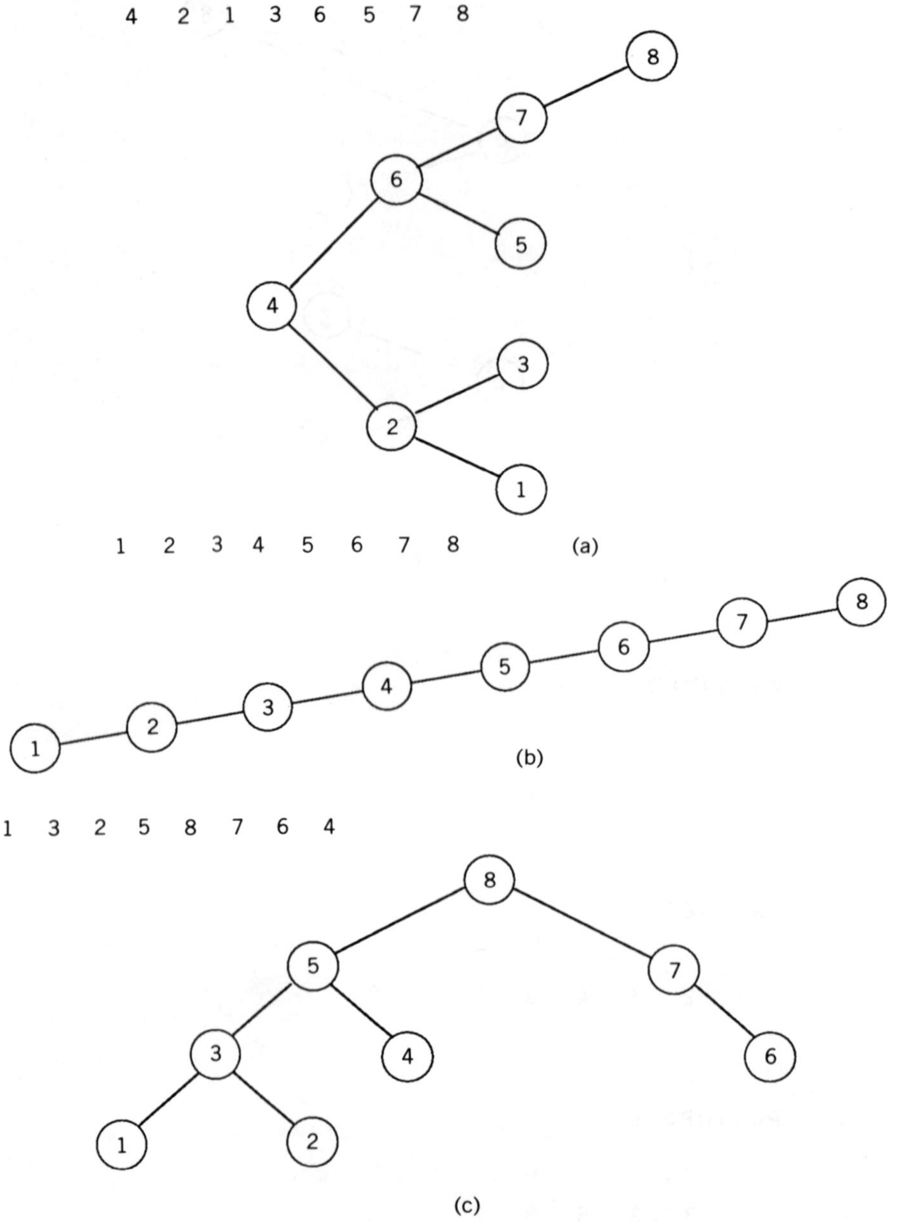

Figure 6.19 Rebuilding trees: (a) preorder; (b) inorder; (c) postorder.

6.19*a*). (The preorder traversal may not reproduce the original list from which the tree was first constructed, but it generates one that reproduces the tree.) This suggests a way to store the tree as a linked list or as a contiguous vector of keys. This approach is very useful because tree storage on a disk is often complicated and expensive as compared to vector storage.

Since the preordered list reproduces its parent tree, it must contain the same information. This means that it could be used to elicit information in place of the tree. This process—preordering the tree and then extracting information about the tree from the list—is sometimes the best way to proceed.

Inordering a tree generates a particularly interesting result (Figure 6.19*b*). A tree constructed on the schema that go-left means less than and go-right means more than is transformed by an inorder traversal into an ascending numerically ordered list. (A tree built on the reverse schema, go-left means more than and go-right means less than, would generate a descending list.) When the additional overhead involved in supporting a tree is unimportant, this suggests an excellent way to sort a list—construct a tree and perform an inorder traversal.

The postordered list rebuilt as a tree also provides an interesting result (Figure 6.19*c*). In the reconstructed tree, the go-left path (from and including the root) contains all the leaves of the original tree. This provides a simple way to determine the leaves of a binary tree.

There are other interesting and useful results obtained when trees are transformed into lists by traversal schemes and rebuilt as trees. The reader should expand the BTREE programs (Figures 6.8 or 6.10) to include traversals and then experiment with various transformations and reconstructions. Try repeated traversals of the same kind and reconstructions, for example, or consider mixed traversals of the same type and reconstructions. Sometimes otherwise difficult tasks can be solved in a simple way using repeated traversals.

6.4 APPLICATIONS

6.4.1 Pattern Matching

The ordered binary tree possesses true shape (as distinguished from topological shape). Therefore, it is appropriate for pattern matching. It is necessary first to be able to express the parents' pattern and the comparison pattern as binary trees. Once this is accomplished, it is easy to determine if the comparison pattern is equivalent to the parent. This property is called *isomorphism*.

Many patterns can be represented as binary trees. The trick depends on attaching proper meanings to go-left and go-right. We have already given the examples of the bead strings and the maze where go-left and go-right have physical significance. The same technique can be used to represent other patterns involving binary choices as binary trees so that they can be pattern matched. More abstract meanings may be attached to go-left and go-right, such as higher or lower priority or probability. An ensemble of n-digit binary numbers could be represented as a binary tree by letting the root equal START, go-left equal 0, and go-right equal 1. If we let go-left represent *logically follows,* and go-right, *does not logically follow,* the logical shape of a text could be represented as a binary tree. These patterns are limited by the fact that the go-left, go-right relationship must be binary. However, the ordered multiway tree (Chapter 7) removes this limitation.

The algorithm for testing isomorphism in the binary tree is straightforward. This assures us that we have chosen an appropriate data structure. We need first to transform the tree into a string that reflects only the shape of the tree. We choose a string because string comparisons are simple and directly supported in most languages. Figure 6.20 shows how this can be done using a modified preorder traversal. In this traversal, we are concerned only with the pattern of the left and right moves required to traverse the tree. Therefore, we build a string that reflects these moves. This is accomplished by concatenating an L to the string for every recursive left call and an R for every right call.

Figure 6.21*a* shows a string derived from its tree by this procedure. It starts with two go-lefts that bring it from the root (3) to the leaf (1). After that, it attempts a go-left that brings it to a NIL followed by a go-right that also encounters a NIL. These actions generate LLLR. The procedure next backtracks a level to node 2. It attempts a go-right that adds an R but encounters a NIL. It back-

```
PROCEDURE PREORD(TP=INTEGER); TRAVERSES PREORDER
  IF TP <> 0 THEN ; TERMINATING CONDITION
  BEGIN
   LL=LL+"L"  ; CONCATENATES L'S
   PREORD T(TP,2) ; RECURSIVE CALL
   LL=LL+"R" ; CONCATENATES R'S
   PREORD T(TP,3) ; RECURSIVE CALL
  END
END
```

(a)

```
PROCEDURE PREORD(T:RP;VAR STS:ST); { TRAVERSE PREORDER}
{$A-}  {ENABLES RECURSION}
  VAR III:INTEGER;
  BEGIN
     IF T <> NIL THEN {TERMINATING CONDITION}
      BEGIN
        STS:=STS+'L';PREORD(T^.LEFT,STS); {CONCATENATES L'S}
        STS:=STS+'R';PREORD(T^.RIGHT,STS); {CONCATENATES R'S}
      END;
  END;
```

(b)

Figure 6.20 Pattern-matching procedures for isomorphism: (a) SBASIC; (b) Pascal.

```
     3  2  1  5  4  6
                                 6
                         5
                                 4
            3
                         2
                                 1
   LLLRRRLLRRLR
                         (a)
     5  4  3  7  6  8
                                 8
                         7
                                 6
            5
                         4
                                 3
   LLLRRRLLRRLR          OK

                         (b)
     3  2  1  5  4
                         5
                                 4
            3
                         2
                                 1
   LLLRRRLLRR            NG

                         (c)
```

Figure 6.21 Pattern-matching isomorphism: (a) parent; (b) sample; (c) sample.

tracks to node 3, where it adds another R, and reaches node 5. The list now contains LLLRRR. This action continues until the entire tree is traversed. Clearly, the resulting string uniquely defines the shape of the tree.

The algorithm is concluded by generating a similar string for the sample. Then, we see if the sample string equals the parent. This operation is directly supported by SBASIC and Pascal. Figure 6.21*b* shows a tree with different nodes than Figure 6.21*a* but with the same structure. Its L–R string is identical to Figure 6.21*a*. Therefore, the two trees are isomorphic. Figure 6.21*c* shows the L–R string of a nonisomorphic tree.

This straightforward algorithm accomplishes a task that might well be dubbed *difficult* by programmers unfamiliar with data structuring. It has been simplified by the proper use of appropriate data structures. First, we represented the patterns as ordered binary trees because these possess shape. Then, we transformed both trees into strings because it is much easier to compare two strings than two trees. In both cases, we chose the data structure appropriate to the required operation. Our goal was to find the data structures that would yield a simple algorithm. If the tree and the list had failed to do so, we would have tried another data structure.

Subisomorphism

Subisomorphism (one tree corresponds to part or parts of another) can also be tested in a straightforward way. We, first, describe this test for a sample limited to one leaf. The preorder procedure is first modified so that it concatenates an N to the list whenever a NIL is encountered. The sample is, then, traversed by this procedure forming an R–L–N string. Every character in this string that is followed by an N is removed, and then every N is removed. This leaves a string that gives the directions (in terms of R–L) from the root of the sample to its terminal leaf. A terminating symbol (*) is added. To test for subisomorphism, we attempt to follow these directions in the parent tree, starting at its root and progressing recursively through all its subtrees. If a subtree is found that allows this to be done without encountering a NIL, the sample is subisomorphic from that root; if not, the sample fails.

Figure 6.22 illustrates this test. Inputs for the parent and sample trees are given in Figures 6.22*a* and 6.22*b*. The two trees are shown in *c* and *d*. The results of the initial preorder traversal of the sample tree and its subsequent reduction are shown in *e* and the results of the test, in *f*. In this case the sample is found to be subisomorphic from node 4.

Figures 6.23 and 6.24 give the SBASIC and Pascal procedures. PREORD is modified by adding IF TP=0 THEN LL=LL+'N' (SBASIC) and IF T=NIL THEN STS=STS+'N'; (Pascal). This adds 'N' to the R–L strings. The string is reduced to a direction string in the main program (not shown). SUBSISO attempts to trace the sample L–R directions in the parent tree and outputs an 'NG' if a NIL is encountered before the sample string is exhausted and an OK if a match is found. RSUBISO applies SUBISO to each subtree until a match is found or the parent tree is exhausted.

Figure 6.22 Subisomorphism tests: (a) parent input; (b) sample input; (c) parent tree; (d) sample tree; (e) processing preorder list; (f) output.

```
          3   2   1   4   6   5   7

                            (a)


       1  3  2

                            (b)


                                          7
                                6
                                          5
                          4
                3
                          2
                                1
                            (c)


                          3
                                2
                1
                            (d)
```

Figure 6.22 *(Continued)*

```
SAMPLE PREORDER


(1)      LNRLLNRNRN

(2)      NRLNNN

(3)      RL*
                         (e)



3         NG

2         NG

1         NG

4         OK
                         (f)
```

The subisomorphic test can be extended to samples with more than one leaf. All paths from the root of the sample to its leaves are found and processed. (This can be done by finding all the leaves of the sample and retracing paths back to the root.) Each path is tested at each subtree of the parent. When all paths succeed from a subtree root, the sample is subisomorphic from that root. We leave this as an interesting project for the reader (Programming Project 6.5).

6.4.2 Balancing Trees

The balanced tree is the data structure of choice for repeated searching. The efficiency of the search operation depends more on the maximum depth of the tree than it does on the number of nodes. However, this efficiency also depends on the condition of balance. The search operation for a completely unbalanced tree (a linked list) is extremely inefficient. The better the balance, the greater the efficiency. Tree balance depends on the arrangement of the keys in the list used to build the tree. We next present an algorithm that will rearrange any key progression so that it will generate a balanced tree.

Our algorithm depends on the fact that a median-ordered list generates a balanced tree. This process can be visualized if you mentally replace the list by a

```
PROCEDURE PREORD(TP=INTEGER) ;FORMS L/R/N LIST
  IF TP=0 THEN LL=LL+'N' ;CONCATENATES 'N'S
  IF TP <> 0 THEN  ;TERMINATING CONDITION
  BEGIN
PRINT LL;
  PRINT T(TP,1)
  LL=LL+"L" ;CONCATENATES 'L'S
  PREORD T(TP,2) ;RECURSIVE CALL LEFT
  LL=LL+"R" ;CONCATENATES 'R'S
  PREORD T(TP,3) ;RECURSIVE CALL RIGHT
  END
END

PROCEDURE SUBISO(X=CHAR;PP=INTEGER) ;TRIES R/L LIST AT 1 SUBTREE
  I=I+1 ;INCREMENTS LIST INDEX
  IF PP=0 THEN PRINT "NG" ; FAILS TEST
  IF (X='*') AND (PP<>0) THEN BEGIN
    S=S+1 ;INCREMENTS COUNTER FOR RSUBISO
    PRINT "OK" ;PASSES TEST
  END
  IF PP<>0 THEN ;TERMINATING CONDITION
    BEGIN
     IF X='L' THEN SUBISO MID$(ST,I,1),T(PP,2) ;TRIES LEFT
     IF X='R' THEN SUBISO MID$(ST,I,1),T(PP,3) ;TRIES RIGHT
    END
END

PROCEDURE RSUBISO(X1=CHAR;PP1=INTEGER) ;TRIES SUBISO AT ALL NODES
  VAR XX1=CHAR
  VAR XP1=INTEGER
   I=1 ;SETS INDEX FOR SUBISO
  XX1=X1 ;TEMPORARY POINTERS TO PROTECT TREE
  XP1=PP1
   IF (PP1<>0) AND (S<>1) THEN ;TERMINATING CONDITION
    BEGIN
     PRINT XP1,;
     SUBISO XX1,XP1 ;CALLS SUBISO AT REACHED NODE
     RSUBISO X1,T(PP1,2) ;MOVES SUBISO TO LEFT NODE
     RSUBISO X1,T(PP1,3) ;MOVES SUBISO TO RIGHT NODE
    END
 END
```

Figure 6.23 Testing for subisomorphism (SBASIC procedures).

length of twine. Selecting the first median node is equivalent to picking up the twine at its center. Two equal lengths will dangle on either side, and the twine tree is balanced. Cut off most of the lengths of twine from both sides, grasp each one of the cutoff segments at its center, and attach each to one of the lengths remaining from the first operation. Now, you have a balanced twine tree composed of a root connected to two balanced subtrees. Performing this operation recursively will construct a balanced twine tree of any depth. A median-ordered list is a result of repeatedly cutting left and right lists in half (or approximately in half). A binary tree constructed from the list is equivalent to attaching these segments to the parent tree at their midpoints. This operation is entirely analogous to constructing the twine tree and therefore has the same result—a balanced tree.

```
PROCEDURE PREORD(T:RP;VAR STS:ST); {FORMS L/R/N LIST}
{$A-}
  BEGIN
      IF T=NIL THEN STS:=STS+'N'; {CONCATENATES 'N'S}
      IF T <> NIL THEN {TERMINATING CONDITION}
      BEGIN
        STS:=STS+'L';PREORD(T^.LEFT,STS); {CONCATENATES 'L'S}
        STS:=STS+'R';PREORD(T^.RIGHT,STS); {CONCATENATES 'R'S}
      END;
  END;


PROCEDURE SUBISO(X:CHAR;P:RP); {TRIES L/R LIST ON TREE}
{$A-}
  BEGIN
   I:=I+1; {INCREMENTS LIST INDEX}
   IF P=NIL THEN WRITELN('NG'); {FAILS TEST}
    IF (X='*') AND (P<>NIL) THEN BEGIN S:=S+1;WRITELN('OK');END; {PASSES TEST}
    IF P<>NIL THEN {TERMINATING CONDITION}
      BEGIN
        IF X='L' THEN BEGIN SUBISO(PT3[I],P^.LEFT);END; {TRIES LEFT}
        IF X='R' THEN BEGIN SUBISO(PT3[I],P^.RIGHT);END; {TRIES RIGHT}
      END;
  END;

PROCEDURE RSUBISO(X:CHAR;P:RP); {TRIES SUBISO  AT ALL SUBTREES}
 {$A-}
  VAR XX:CHAR;XP:RP;
    BEGIN
      XX:=X;XP:=P; {TEMPORARY POINTERS TO PROTECT TREE}
      I:=1; {SETS INDEX FOR SUBISO}
       IF (P<>NIL) AND (S<>1) THEN {TERMINATING CONDITIONS}
        BEGIN
          WRITE(XP^.KEY,'        '); {DISPLAYS SUBTREE ROOT}
          SUBISO(XX,XP); {CALLS SUBISO}
          RSUBISO(X,P^.LEFT); {MOVES TO LEFT NODE}
          RSUBISO(X,P^.RIGHT); {MOVES TO RIGHT NODE}
        END;
    END;
```

Figure 6.24 Testing for subisomorphism (Pascal procedures).

The algorithm should now be obvious. Build a tree from a linked list, ignoring balance (or start with an unbalanced tree generated by some other procedure). Median ordering requires a numerically ascending list. Achieve this by an inorder traversal of the tree. Rearrange this list into median order, and reconstruct the tree.

The reader would have a greater appreciation of the conceptual simplicity of this algorithm were we to discuss at length some alternate procedures, presently proposed. These involve building unbalanced trees and then moving internal nodes about in a very complicated way. The binary tree is much like the real tree, however. It is easy to snip off (delete) twigs or leaves from the branches of the tree and, if desired, to attach (add) these elements to other branches. But, it is very difficult to remove internal sections of a branch. Existing tree balance algorithms attempt to do this and so misuse the tree structure. The difficulties that result are hardly surprising.

Our algorithm uses data structure correctly. When we need to rearrange nodes, we transform the tree to a linked list. The linked list is the appropriate structure for adding, deleting, or rearranging nodes. Since our ultimate purpose is to perform an efficient search, we subsequently transform the list to a tree.

Figures 6.25 and 6.26 show SBASIC and Pascal procedures that produce balanced binary trees, and Figure 6.27 shows a sample output. These procedures are used in conjunction with the tree-building procedures of Figures 6.8 and 6.9. Presented in these figures are only the required modifications of existing procedures.

Figure 6.25 Procedures for balancing trees (SBASIC).

```
PROCEDURE BLIST(R0,R1,R2=INTEGER);BUILDS DOUBLY LINKED LIST
 N(R1,1)= R1; SETS KEY
 N(R1,3)=R2 ; SETS RIGHT POINTER
 N(R1,2)=R0; SETS LEFT POINTER
END


PROCEDURE INORD(TP=INTEGER) :TRAVERSES INORDER
  IF TP <> 0 THEN
  BEGIN
   INORD T(TP,2) ; LEFT RECURSIVE CALL
   I=I+1 ; INCREMENTS I
   A(I)=T(TP,1);CREATES  VECTOR USED TO BUILD LIST
   INORD T(TP,3); RIGHT RECURSIVE CALL
  END
END

PROCEDURE MED(LSPTR,MDORDPTR=INTEGER); GENERATES MEDIAN ORDERED LIST
VAR JJ,MPOS,S,J,=INTEGER
PROCEDURE BUILD ; BUILDS EMPTY MATRIX FOR MEDIAN ORDERED LIST
  FOR J=0 TO 30; SCANS MAXIMUM MATRIX SIZE
    MEDLST(J,1)=J ; SETS KEYS
  NEXT J
    LSPTR=1 ;SETS POINTER TO NUMERICALLY ORDERED LIST
    MDORDPTR=0 ;CREATES POINTER TO EMPTY MEDIAN ORDERED LIST
   MEDLST(0,3)=0;CREATES DUMMY HEAD NODE
END

PROCEDURE INSERTAIL(NN=INTEGER); INSERTS NODES TAIL FIRST INTO MEDIAN LIST
  VAR TEMP=INTEGER
    TEMP=0; SETS TEMPORARY POINTER TO DUMMY NODE
    WHILE MEDLST(TEMP,3) <>0 DO TEMP=MEDLST(TEMP,3);FINDS LAST NODE
    MEDLST(NN,3)=0 ;SETS LAST RIGHT POINTER TO NIL
    MEDLST(NN,2)=TEMP ;POINTS LEFT POINTER TO PREVIOUS LAST NODE
    MEDLST(TEMP,3)=NN ;POINTS PREVIOUS NODE TO NEW END NODE
END

PROCEDURE MEDIAN(LSIZE,LLSTPR=INTEGER) ;SETS UP MEDIAN ORDERED LIST IN A MATRIX MEDLST
  VAR NNN,SIZEL,SIZER,RP,LLL=INTEGER
    REM FIND LIST SIZES AND MEDIAN POSITION
   LLL=LLSTPR ;INTERNAL POINTER TO NUMERICALLY ORDERED LIST
   IF LSIZE <> 0 THEN ;TERMINATING CONDITION
   BEGIN
    SIZER=FINT(LSIZE/2) ;SIZE OF RIGHT LIST
    SIZEL=SIZER ;SIZE OF LEFT LIST
    IF FINT(LSIZE/2)=LSIZE/2 THEN SIZEL=SIZER-1 ;IF LIST IS EVEN, MODIFY LEFT SIZE
    NNN=SIZEL+1 ;FIND POSITION OF MEDIAN NODE
```

Figure 6.25 (Continued))

```
          MTRAVERSE NNN,LLSTPR ;FIND POINTER TO MEDIAN NODE
          REM SPLIT LIST IN TWO
          IF MPOS<>0 THEN N(MPOS-1,3)=0 ;ISOLATE LEFT LIST
          RP=MPOS+1 ;POINTER TO FIRST NODE IN RIGHT LIST
          N(RP,2)=0 ;LEFT POINTER OF FIRST RIGHT LIST NODE, NILLED
          IF MPOS<>0 THEN N(MPOS,3)=0 ;RIGHT POINTER OF MEDIAN NODE NILLED
          IF MPOS<>0 THEN N(MPOS,2)=0 ;LEFT POINTER OF MEDIAN NODE,NILLED
          INSERTAIL MPOS ;INSERT MEDIAN NODE IN MEDIAN ORDERED LIST
          MEDIAN SIZEL,LLL ;RECURSIVE CALL LEFT
          MEDIAN SIZER,RP ; RECURSIVE CALL RIGHT
         END
      END

      BEGIN ; MAIN PART OF MED PROCEDURE
       BUILD ;BUIDLOS EMPTY MEDIAN ORDERED MATRIX
        MEDIAN JJ,LSPTR ;REARRANGES NUMERICALLY ORDERED LIST INTO MEDIAN ORDER
        PRINT
        PRINT "MED ARRAY"; DISPLAYS MEDIAN ARRAY
        PRINT
        FOR I=0 TO 10 ;ROWS
          FOR K=1 TO 3 ;COLUMNS
           PRINT MEDLST(I,K); ;MEDIAN ORDERED ARRAY
          NEXT K
         PRINT ;ENDS LINE AT END OF EACH ROW
        NEXT I
      PRINT "END NUMLIST"
      PRINT
     END
END
```

Figure 6.26 Procedures for balancing trees (Pascal).

```
PROCEDURE    BUILSL(VAR   P:RP;NKEY:INTEGER); (BUILDS DOUBLY LINKED LIST)
   VAR Q:RP;
    BEGIN
       NEW(Q); (RETRIEVES SOURCE NODE FROM HEAP)
       Q^.RIGHT := P; (SETS POINTER FIELD OF NEW NODE P's TARGET)
       IF P<>NIL THEN P^.LEFT:=Q; (SETS LEFT POINTER)
       Q^.KEY:= NKEY; ( FILLS KEY FIELD)
       Q^.LEFT:=NIL; (TERMINATES LEFT POINTER OF FIRST NODE)
       P:= Q;  (POINTS TO INSERTED NODE)
    END;

PROCEDURE INORD(T:RP); (BUILDS ASCENDING NUMERICALLY ORDERED LIST)
($A-)
  VAR III:INTEGER;
  BEGIN
     IF T <> NIL THEN ( TERMINATING CONDITION)
      BEGIN
        INORD(T^.LEFT); ( GO-RIGHT)
        BUILSL(PR,T^.KEY); (BUILDS INORDERED LIST)
        INORD(T^.RIGHT); ( GO-LEFT)
      END;
  END;
```

```
PROCEDURE MEDLIST(LRPTR:RP;VAR MDORDPTR:RP);
{MEDIAN ORDERS NUMERICALLY ORDERED LIST}
{$A-}
VAR MDPTR,TEMP,TEM:RP;SIZE:INTEGER;

PROCEDURE MTRAVERSE(SIZE:INTEGER;X:RP; VAR Y:RP);{OUTPUTS POINTER TO MEDIAN NODE}
 VAR K:INTEGER;
{SIZE-LENGTH OF LIST; X-POINTER TO ORIGINAL LIST; Y-POINTER TO MEDIAN ORDERED LIST}
     BEGIN
       K:=SIZE;
       Y:=X; {SETS MEDIAN POINTER TO BEGINNING OF LIST}
       WHILE K<>1 DO
         BEGIN
            Y:=Y^.RIGHT; {MOVES RIGHT}
            K:=K-1; {DECREMENTS K}
         END;
     END;

PROCEDURE INSERTTAIL(VAR X:RP); {INSERTS MEDIAN NODE TAIL FIRST}
   VAR TEMP:RP;
     BEGIN
       TEMP:=MDORDPTR; {PREVENTS CHANGING MDORDPTR}
       WHILE TEMP^.RIGHT<>NIL DO TEMP:=TEMP^.RIGHT;{FINDS LAST NODE IN LIST}
       X^.RIGHT := NIL; {RIGHT POINTER OF NEW NODE SET TO NIL}
       TEMP^.RIGHT:=X; {POINTS LAST NODE OF OLD TAIL NODE TO NEW NODE
       X^.LEFT:=TEMP; {POINTS LEFT POINTER OF NEW NODE TO OLD TAIL NODE}
     END;


PROCEDURE MEDIAN(LLRPTR:RP;SIZEE:INTEGER); {CONSTRUCTS MEDIAN ORDER LIST}
{$A-}
  VAR SIZEL,SIZER:INTEGER;RIGHTP,TP,MMDPTR:RP;
  BEGIN
  IF (LLRPTR<>NIL)  THEN {TERMINATING CONDITION}
      BEGIN
       {FINDS POSITION OF MEDIAN NODE}
       IF ODD(SIZEE) THEN BEGIN SIZEE:=SIZEE DIV 2 +1;SIZEL:=SIZEE -1;
       SIZER:=SIZEL; END
       ELSE BEGIN SIZEE:=SIZEE DIV 2; SIZEL:=SIZEE -1;SIZER:=SIZEE;END;
       MTRAVERSE(SIZEE,LLRPTR,MMDPTR); {FINDS POINTER TO MEDIAN NODE}
       {SPLITS LIST IN TWO}
       RIGHTP:=MMDPTR^.RIGHT;{SETS POINTER TO RIGHT LIST}
       IF RIGHTP<>NIL THEN RIGHTP^.LEFT := NIL; {TERMINATES LEFT SIDE OF RIGHT LIST}
       TP:=MMDPTR^.LEFT; {CREATES A TEMPORARY POINTER TO END OF LEFT LIST}
       IF TP<>NIL THEN TP^.RIGHT:= NIL ELSE LLRPTR:=NIL; {ISOLATES MEDIAN NODE}
       {LRPNTR POINTS LEFT LIST, RIGHTP POINTS TO RIGHT LIST.
       SIZEL IS LSIZE OF LEFT LIST, SIZER, OF RIGHTLIST}
       INSERTTAIL(MMDPTR); {iINSERTS NODE IN MEDIAN LIST}
       MEDIAN(LLRPTR,SIZEL); {LEFT RECURSIVE CALL}
       MEDIAN(RIGHTP,SIZER); {RIGHT RECURSIVE CALL}
   END;
  END;

BEGIN  {MAIN PART OF MEDIAN PROCEDURE}
   NEW(MDORDPTR); {CREATES DUMMY NODE FOR MEDIAN ORDERED LIST}
   MDORDPTR^.RIGHT:=NIL;
   MDORDPTR^.KEY := 0;
   MEDIAN(LRPTR,N); {CALLS MEDIAN}
END;
```

```
8 5 6 2 3 9 7 1 4

           9

     8

                     7

                 6

           5

                          4

                     3

                 2

                     1

              (a)
```

```
                     9

                 8

           7

                 6

   5

                     4

                 3

           2

                 1

              (b)
```

Figure 6.27 Output of tree balancing program: (a) original tree; (b) balanced.

Both programs require small modifications in the list-building procedures BLIST for SBASIC and BUILSL for Pascal. These are needed because the median-ordering procedure requires a doubly-linked list. In both cases this is accomplished by adding a left link that points back to the preceding node. In the SBASIC case, the list is constructed from an existing vector of keys. This is a departure from our previous techniques which mimicked the Pascal pointers, but it is a *different, not a better,* way. The Pascal list-building procedure follows the conventional approach.

The meaning of *Visit* was modified in both INORD procedures. Now, in the SBASIC case, visit means insertion into a vector of keys. In the Pascal case, it now means supplying a pointer to the visited node. In both cases, we exploit the straightforward way in which an inorder traversal generates a sorted list.

Notice how the MED and MEDLIST procedures were modified. In Figures 5.7 and 5.9 these were complete programs. We did not break them up into component procedures in Figures 6.25 and 6.26. Instead, we transformed each program into a procedure by changing the first line of each into a procedure declaration. This illustrates the *block* structure of SBASIC and Pascal. It is an extremely useful property that permits the programmer to use entire programs as components of other programs with minimum alteration.

Often, a tree is built piecemeal. For example, in a symbol table in a compiler, nodes contain the names of variables and their properties. In order to support efficient searching, a tree is built from these nodes as they become available, but before a node is added to the tree, the tree must be searched to see if the symbol and its properties have already been entered. If so, the symbol is abandoned; if not, the symbol is added at the appropriate place. The problem is how to add nodes to a tree while retaining balance.

Here, it is crucial to use the appropriate data structures. The tree must be used for searching and the list for adding, deleting, and rearranging nodes. With this in mind the algorithm is almost obvious. Add nodes to the tree until it becomes unbalanced enough to affect search efficiency significantly. Then, use an inorder traversal to generate a numerically ordered list, and then transform to median-order and rebuild the tree. (We need a measure of unbalance here to trigger the rebalancing process.)

It is often necessary to add or delete a node (or nodes) from a tree while not affecting balance. Attempting this on a tree introduces complications. Better to transform the tree to an ordered list and perform the additions or deletions on the list. Subsequently, median-order the list and rebuild the tree.

6.4.3 Transformations of Algebraic Notation

There are three kinds of algebraic notation in general use. They are *infix, prefix,* and *postfix.* Infix notation is the conventional one: (a+b)*(c+d). Parenthesis are required to prevent ambiguity. Parenthesis are not required in prefix and postfix notation. In prefix notation, each term consists of a binary operator (+, −, *, /, ∧) followed by two elements (a, b, c, . . .) or numbers. In postfix notation, each term consists of two elements or numbers followed by a binary operator. (Unary operators also exist, but they can be absorbed into their elements.) Terms may be nested and elements may be composed of terms that must be evaluated before they may participate in the next stage of evaluation.

These algebraic notations are best explained by an example. We show next an infix notation followed by its pre- and postfix versions:

Infix: (a+b)*(b/c)
Prefix: *+ab/bc
Postfix: ab+bc/*

The prefix example is interpreted by starting at the left and searching for a binary operator followed by two elements. The first such term is +ab. This term is evaluated if numeric (here we assign the symbol X to this term). The next such term is /bc. We assign Y to this term. This gives

```
*XY
```

which can now be evaluated. The postfix example is interpreted by starting at the left and searching for two elements followed by a binary operator. The first such term is ab+ (X) followed by bc/ (Y). This gives

```
XY*
```

which can now be evaluated.

The chief advantage of pre- and postfix notations is their freedom from parenthesis. This makes their expressions more compact than the infix case and more easily handled by the computer. For example, a postfix expression can be evaluated by using two lists. The original expression is placed in one list, while the other is initially empty. Symbols are peeled off the first and examined. If they are not binary operators, they are placed in the second list. When an operator is found, the previous two elements can be removed from the second list, the appropriate operation performed, and the result placed back in the second list. After a single pass has evaluated all the primary terms, the operation is repeated, moving elements from the second list back to the original one. This process is repeated until the expression is completely evaluated.

Notational transformations are efficiently performed by structuring the expression as a binary tree and then traversing it. An inorder traversal gives an infix expression, but without parenthesis. A preorder traversal gives a prefix result, and a postorder traversal gives a postfix result.

Our first task is to construct the tree. A sample expression tree is shown in Figures 6.28*d* and 6.28*e*. Each subtree (root plus two nodes) is composed of a binary operator and its referents. The referents may be either elements or operator-referents subtrees. Figure 6.28*d* shows a complete expression tree in which a

Figure 6.28 Output of notation transformation program: (a) input; (b) input reversed; (c) output of median-ordering procedure; (d) balanced tree; (e) tree after removing zeros; (f) results of traversals.

```
 NO. OF KEYS

7

ENTER KEYS AND SYMBOL IN REVERSE ORDER

D7 +6 C5 *4 O3 +2 A1
```

(a)

```
1 A  2 +  3 O  4 *  5 C  6 +  7 D
```

(b)

```
4 *  2 +  1 A  3 O  6 +  5 C  7 D
```

(c)

```
                    D

          +

                    C

  *

                    O

          +

                    A
```

(d)

Figure 6.28 *(Continued)*

(e)

```
PREORDER   * A + C D

INORDER    A * C + D

POSTORDER  A C D + *
```

(f)

0 has been added to achieve completeness. Figure 6.28*e* shows the tree with the 0 and its associated operator removed. The second tree is the one we want.

The expression tree is easily implemented. First, 0's must be added to the infix expression so that it is balanced around its highest level operator. Parenthesis are added as needed to avoid ambiguity. For example, the unbalanced expression

```
a*b/d
```

is completed by adding a 0 to the a, giving

```
(a+0)*(b/d)
```

The unbalanced expression

```
(a*(b+c))/(a+c/d)
```

becomes

```
((a+0)*(b+c))/((a+0)+(c/d))
```

Next, the elements and operators are numbered consecutively from left to right (parenthesis are ignored). A doubly-linked list is built, containing the number as the key and the symbol as content. (Note in Figure 6.28*a* and 6.28*b*, the nodes are 1A, 2+, 30, 4*, 5C, 6+, and 7D.) The resulting list in numerical ascending order is then median-ordered. This list is searched, and whenever a 0 is encountered, its node and the node, two places to the left, are deleted. (If the 0 is always added to the right of the element, its associated operator will always be two nodes to the left.) A tree displaying symbols instead of keys is built from this list. Figure 6.28*b* shows the data for the input list. Figure 6.28*c* shows the key and content fields after the input has been median-ordered but still contains 0's. Figure 6.28*d* shows the complete expression tree, and Figure 6.28*e* shows the reduced tree (0's and associated operators removed).

The tree of 6.28*e* may now be traversed. Preorder, inorder, and postorder traversal yield prefix, infix (with ambiguities), and postfix expressions. These results are shown in Figure 6.28*f*.

Figures 6.29 and 6.30 display the additional SBASIC and Pascal procedures needed for the notation transformation programs. The procedure REDUCE

```
PROCEDURE DDELETE(T,X=INTEGER) ;DELETES A GIVEN NODE
  VAR Q,QR,QL=INTEGER
   Q=T ;TEMPORARY POINTER
   WHILE Q<>X DO  Q=N(Q,3) ;FINDS TARGET
   QR=N(Q,3) ;POINTER TO RIGHT NODE
   QL=N(Q,2) ;POINTER TO LEFT NODE
   N(QL,3)=QR ;LEFT NODE POINTED TO RIGHT NODE
   N(QR,2)=QL ;RIGHT NODE POINTED TO LEFT NODE
   N(Q,3)=0 ;DISCONNECTS RIGHT POINTER OF TARGET
   N(Q,2)=0 ;DISCONNECTS LEFT POINTER OF TARGET
END


PROCEDURE REDUCE(T=INTEGER) ;REMOVES 0'S AND ACCOMPANYING OPERATORS
  VAR TM,TM1=INTEGER
   TM=T ;TEMPORARY POINTER TO LIST
   WHILE TM<>0 DO
     BEGIN
      IF S(TM)='0' THEN
        BEGIN
          TM1=N(TM,2) ;MOVES POINTER 1 NODE TO LEFT
          TM1=N(TM1,2) ;MOVES POINTER 1 MORE NODE TO LEFT
          DDELETE T,N(TM,1) ;DELETES 0
          DDELETE T, N(TM1,1) ;DELETES OPERATOR
          TM=T ;RETURNS TO START OF LIST
        END
       TM=N(TM,3) ;MOVES TO NEXT NODE
     END
END
```

Figure 6.29 Additional procedures for notation transformation program (SBASIC).

```
PROCEDURE DDELETE(T:RP;X:INTEGER); {DELETES DOUBLY LINKED NODES}
 VAR Q1,QR,QL:RP;
 BEGIN
   Q1:=T; {TEMPORARY POINTER SET}
   WHILE Q1^.KEY <>X DO Q1:=Q1^.RIGHT; {FIND TARGET NODE}
   QR:=Q1^.RIGHT; {POINTS TO FOLLOWING NODE}
   QL:=Q1^.LEFT; {POINTS TO PRCEDING NODE}
   QL^.RIGHT:=Q1^.RIGHT; {POINTS PRECEDING NODE TO FOLLOWING NODE}
   QR^.LEFT:=Q1^.LEFT; {POINTS FOLLOWING NODE TO PRECEDING NODE}
   Q1^.RIGHT:= NIL;Q1^.LEFT:=NIL; {DISCONNECTS TARGET NODE}
END;

PROCEDURE REDUCE(T:RP); {REMOVES 0'S FROM LISTS}
VAR TM,TM1:RP;
BEGIN
  TM:=T; {SETS UP TEMPORARY POINTER}
  WHILE TM<>NIL DO
     BEGIN
     IF TM^.CONT = '0' THEN
         BEGIN
           TM1:=TM^.RIGHT;TM1:=TM1^.RIGHT;  {MOVES  NODES RIGHT}
          DDELETE(TM,TM^.KEY); {DELETES 0}

           DDELETE(TM1,TM1^.KEY); {DELETES OPERATOR ASSOCIATED WITH 0}
           TM:=T; {RETURNS TO BEGINNING OF LIST}
          END;
      TM:=TM^.RIGHT; {MOVES TO NEXT NODE ON LIST}
     END;
   END;
```

Figure 6.30 Additional procedures for notation transformation program (PASCAL).

eliminates the 0's and associated operators. The procedure DDELETE is called by REDUCE and deletes the designated nodes. The other procedures—building the doubly-linked list, median-ordering the numerical ascending-ordered list, constructing and displaying the tree, and performing the various traversals—are from the library of previously composed procedures, slightly modified in some cases.

REDUCE moves down the balanced median-ordered list until it finds a 0 in the content field. Then, for SBASIC it sets up an auxiliary pointer two nodes to the left of the target. Since the Pascal procedure uses an inverted median-ordered list, it sets up an auxiliary pointer two nodes to the right. DDELETE is called twice—once to delete the 0 and then to delete the accompanying operator. DDELETE starts at the beginning of the list for the SBASIC procedure and searches to the right until it finds the target. Then, it detaches the node from the list. The Pascal procedure always searches to the right. Therefore, the DDELETE search is started from the 0 node. Neither approach is inherent to the languages. The list need not have been reversed for Pascal. They are simply artifices arising from arbitrary choices. The list is then used to construct the expression tree.

The addition of a character as content in the otherwise numeric node has created a problem for the SBASIC program. The Pascal node can contain any combination of types, but the SBASIC node, being a row in a matrix, cannot. Making strings out of the list and tree matrices would have necessitated extensive changes in all procedures. Instead, a string vector S was introduced and used to contain the symbols. S is tied to the rest of the node by its index, S(1), which contains the symbol for node 1.

6.5 SUMMARY AND CONCLUSIONS

The ordered binary tree has proved to be an extremely useful and versatile structure. Its range of applications arise from its fundamental properties. It possesses shape; therefore, it is applicable to the important class of tasks based on pattern matching. The go-left, go-right decisions provide efficient and direct search directions. These characteristics make it the structure of choice for most tasks involving searching. The various modes of traversing (transforming the tree into a list) generate interesting and surprisingly useful results. Among them is the use of inorder traversal for a highly efficient, yet straightforward, sort algorithm. We described one interesting application of traversal, the transformation of algebraic notations, but there are many more equally fascinating applications.

There are important kinds of binary trees other than those we have been able to cover. The nodes of a binary tree may contain three pointer fields instead of two, the additional field pointing back to the parent node. This structure provides a simple way to trace paths from leaves to the root. Leaves are found (by traversal), and then the parent pointer is followed back to the root. This idea is extended and used in *threaded* binary trees. In this structure the back pointer is not limited to pointing to the parent node but may point to any node desired.

The ease with which root-leaf paths can be traced in the binary tree fills a gap. The digraph provides an excellent way to determine if paths exist between any given nodes, but it is inappropriate for finding the nodes in a path. When this capability is needed, the adjacency matrix should be transformed into a tree. In general, the most interesting programs will contain several data structures, and the programmer will always opt for the one that most simplifies his task.

PROGRAMMING PROJECTS

6.1 A maze consists of a single entrance and binary forking paths. Paths do not intersect, and each fork leads to a unique path. Compose a program that will find one or more exits. Do not use trial and error.

6.2 A check must pass through a series of ten tests to determine its final handling. Compose a program that will perform this task.

6.3 It is sometimes possible to identify something by playing a game of Twenty Questions. For example, a phonetic sound might be identified by asking if its duration is *long* or *short*, if its pitch is *low* or *high*, etc. Dream up a double task of this type, and compose the program.

6.4 Compose a program that will find all the paths from the root of a tree to its leaves. *Hint:* Structure nodes with pointers back to parents and use traversals to find leaves.

6.5 Compose a program that will test for subisomorphism between a parent tree and a sample with more than one root.

6.6 Define a measure of unbalance (e.g., average number of levels/minimum number of levels for a balanced tree). Compose a program that adds nodes to a tree (1, 2, 3, . . . , at a time) without duplication and rebalances the tree when the measure of balance is exceeded.

6.7 Compose a program that will evaluate expressions entered in infix notation.

7 Multiway Trees and Forests

7.1 GENERAL CHARACTERISTICS AND APPLICATIONS OF THE MULTIWAY TREE

Trees in which the number of descendants may be greater than 2 are called *multiway trees*. These may be ordered or unordered, but, in general, the ordered tree is more interesting. Figure 7.1 shows a multiway tree. The terms *level, subtree, parent, descendant, sibling,* and *leaves* have the same meanings here as for the binary tree. The concept of *balance* also applies. A *complete* tree is one in which all parent nodes have the maximum number of direct descendants. (Remember leaves are not parents.) In a *balanced* tree, for each node, the number of nodes in its left and right subtrees differs by 1 at most. (Some authors refer to this condition as *perfectly balanced,* reserving *balance* for a less stringent condition.)

Like the binary tree, the ordered multiway tree possesses a true shape. Moreover, since the number of pointers leaving a node can be large, the number and gradations of meanings assigned to these pointers can be more extensive. The limitation to binary meanings no longer applies. For this reason, multiway trees have wide application to pattern matching tasks more complex than those previously studied.

Multiway trees can be traversed with interesting and useful results. Traversal can be accomplished in two ways: directly as with the binary tree, but with a recursive call for each pointer, or by transforming the multiway into a binary tree. For multiway trees with more than three descendants, transformation is a more practical procedure. This transformation is interesting in itself, for al-

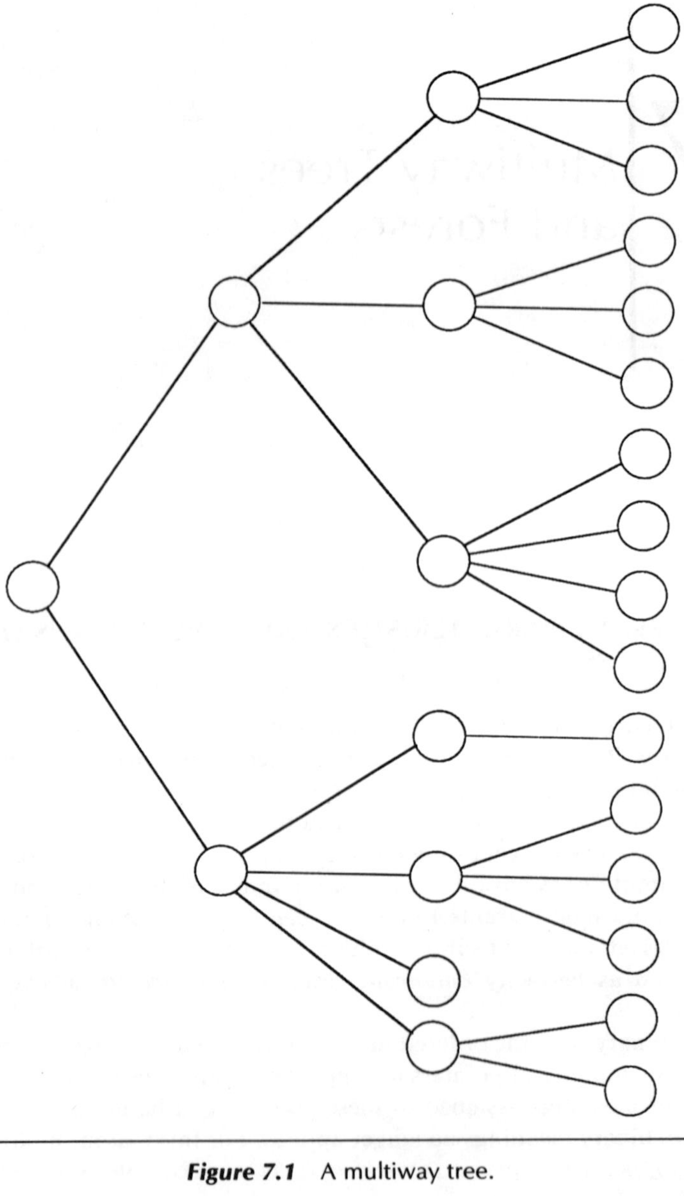

Figure 7.1 A multiway tree.

though some information might be lost, other information is made more accessible. Sometimes this is the solution to an otherwise difficult problem.

A multiway tree modified by replacing its nodes by *pages* (blocks of information) is called a *B-tree*. This structure can facilitate retrieving data from a disk. Because of the relatively small memories of microcomputers, users must often incorporate disk storage and retrieval into their programs. The B-tree when properly balanced can minimize disk access time. Therefore, it is particularly important to such users.

Other multiway tree structures abound. Groups of multiway trees can be combined into *forests.* An *indexed* multiway tree is created by permitting only a limited number of pointers out of a node but letting each pointer assume a number of positions. Combinations of normal and indexed multiway trees called *BB-trees,* and *hedges* are also possible and find important use.

The multiway tree is the most complex structure we have studied so far. For this reason, it can assume many structural variations. This is all to the good. It means that we have a versatile structure capable of matching the structures of a wide assortment of tasks. It means that we have a structure with potentially wide and useful application.

7.2 CONSTRUCTING THE MULTIWAY TREE

The structure of the multiway tree usually reflects its keys. (This is also true for the binary tree.) In applications involving searches, the keys must relate to the contents, but in other applications, the keys may merely serve to direct tree construction in a desired way. The expression tree (Chapter 6) is an example of the latter. There, the keys only reflected the position of the algebraic element in the infix expression.

The ternary tree (a multiway tree with a maximum of three descendants per parent) may be constructed by assigning keys. The desired tree is drawn, and keys are assigned solely to guide the correct placement of nodes in the tree-building procedure. However, this scheme does not work well for higher-order multiway trees. There it is better to transform the multiway into a binary before construction. We give examples of both construction procedures.

7.2.1 Constructing the Ternary Tree

As an example, we build a *ternary symbol* tree. This is a tree from which a complete set of unique and meaningful symbols can be derived. The tree is ternary because each node has a maximum of three pointer directions: left, down, and right. The ternary tree has many useful applications, but we will concentrate on the building procedure.

The required tree and the derived symbol set are shown in Figure 7.2. We choose a simple and arbitrary set of symbols to illustrate the technique. Starting from the root (S), go-left leads to A and go-right to B. These symbols are contained in the content field of the left and right nodes. At the next level go-left leads to a or d, go-down leads to b or e, and go-right leads to c or f. The intermediate symbols A and B may be assigned general significance, but the shape of the symbols a through f depend on the entire path from root to leaf. It can be seen that this technique guarantees the uniqueness of each terminal symbol.

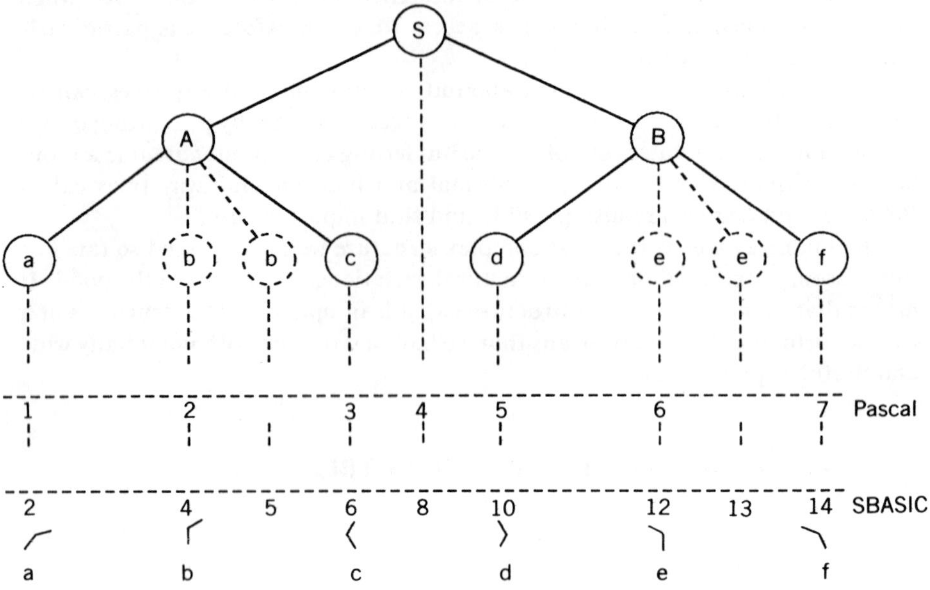

(a)

Median order									
Pascal	4	2	1	2	3	6	5	6	7
	S	A	a	b	c	B	d	e	f
SBASIC	8	4	2	5	6	12	10	13	14
	S	A	a	b	c	B	d	e	f

(b)

Figure 7.2 Assigning keys to the ternary tree: (a) ternary tree; (b) median order.

To build this tree, we assign keys to each node so that a tree built on the basis of the meanings assigned to go-left, go-down, and go-right will reproduce the tree. There are no other restrictions on the choice of keys. Figure 7.2 shows a simple scheme for assigning keys. The tree must be carefully drawn so that nodes are properly located. For example, nodes a and d must be to the left of A and B, respectively; b and e, directly below A and B; c must be to the right of A but to the left of S; and d to the left of B but to the right of S. This is the normal way to draw trees. Then, assuming that all nodes have been projected down to a horizontal axis, assign integers from left to right incrementing by 1. A and b are assigned the same number as are B and e. The resulting ascending numerically ordered set of keys must now be transformed to median order. This can in simple cases be done by hand. Otherwise, the procedure for median ordering can be used. Let go-left mean *less than,* go-right mean *more than,* and go-down mean *equal to,* and construct the tree using a variation of the tree-building procedure BTREE.

This scheme works for Pascal but must be modified for SBASIC. In Pascal, pointers are addresses independent of keys. Therefore, trees can be built, although they have nodes with identical keys. In the scheme, we use to build trees in SBASIC, nodes are located by their keys. Therefore, we cannot permit more than one node with the same key. It is certainly possible to modify the SBASIC scheme so that locations are independent of nodes and use the same Pascal method for assigning keys. However, we can stay with our scheme by slanting the go-down link slightly to the right of its parent node. Starting from the left, the keys are incremented by 2, except for the go-down link. This is incremented by 1. (The link following the go-down may also be incremented by 1.) The results of this procedure are also shown in Figure 7.2.

Figures 7.3 and 7.4 show SBASIC and Pascal procedures for building the ternary tree. These procedures are modifications of existing ones. They illustrate again the efficiency of recursion when applied to a recursive structure, in this

```
PROCEDURE BMLIST(R1=INTEGER) ;BUILDS SINGLY-LINKED LIST WITH 3 POINTERS
 N(R1,1)= R1 ;SETS KEY
 N(R1,4)=N(P,4)  ;SETS RIGHT POINTER TO P'S TARGET
 N(R1,3)=0 ;NILS DOWN POINTER
 N(R1,2)=0  ;SETS LEFT POINTER TO NIL
 N(P,4)=R1 ;POINTS P TO NEW NODE
END

PROCEDURE BTNTREE(TP,Y,R = INTEGER) ;BUILDS TERNARY TREE
  IF TP =0 THEN ;TERMINATING CONDITION
   BEGIN
    TP=X ;SETS ROW OF TREE MATRIX =X
    T(TP,1)=X ;SETS KEY = X
    T(Y,R)=TP ;SETS POINTER FIELD OF PARENT NODE
   END
  ELSE BEGIN
        IF X < T(TP,1) THEN
         BEGIN
          R=2 ;STORES POINTER FIELD OF PARENT NODE
          Y=T(TP,1) ;STORES KEY (ROW ) OF PARENT NODE
          BTREE X,T(TP,2),Y,R ; RECURSIVE CALL LEFT
         END
        IF X=T(TP,1)+1 THEN
         BEGIN
          R=3 ;STORES POINTER FIELD OF PARENT NODE
          Y=T(TP,1) ;STORES KEY OF PARENT NODE
          BTREE X,T(TP,3),Y,R ;RECURSIVE CALL DOWN
         END
        IF X > T(TP,1)+1 THEN
         BEGIN
           R=4 ;STORES POINTER FIELD OF PARENT NODE
           Y=T(TP,1) ;STORE KEY OF PARENT NODE
           BTREE X,T(TP,4),Y,R ;RECURSIVE CALL RIGHT
         END
       END
END
```

Figure 7.3 Procedures for building ternary tree (SBASIC).

```
PROCEDURE BMLIST(VAR P:RP;NKEY:INTEGER); {BUILDS TERNARY NODES}
   VAR Q:RP;
    BEGIN
      NEW(Q); {RETRIEVES SOURCE NODES FROM HEAP}
      Q^.RIGHT := P; {SETS POINTER FIELD TO P}
      Q^.KEY:= NKEY; {SETS KEY}
      Q^.DOWN:=NIL; {NILS DOWN FIELD}
      Q^.CONT:=B[I]; {SETS SYMBOL}
      P:= Q;  {POINTS P TO INSERTED NODE}
    END;

PROCEDURE BTNTREE(X:INTEGER;D7 VAR PQ:RP); {BUILDS TERNARY TREE}
 {$A-} {ENABLES RECURSION}
 VAR PS:RP;
        BEGIN
       IF PQ=NIL THEN PQ:=PW
       ELSE
        BEGIN
         IF X < PQ^.KEY THEN BTNTREE(X,PQ^.LEFT); {LEFT CALL}
         IF X = PQ^.KEY THEN BTNTREE(X,PQ^.DOWN); {DOWN CALL}
         IF X > PQ^.KEY THEN BTNREE(X,PQ^.RIGHT); {RIGHT CALL}
        END;
   END;


PROCEDURE TPREORD(T:RP); {TRAVERSES TERNARY TREE IN PREORDER}
{$A-}
  BEGIN
     IF T <> NIL THEN
      BEGIN
        WRITE(T^.KEY,T^.CONT,'  '); {DISPLAYS KEYS AND SYMBOLS}
        TPREORD(T^.LEFT); {TRAVERSES LEFT}
        TPREORD(T^.DOWN); {TRAVERSES DOWN}
        TPREORD(T^.RIGHT); {TRAVERSES RIGHT}
      END;
  END;
```

Figure 7.4 Procedures for building ternary tree (Pascal).

case, the ternary tree. Singly-linked lists with the needed number of pointer fields are constructed by BMLIST. The SBASIC procedure simulates the pointer technique of Pascal and sets up a singly-linked list with left and down pointers NILLed. The associated symbols are contained in a separate vector to allow the matrix to be of type INTEGER. The Pascal list builder is the old BUILSL with a *down* pointer added. Since Pascal records need not be homogeneous, the symbol is conveniently contained in a contents field of type STRING or CHAR.

The tree construction procedures BTNTREE are also simple modifications of the binary tree construction procedures BTREE. The change can be easily made. For Pascal, an IF X:=PQ^.KEY THEN BNTREE(X,PQ^.DOWN) statement is added to take care of the go-down case. For SBASIC the middle IF X=T(TP,1)+1 THEN. . . statement takes care of the go-slightly-right link.

Multiway trees are not easy to display. Therefore, we use other means to verify our tree constructions. For SBASIC, the tree matrix (Figure 7.5*a*) provides suffi-

```
INPUT LIST

8S 4A 2a 5b 6c 12B 10d 13e 14f


TREE MATRIX

KEY  L   D   R   S

 0   0   0   0
 2   0   0   0   a
 0   0   0   0
 4   2   5   6   A
 5   0   0   0   b
 6   0   0   0   c
 0   0   0   0
 8   4   0   12  S
 0   0   0   0
 10  0   0   0   d
 0   0   0   0
 12  10  13  14  B
 13  0   0   0   e
 14  0   0   0   f
 0   0   0   0

                                 (a)

ENTER KEYS IN REVERSE ORDER  FOLLOWED BY SYMBOL

7 f 6 e 5 d 6 B 3 c 2 b 1 a 2 A 4 S

CORRECT ORDER

4S   2A   1a   2b   3c   6B   5d   6e   7f

PREORDER

4S  2A  1a  2b  3c  6B  5d  6e  7f


                                 (b)
```

Figure 7.5 Output of ternary tree programs: (a) SBASIC; (b) Pascal.

cient verification. The matrix columns are identified (L—left, D—down, and R—right) and the respective symbols shown under S. The tree root is obviously S since no node points to it. (The reader should double-check that this is the desired tree.) The Pascal verification exploits the fact that a preorder traversal of a tree uniquely identifies the tree. This is true for all trees binary or multiway. Therefore, we have modified the preorder traversal procedure by adding a go-down path which is followed when a key equals its parent key. The results of this traversal (Figure 7.5*b*) verify the tree construction.

7.2.2 Constructing Higher-Order Multiway Trees

It is not feasible to construct the multiway tree of order higher than three, in its original form. The problem lies in the comparison-decision operation. For the ternary tree, the decision is a simple one: go-left if less, go-down if equal, and go-right if greater. For higher-order trees, this decision must be based on more complex and quantitative relations. A fourth-order tree might require a go-extreme-left if the ratio of the subtree node to the test node is less than $1/4$, go-left if between $1/4$ and $1/2$, go-right if between 1 and 2 and go-extreme-right if greater than 2. It is no easy task to select keys that satisfy this requirement and all others at the same time. This task becomes impractical as tree order increases.

Instead, we exploit the fact that the multiway tree can be transformed into a binary tree with perhaps no significant loss of information. In this form, it is easy to assign the required keys. (Other binary operations—traversal and search—have useful and powerful application to the multiway tree in this form.)

Figure 7.6 shows the procedure for transforming a multiway tree into a binary one. Figure 7.6*a* shows the original multiway tree. Figure 7.6*b* is formed by connecting the root of each subtree by a go-down link to its leftmost direct descendant (first sibling). Then, all siblings (descendants of the same parent) are connected by horizontal links. This process is carried out recursively for all nodes. Rotating the result a few degrees clockwise so that the go-down links become go-left links and the horizontal links become go-right links and adjusting the relative position of the nodes, gives the binary tree of Figure 7.6*c*.

Figure 7.7 shows a simple procedure for assigning keys. In Figure 7.7*a*, we start at the left and assign the leftmost node a key of 1. Moving right, we assign a key incremented by 1 to each successive node as it is reached. To use this method, we must first make sure that the nodes are correctly positioned as shown. However, it is not necessary to rotate the transformed multiway tree to assign keys. Figure 7.7*b* shows a simpler way using the unrotated version. Starting at the left, assign key numbers incrementing by 1 to the first set of terminal siblings (leaves). When this set is completed, assign the next key number to its parent. Perform this same operation on all sets of siblings, continuing to increment by 1. The root node, when reached, can be assigned any number larger than those previously assigned, though sometimes it is useful to use the incrementing scheme of the next lowest level. This would give a root key of 25 instead of 21 for Figure 7.7*b*.

Figure 7.8 shows how this key assignment scheme is applied to trees of any depth. Figure 7.8*a* shows a subtree in a tree of any depth. As before, we start at the leaves and increment by 1 for each terminal sibling set. Also as before, we assign an incremented key to the parent whenever a sibling set is completed. Note, however, that this scheme applies recursively at all levels. When the intermediate sibling set (e.g., 4, 8, and 12) is completed, we increment its parent key to 16 before continuing. (In this example, we use the direct descendant's increment for the parent.)

Figure 7.8*b* shows the results of a manual preorder traversal performed di-

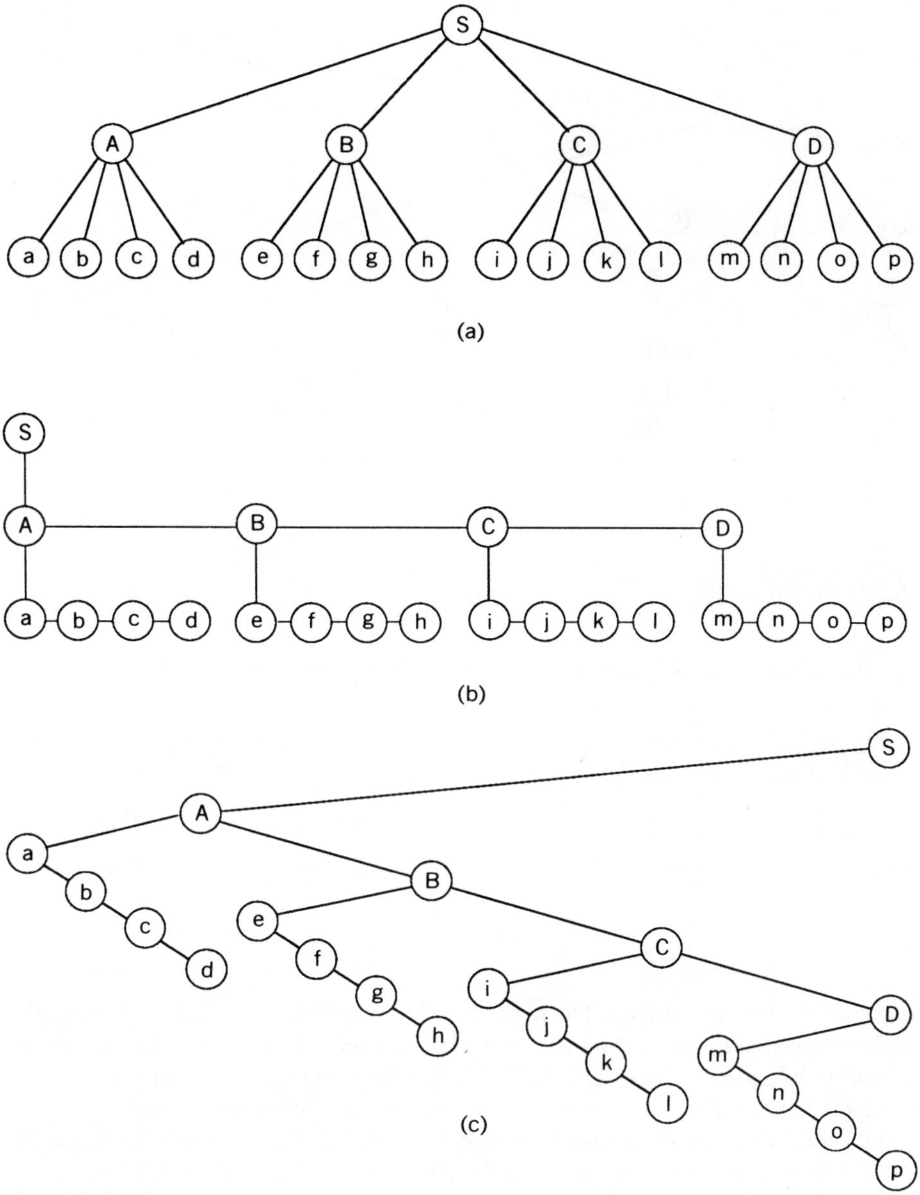

Figure 7.6 Multiway to binary tree transformation: (a) multiway tree; (b) binary transformation; (c) rotated.

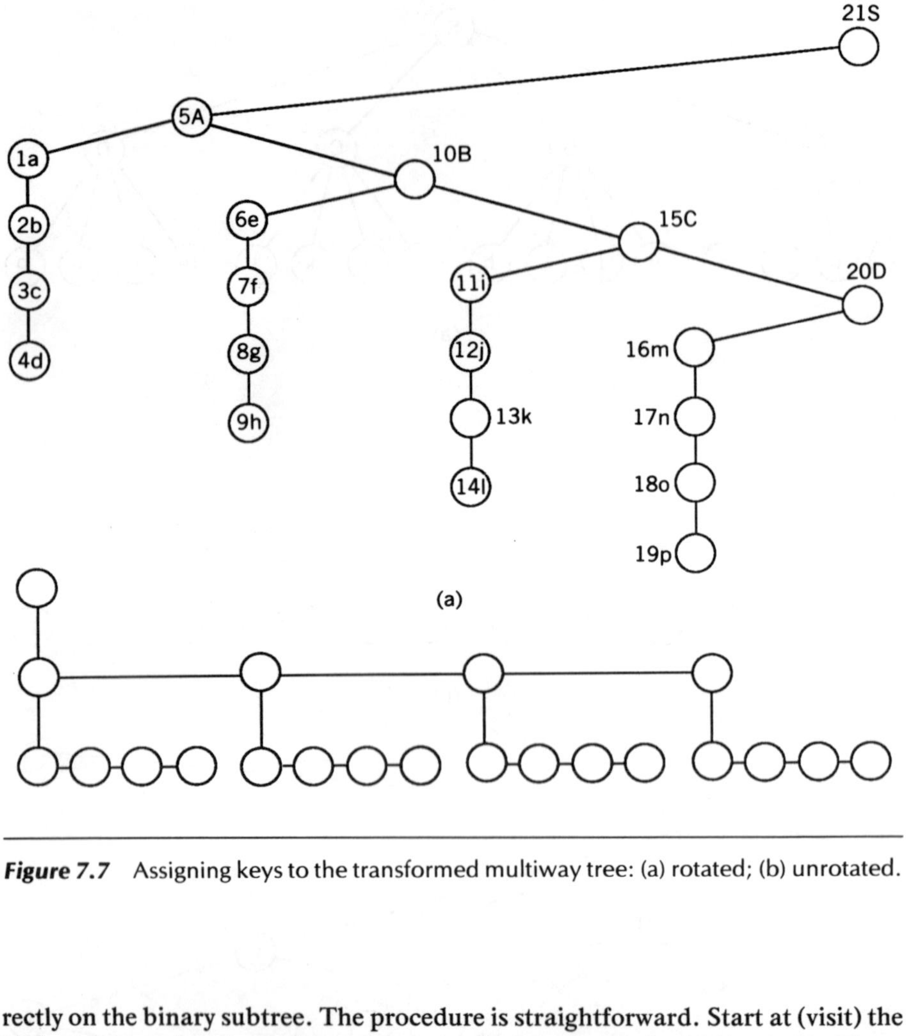

Figure 7.7 Assigning keys to the transformed multiway tree: (a) rotated; (b) unrotated.

rectly on the binary subtree. The procedure is straightforward. Start at (visit) the highest leftmost node, and move down to the leftmost leaf, visiting each node as encountered. Move to the right end of the sibling set, visiting each node as encountered. Repeat this operation recursively for the entire structure.

Once keys are assigned and traversed in preorder, the resulting list becomes the input data for a binary tree construction procedure. Figure 7.9 shows the results obtained from the BTREE program applied to the preordered list derived from Figure 7.7*b*. (We have added the circles and links for clarity.) Each circle contains the node symbol appended to the key. The results verify our method.

The binary version of the multiway tree is an exact representation only when the multiway tree is *complete*. Recall this means that each nonterminal node has a complete set of descendants. In a complete set, the first, second, etc., siblings

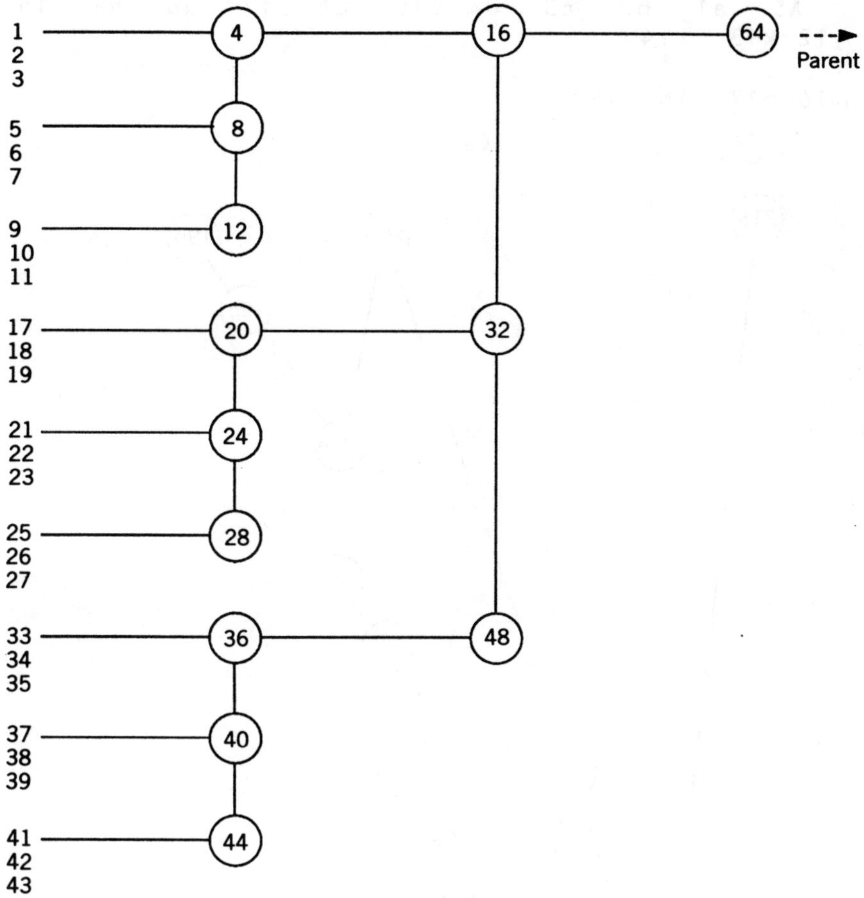

(a)

64 16 4 1 2 3 8 5 6 7 12 9 10 11 32 20 17 18 19 24
21 22 23

28 25 26 27 48 36 33 34 35 40 37 38 39 44 41 42 41

(b)

Figure 7.8 Assigning keys to subtrees: (a) binary transformation; (b) preorder traversal.

```
ENTER SYMBOLS FOLLOWED BY KEYS

S21    A5   a1   b2   c3   d4  B10   e6   f7   g8   h9  C15
i11  j12  k13   l14

D20  m16  n17  o18  p19
```

(a)

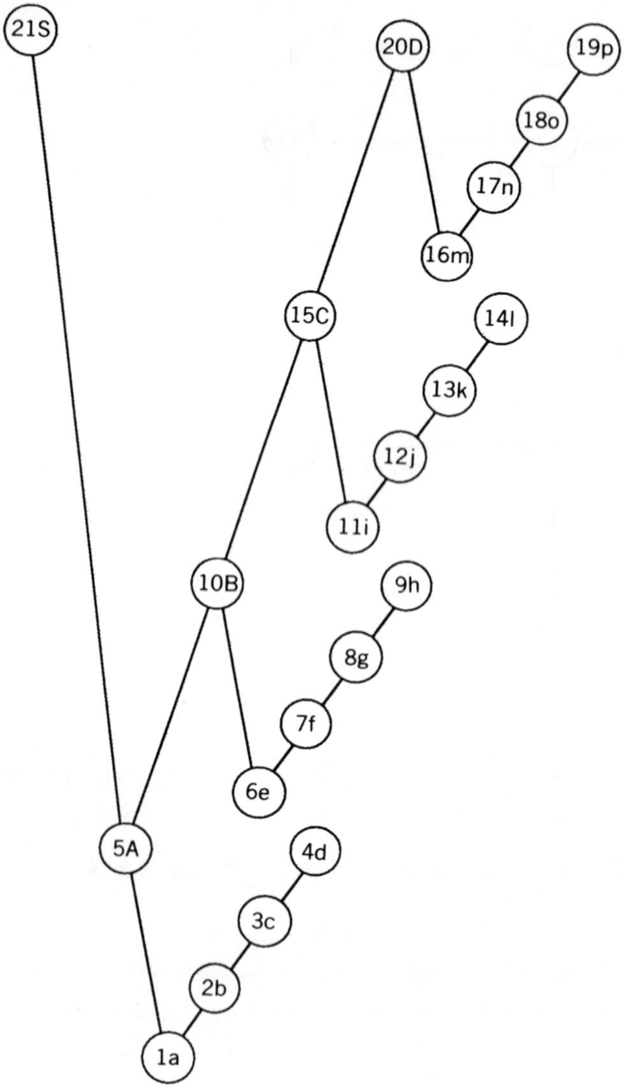

(b)

Figure 7.9 Output of multiway tree construction program: (a) input; (b) output.

are targeted by the first, second, etc., pointers of the parent. In an incomplete set, this can not be determined. For example, if a node with four pointer fields has two siblings, they could be targeted by any two of the parent's pointers.

Sometimes the lost information is unimportant. Suppose, for example, that the go-down link represents *son of* and the horizontal link represents *increasing age*. Then no information is lost if the set of sons is incomplete. In cases such as these, memory can be saved by leaving the multiway tree incomplete.

However, sometimes the lost information is crucial. For example, if in a fourth-order tree, each link represented a different color. Then, we could not determine the color of a descendant within an incomplete sibling set. In such cases, the original tree must be completed by adding dummy nodes.

7.3 MULTIWAY TRAVERSAL

Traversing multiway trees yields interesting and useful results. The ternary tree can be traversed directly as discussed. The multiway tree can also be traversed directly manually, but the computer can most efficiently traverse the tree in its binary form. There are unique and useful relationships between the results of traversing the tree in its multiway form and in its binary form. To illustrate, we perform preorder, inorder, and postorder traversals on the multiway tree of Figure 7.6*a* by hand using the parallel processing schema, and on its binary version (Figure 7.6*b*) by computer:

```
PREORDER
    Multiway: SAabcdBefghCijklDmnop
    Binary: SAabcdBefghCijklDmnop

INORDER
    Multiway: abAcdefBghSijCklmnDop
    Binary:   abcdAefghBijklCmnopDS

POSTORDER
    Multiway: abcdAefghBijklCmnopDS
    Binary:   dcbahgfelkjiponmDCBAS
```

Preorder traversal of the multiway tree and its binary version produce identical results. This is a useful relationship. All multiway trees can be traversed preorder by transforming them into binary form and using conventional binary preorder traversal. Inorder traversal of the binary version produces the same result as postorder traversal of the multiway form. This is also a useful relationship. We are left with two apparently unrelated results: inorder traversal of the multiway and postorder traversal of the binary. Remember them. They may someday provide exactly the transformation you need to solve a task.

7.4 SEARCHING THE MULTIWAY TREE

The multiway tree may be searched, but not as efficiently as the binary one. The search is of course conducted on the binary version and differs in no way from a conventional binary search. However, the binary version is rarely balanced. Therefore, the efficiency of the search is less than optimum. If the exact position of the node must be known, then the tree must be completed with dummy nodes as required. Otherwise, it need not be complete.

Multiway trees may often be too large to be retained in core memory, especially in microcomputers. The binary version of the tree may be modified to provide a convenient disk-storage structure. In this structure each sibling set is contained in a file record. Each record contains the keys and content fields of each sibling in the set. Figure 7.10 shows a sample of this structure. The first number in each cell is the key, and the second character is the content. Each record has the same structure although the number of cells may vary.

If keys are assigned in the conventional way, the records will contain the keys shown in Figure 7.10. (This tree has been derived from Figure 7.9.) Notice that each key is one higher than the highest key of its direct descendants (except of course for leaves). The first cell (21 S) is one higher than its highest direct descendant cell (20 D), the second cell in the sibling set attached to 21 S has a key of 10 which is one higher than its highest direct descendant cell, and so on.

This relationship directs the search. Each record is assigned a record number equal to the key of its parent node. A search is then conducted by first retrieving the root of the tree and then comparing its key against the target key. If the target key is higher, its node is not contained in the tree. If it is lower, the record given by the root key is retrieved. The target key is compared against each cell of

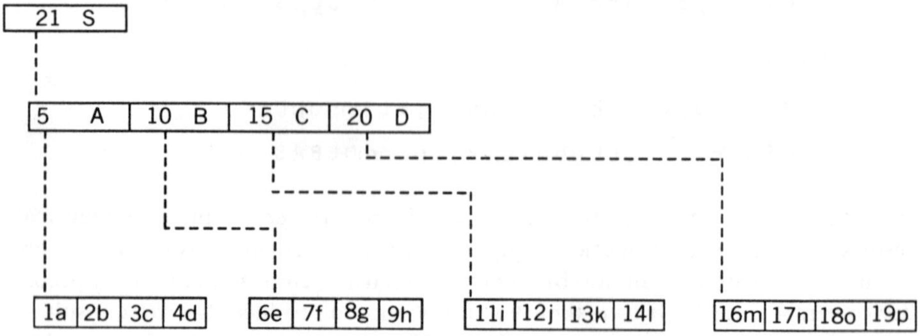

Figure 7.10 Structure of a disk-based multiway tree.

the retrieved record. If it is lower than the first key, the record given by this key is retrieved, and the process is continued; if not, succeeding cells are visited until one is found that has a higher key than the target. The associated record is then retrieved, and the process continued until either the target is found or the tree is exhausted.

This structure permits the computer to search or otherwise use trees of sizes limited only by disk logistics. It also eliminates pointers and stores data efficiently. In BASIC the information for each record would be stored in two arrays, one for the keys and the other for the characters. In Pascal, both keys and characters would be contained in a single record.

7.5 PATTERN MATCHING

The pattern-matching capability of the computer is dramatically enhanced by the multiway tree. The dyadic limitation of the binary tree on link meanings is removed. Links may now represent many shades of meaning, both qualitative and quantitative. As a result, the kinds of patterns expressible as multiway trees are limited only by logistical considerations. For example, in a four-link tree representing a manufacturers bead string inventory, the leftmost link might signify a connection to a smaller bead of another color; the next left link, a connection to a smaller bead of the same color; the next, to a larger bead of another color; and so on. In a multiway tree representation of the probabilities of events, links can represent *less than 25%, between 25 and 50%, between 50 and 75%, and between 75 and 100%* probability. A job control tree might use links signifying *must be done before, can be done at the same time, must be done after,* or *is unrelated to.*

Many straight-line patterns can be represented as multiway trees. Figure 7.11 shows a geometric pattern and its representation as a multiway tree and a binary-transformed multiway tree. A ternary tree is required here, with the leftmost link signifying *down-right,* a middle vertical link signifying *horizontal,* and a rightmost link signifying *up-right.* Links must be given a direction so that they conform to the tree convention. (Undirected links can be represented by bidirectional lines.) Dummy nodes must be inserted into the tree to mark unused links. Note also that the resulting tree may contain multiple nodes with the same key. Therefore, these keys cannot be used to build the tree. They may be retained as content, but other keys must be assigned as described previously.

The ability to represent geometric patterns is important. We have held throughout this text that the underlying structure of any programming task can be represented as a geometric structure. Therefore finding that these patterns can be represented by a tree is significant and suggests solutions to many programming tasks. For example, Figure 7.11*a* might represent a maze. Transforming this into a tree permits us to find paths to any exit (leaf) in a straightforward way. We construct the tree with back pointers to parent nodes, locate the desired leaf, and follow the back pointers to the root. The geometric diagram

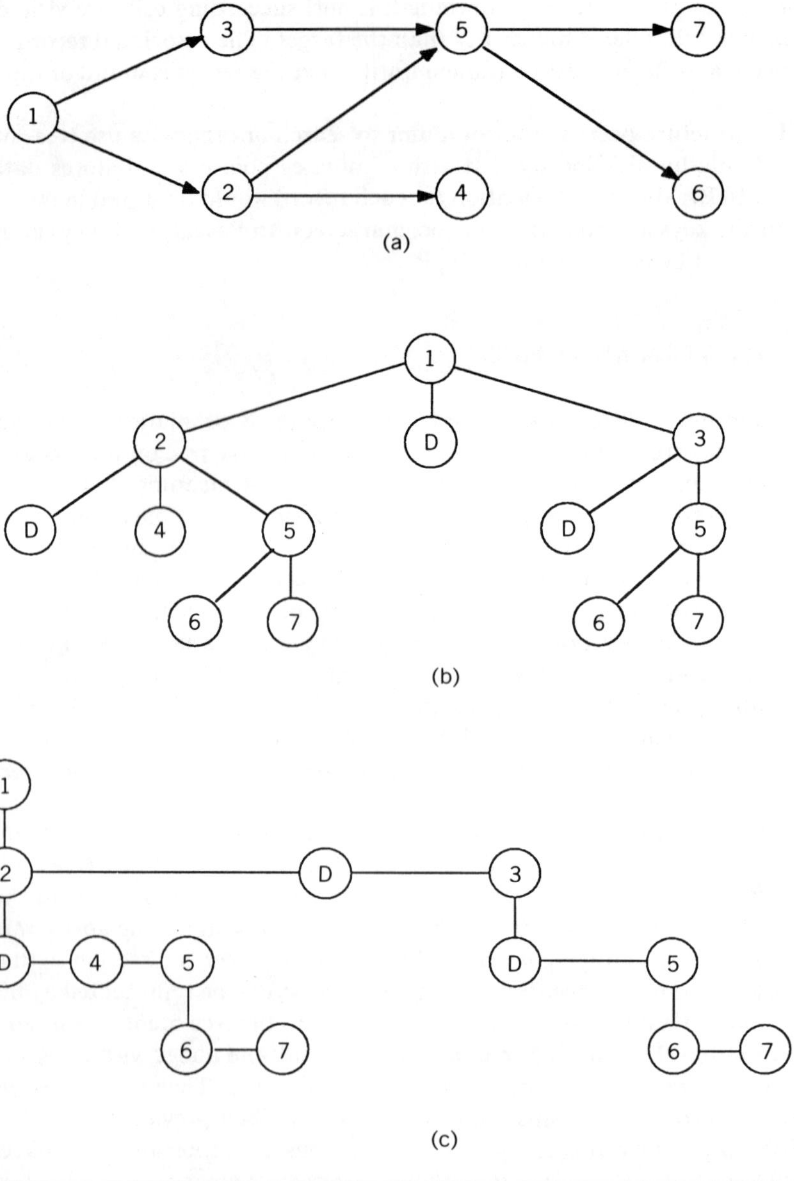

Figure 7.11 Multiway tree representation of a geometric pattern: (a) pattern; (b) multiway tree; (c) binary version.

may represent useful mathematical and analytic relations and a tree representation may well be the transformation that leads most directly to computerization.

The question usually asked in pattern-matching tasks is: Is one structure isomorphic or subisomorphic to another? In this case, the contents of the nodes do not warrant consideration. Relations between nodes as embodied in the links constitute the pertinent information. For example, in the bead string inventory case, the nodes would be treated simply as *beads*. Their links would express the significant relations between the beads. We do not need to know the size or color of any bead to compare this structure to any other. The same is true for the probability example. In another application, we might need to know the nature of the event to which probability is assigned but not for isomorphic and subisomorphic testing. When structures are of interest, we might very well compare the structure of a bead string to that of a transportation system. This is one case where apples may usefully be compared with pears.

Once the multiway tree is established, it can be transformed into its binary version, and the procedures described in Chapter 6 for testing isomorphism may be applied. However, because dummy nodes have been added to the tree and the sample to retain link positions, some additional operations are required to test for subisomorphism. First, the locations of the real nodes of the sample must be recorded when its L-R-N string is formed, and, second, a test must be made to see if any of these real nodes coincide with the dummy nodes of the tree when it is tested for subisomorphism at a node. If so, the test fails at that node.

7.6 APPLICATIONS

The multiway tree is a complex and versatile structure. This means that it has the potential to match the structures of a wide variety of tasks. Its applications are similar to those of the binary tree, but it escapes the binary relation limitation. It cannot only represent shapes based on a *less than/more than* criteria but those arising from multiordered relations.

Multiway trees created by multiordered relations basically match the structure of context-dependent tasks. A context-dependent task is one in which future *moves* are limited by all preceding ones (history). The game of chess provides a good example. The possible moves in a chess game at any point depend on the present positions of the pieces. In turn, these positions depend on all past moves. Multiway trees are appropriate for computer games of skill. The task of verifying all acceptable permutations of symbolic equations is another context-based task for which the multiway tree is appropriate. The acceptability of a symbol at any position in the equation depends on what precedes it. Computer speech recognition—a task requiring the *listener* to match an ambiguous acoustic signal against context limitations—is another. There are numerous opportunities to exploit the multiway tree in context-based tasks.

7.6.1 Spelling Checker

Spelling is an obviously context-based task. The acceptability of a letter at any location depends on preceding letters of the word. Many commercial spelling checkers rely on a word list (dictionary) and carry out direct comparisons. The problem of supporting large dictionaries can be alleviated by storing roots, prefixes, and suffixes, but basically the dictionary structure is inappropriate, wasteful, and slow. We present an algorithm that springs almost full-blown from the multiway tree structure. As expected, this algorithm is concise, versatile, and efficient.

Our spelling-checker algorithm uses a transformed multiway tree to represent the vocabulary. Words are checked by seeing if each letter can be reached in the tree along a path that includes all previous letters. For example, for the word *cat,* we see if *c* can be reached in the tree without passing through other letters. Then we see if *a* can be reached via a path that includes *c.* We do the same for *t.* If this is the end of the word (indicated in our example by an *), then the word is correct.

The multiway tree clearly provides an efficient way to store a vocabulary. All words with the same initial sequences share the same path and use the same letters. For example, the words *cat, cats, catch, catches, catching, cattle,* and *catapult* share the initial sequence *cat.* Words like *catch, catches, catcher,* and *catching* share the first four letters and require about ten symbols plus four termination symbols. Dictionary storage without space-saving artifices requires 27.

The multiway tree checker is faster than dictionary comparisons. The worst case search for the dictionary is closely related to the size of the vocabulary. Although lexical ordering and other strategies reduce the number of search comparisons required, the number is usually very large. The example that we will present next requires a maximum of 23 symbol comparisons if they are performed by direct comparison. The maximum number of comparisons for the tree checker is given by the maximum depth of the transformed tree. In our example, the maximum number equals 8. For large vocabularies, the speed advantage of the tree checker over the dictionary could be significant.

Spelling checkers will almost always be disk based because of the required large vocabularies. The search tree described in Section 7.4, and illustrated in Figure 7.10, can easily be used in this algorithm, for it solves the problem of disk basing.

To present the underlying principles of the spelling checker in a simple way, we have used nonsense words in a very restricted vocabulary. The entire vocabulary consists of the words *aa, aaa, aac, ac, acb, acc, cb, ca,* and *cc.* Figure 7.12 shows the multiway tree used. Keys have been assigned to the nodes of this tree, using the methods discussed earlier in this chapter. The * indicates the end of a word.

Let us trace two words through the tree. *S* is the start of the tree and is not part of any word. Trace *acb.* We proceed by first checking the direct descendants of S21 for *a.* The first *a* is found directly below S (a13). The next letter *c* is

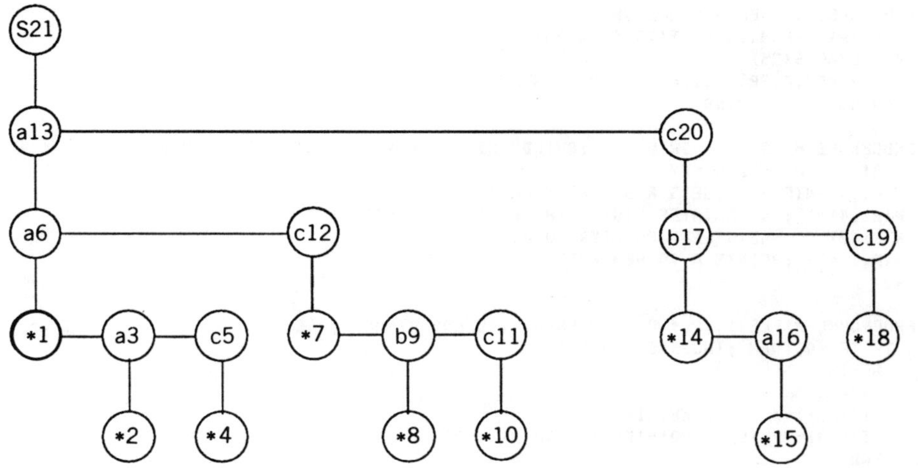

Figure 7.12 Transformed multiway tree for spelling checker.

found by searching horizontally through the direct descendants of a13. We locate *c* at c12. Next we check the direct descendants of c12 and search for *b*. This is found at b9. Since the first descendant of b9 is *8 and the word ends there with *, *acb* is accepted. The word *abc* would fail at the direct descendant level a6—c12, since *b* would not be found there.

Figures 7.13 and 7.14 show SBASIC and Pascal spelling-check programs. Both receive data for the transformed tree as symbol-key pairs. This is used to build a linked list. (Although we have modified existing procedures that build doubly-linked lists, singly-linked ones would do.) These lists are used to build binary trees using BTREE. CHECK is the new procedure that traces words through the tree. Arguments of CHECK consist of PP, a pointer initially to the root node but subsequently to subtrees, and X, the successively peeled off characters of the word. First a move left (down) positions the search at the leftmost descendant of the root. These descendants are searched for the first character of the word. In our example, there are two acceptable letters, *a* and *c*. The WHILE statement performs this search. If a match is not found, the loop ends with the pointer at NIL (Pascal) or 0 (SBASIC). The following IF statement is true, and the procedure reports an error. If a match is found, the pointer is at the matched node in the tree. The ELSE statement is implemented, and CHECK runs recursively with PP at the matched node and X, the next character of the word. OK is reported when * is reached simultaneously for the tree and the word (last symbol).

The node structure of the Pascal program is conventional, but there are some elements of the SBASIC node worth mentioning. The SBASIC nodes are rows in a matrix and as such only support homogeneous elements, in this case integers.

```
REM  SPELL, CHECKS SPELLING
 DIM INTEGER N(25,4) T(25,4) A(25)
 DIM CHAR S(25)
 VAR N,KEY,P,RR,YY,I,K,LP,TTP = INTEGER
 VAR WORD,ST=STRING

PROCEDURE MLIST1(R1=INTEGER) ;BUILDS SINGLY-LINKED LIST WITH 3 POINTERS
 N(R1,1)= R1 ;SETS KEY
 N(R1,3)=N(P,3)  ;SETS RIGHT POINTER TO P'S TARGET
 N(R1,4)=I ; ASSOCIATES LIST WITH CHARACTER VECTOR
 N(R1,2)=0  ;SETS LEFT POINTER TO NIL
 N(P,3)=R1 ;POINTS P TO NEW NODE
END

PROCEDURE BTREE(X,TP,Y,R = INTEGER) ;BUILDS BINARY TREE
  IF TP =0 THEN ;INSERTS NEW NODE
   BEGIN
    TP=X
    T(TP,1)=X ;SETS KEY IN NEW NODE
    T(Y,R)=TP ;SETS POINTER IN PARENT NODE
   END
  ELSE BEGIN
        IF X < T(TP,1) THEN ;LEFT CONDITION
         BEGIN
           R=2 ;SETS LEFT FLAG
           Y=T(TP,1) ;RECORDS PARENT
           BTREE X,T(TP,2),Y,R ;LEFT CALL
         END
        IF X > T(TP,1) THEN ;RIGHT CONDITION
         BEGIN
           R=3 ;SETS RIGHT FLAG
           Y=T(TP,1) ;RECORDS PARENT
           BTREE X,T(TP,3),Y,R ;RIGHT CALL
         END
       END
END

PROCEDURE CHECK(PP=INTEGER;X=CHAR) ;CHECKS SPELLING
  PP=T(PP,2) ;MOVES DOWN TO DESCENDANT
  IF (S(N(PP,4))= '*') AND (X ='*') THEN PRINT "OK"
  ELSE
    BEGIN
      WHILE (S(N(PP,4))<>X) AND (PP<>0) DO PP=T(PP,3);TERMINATING CONDITION
      IF PP= 0 THEN PRINT "ERROR"
      ELSE
       BEGIN
         I=I+1 ;INCREMENT I TO MOVE TO NEXT LETTER IN WORD
         CHECK PP, MID$(WORD,I,1) ;RECURSIVE CALL
       END
    END
END

REM MAIN
P=0 ;CREATE EMPTY LIST
REM BUILDS LIST
INPUT "NO. OF KEYS THEN KEYS FOLLOWED BY SYMBOL ";N
FOR I=1 TO N
  INPUT A(I),S(I)
  MLIST1 A(I) ;CALLS LIST BUILDER
NEXT I
```

Figure 7.13 Spelling checker (SBASIC).

```
LP=N(P,3) ;SETS POINTER AT BEGINNING OF LIST
TTP=LP ;SETS ROOT AS FIRST NODE
WHILE N(LP,3) <> 0 DO
 BEGIN
  YY=0 ;SETS PARENT NODE AT 0--CONDITION FOR ROOT
  RR=0 ;SETS POINTER FLAGS AT 0--CONDITION FOR ROOT
  T(TTP,1)=TTP ;SETS ROOT KEY
  BTREE N(LP,1),TTP,YY,RR ;CALLS BTREE
 END
10 INPUT "WORD ENDING WITH *";WORD ;ACCEPTS TEST WORD
I=1 ;INITIALIZE I
CHECK TTP, MID$(WORD,I,1) ;CALL SPELLING CHECKING PROCEDURE
GOTO 10 ;GO BACK FOR ANOTHER WORD
END
```

Figure 7.14 Spelling checker (Pascal).

```
PROGRAM SPELL(INPUT,OUTPUT); {CHECKS SPELLING}
  LABEL HERE;
  TYPE
  RP=^NODE;
  NODE = RECORD
           KEY:INTEGER ;
           CONT:CHAR;
           RIGHT:RP ;
           LEFT:RP;
         END;
  ST =STRING[5];
  VAR SYMB:CHAR;PM,MT,ROOT,PL,TP,PP,PW:RP;N,NN,BB,I,K:INTEGER;
      A:ARRAY[1..50] OF INTEGER; B:ARRAY[1..50] OF CHAR; WORD:ST;

PROCEDURE BUILS(VAR P:RP;NKEY:INTEGER;SY:CHAR); {BUILDS LINKED LIST}
   VAR I:INTEGER;Q:RP;
    BEGIN
       NEW(Q); {RETRIEVES SOURCE NODE FROM HEAP}
       Q^.RIGHT := P; {SETS POINTER TO P}
       IF P<>NIL THEN P^.LEFT :=Q; {SETS LEFT POINTER}
       Q^.KEY:= NKEY; {SETS KEY}
       Q^.CONT:=SY; {SETS CONTENTS FIELD}
       Q^.LEFT:=NIL; {SETS LEFT POINTER OF 1ST NODE TO NIL}
       P:= Q;  {POINTS P TO INSERTED NODE}
    END;

PROCEDURE BTREE(X:INTEGER; VAR PQ:RP); {BUILDS BINARY TREE}
 {$A-}
 VAR PS:RP;
         BEGIN
        IF PQ=NIL THEN PQ:=PW
        ELSE
           BEGIN
 IF X < PQ^.KEY THEN BTREE(X,PQ^.LEFT); {LEFT CALL}
 IF X > PQ^.KEY THEN BTREE(X,PQ^.RIGHT); {RIGHT CALL}
           END;
        END;
```

Figure 7.14 *(Continued)*

```
PROCEDURE CHECK(SP:RP; X:CHAR); {CHECKS SPELLING}
  {$A-}
    BEGIN
     SP:=SP^.LEFT; {MOVES DOWN TO DESCENDANTS}
      IF (SP^.CONT='*') AND (X='*') THEN WRITELN('OK') ELSE
        BEGIN
         WHILE (SP^.CONT<>X) AND (SP<>NIL) DO SP:=SP^.RIGHT;{SEARCHES DESCENDANTS FOR X}
         IF SP=NIL THEN WRITELN('ERROR') {IF DESCENDANT NOT FOUND REPORTS ERROR}
         ELSE BEGIN {DESCENDANT FOUND GOES TO NEXT DESCENDANT}
                I:=I+1;CHECK(SP,WORD[I]);
               END;
        END;
    END;

{MAIN}
  BEGIN
    WRITELN('NO. OF KEYS');READLN(N); {ENTER TREE DATA}
    PP:=NIL; WRITELN('ENTER  SYMBOL-KEY IN REVERSE ORDER');
    FOR I:=1 TO N DO BEGIN READ(B[I],A[I]);
    WRITE(' ');BUILS(PP,A[I],B[I]);END; {BUILDS LINKED LIST FROM DATA}
    PW:=PP;WRITELN;
    WHILE PW<>NIL DO BEGIN WRITE(PW^.KEY:3,' ',PW^.CONT,' ');
    PW:=PW^.RIGHT;END;WRITELN; {DISPLAYS LIST}
    MT:=PP; {TEMPORARY POINTER TO ROOT OF TREE}
    ROOT:=NIL; {ESTABLISH ROOT OF TREE}
    WHILE MT<> NIL DO
    BEGIN
     PW:=MT; {TEMPORARY POINTER TO FIRST NODE IN LIST}
     MT:= MT^.RIGHT; {MT POINTS TO SECOND NODE IN LIST}
     PW^.LEFT:=NIL; PW^.RIGHT:=NIL; {NODE TERMINATED IN NILS}
     BTREE(PW^.KEY,ROOT); {CALL BTREE TO INSERT NEW NODE}
    END;
   HERE: WRITELN('ENTER WORD, END WITH *'); {ENTER TEST WORDS}
   WRITELN;READLN(WORD);
   I:=1; CHECK(ROOT,WORD[I]); {CALL SPELLING CHECK PROCEDURE}
   GOTO HERE; {RETURN FOR NEXT WORD}
 END.
```

Therefore, the symbols are contained in an associated character vector. The matrix and the vector are associated by adding a fourth column to the matrix; this column contains the index number of the associated symbol. In CHECK the required symbol is found by S(T(PP,4)). PP is the target row, 4 the index field, and S the character vector. T(PP,4) then gives the correct index of S.

Figure 7.15 shows some sample input and output. In our example, the tree contains 21 nodes. This is input as the pairs 21 S, 11 C, etc. This data builds the multiway tree. A preorder traversal of the tree is listed to verify the construction. Sample words are entered next, and the results shown. Obviously, more work needs to be done to produce a commercially acceptable spelling checker, but the essential algorithm is concise and extremely efficient. This is what we have come to expect when data structures are used appropriately.

```
NO. OF KEYS
21

INPUT
 21 S  13 a   6 a   1 *   3 a   2 *   5 c   4 *  12 c   7 *   9 b
 8 *  11 c  10 *  20 c  17 b  14 *  16 a  15 *  19 c  18 *

PREORDER
Saa*a*c*c*b*c*cb*a*c*

ENTER WORD, END WITH *

ac*
OK

aab*
ERROR

acc*
OK

aca*
ERROR

aa*
OK

aa*
OK

cb*
OK

cbb*
ERROR

cba*
OK

cc*
OK
```

Figure 7.15 Output of spelling checker.

7.6.2 A Symbolic Equation Checker

A symbolic equation checker is an obvious offshoot of the spelling checker. The symbolic equation is treated simply as a word to be checked. However, because the length of the equation is always known, the termination symbol (*) can be omitted. Also, it is more important in this application to indicate the error and its location.

Figure 7.16 displays the transformed multiway tree for the equation

$$Y = AX + BZ$$

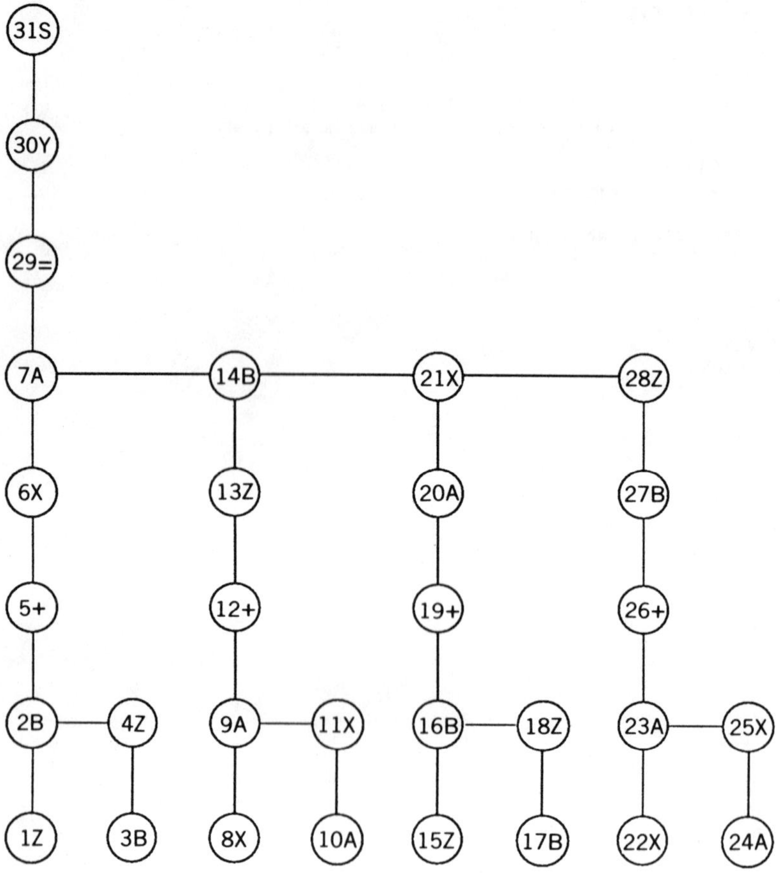

(a)

31S 30Y 29= 7A 6X 5+ 2B 1Z 4Z 3B 14B 13Z 12+ 9A 8X
11X 10A 21X 20A19+ 16B 15Z 18Z 17B 28Z 27B 26+ 23A

22X 25X 24A

(b)

Figure 7.16 Tree representation of all acceptable permutations of Y = AX + BZ: (a) transformed tree; (b) entry data.

and the entry data required to build the tree. The programmer must work out all acceptable permutations of the equation in order to construct the tree. There are eight such permutations in our example. They are:

1. Y = AX + BZ
2. Y = BZ + AX
3. Y = XA + ZB
4. Y = ZB + XA
5. Y = XA + BZ
6. Y = BZ + XA
7. Y = ZB + AX
8. Y = AX + ZB

The tree is constructed from these permutations by noting which symbols can follow each other and establishing all such connections in the tree. For example, the first letter is always Y. Therefore, the start symbol (S) leads directly to and only to Y. The same is true on the next level for "=." Therefore, Y leads directly to and only to "=." Direct descendants of the "=" symbol are A, B, X, or Z, as shown in the figure. X is the only direct descendant of A, Z of B, A of X, and B of Z. All these siblings must be followed by "+." Therefore, A, X, and "+," B, Z, and "+," X, A, and "+," and Z, B, and + are each connected by down links. The AX + path can be followed by either B or Z. Therefore, this "+" has two descendants (B and Z). The rest of the tree is treated similarly. Once this is done, the keys can be assigned in the conventional way.

Figure 7.17 shows the modifications in the CHECK procedures required by the symbolic equation checker. Since the length of the equation is known, the procedure terminates when the counter (I) exceeds this number or an error is encountered. The error output statement has also been modified to display the location of the error and the incorrect entry. Figure 7.18 shows the output of the program and verifies its operation.

There is of course a simple alternate way to check symbolic equations. Record each permutation as a string, and check input against each string. Using string functions, the test equation can be checked symbol by symbol against the permutations, and errors can be indicated. However, the multiway tree checker has several advantages over this direct approach.

The tree checker can save memory. There are 31 symbols in our tree as compared to 56 in the alternate method, but this advantage may be wiped out by the overhead required to store keys and pointers. The memory economy therefore is unimpressive in this case. However, adding one more term (+CW) increases the symbol count in the alternate method to 480, while only increasing the nodes to 158. This advantage increases with the size of the equation.

When partials of the equation are also checked, the tree advantage increases further. In the direct method, it is difficult to check any partial because the context surrounding the partial must be known. Although special functions and

```
PROCEDURE CHECK(PP=INTEGER;X=CHAR) ;CHECKS SYMBOLIC EQUATIONS
 PP=T(PP,2) ;MOVES DOWN TO DESCENDANT
 IF I=LN+1 THEN PRINT "OK"
 ELSE
   BEGIN
     WHILE (S(N(PP,4)) <> X) AND (PP <> 0) DO
      BEGIN
      PP=T(PP,3) ;MOVES RIGHT
     END
     IF PP= 0 THEN PRINT "ERROR AT ";I;" TH ELEMENT ";S(I)
     ELSE
      BEGIN
        I=I+1
        CHECK  PP,  MID$(WORD,I,1) ;RECURSIVE CALL TO NEXT  SUB-TREE
      END
   END
END
```

(a)

```
PROCEDURE CHECK(SP:RP; X:CHAR); {CHECKS SYMBOLIC EQUATIONS}
  {$A-}
    BEGIN
     SP:=SP^.LEFT; {MOVES DOWN TO DIRECT DESCENDANTS}
      IF I=LN+1 THEN WRITELN('OK') ELSE
       BEGIN
        WHILE (SP^.CONT<>X) AND (SP<>NIL) DO SP:=SP^.RIGHT; {SEARCHES DESCENDANTS}
        IF SP=NIL THEN WRITELN('ERROR AT ', I,'TH CHARACTER  ',WORD[I]){DISPLAYS ERROR}
        ELSE BEGIN
               I:=I+1;CHECK(SP,WORD[I]); {RECURSIVE CALL TO NEXT SUB-TREE}
              END;
       END;
    END;
```

(b)

Figure 7.17 Procedures for checking symbolic equations: (a) SBASIC; (b) Pascal.

strategies may handle this problem, it introduces the kinds of complications we are trying to avoid. The tree checker can be modified to handle partials by entering the length of the partial (LN) along with the partial itself. LN then terminates the checking procedure at the end of the partial. Partial terms are already included in the tree. Therefore, it costs nothing to check them. This increases the memory advantage of the tree checker.

The tree checker is much faster than the direct method. For the direct method, the worst case for our example requires 56 comparisons to determine if an equation is acceptable (target in last string) and the best case requires only seven comparisons. For the tree checker, the worst case ($Y = ZB + XA$) requires 12 comparisons (the maximum depth of the transformed tree), and the best case, eight comparisons. (This is found from Figure 7.16.) This advantage increases rapidly with the size of the equation.

```
NO. OF KEYS AND LENGTH OF EQUATION
31 7

INPUT
31 S   30 Y   29 =    7 A    6 X    5 +    2 B    1 Z    4 Z    3 B   14 B
13  Z  12 +    9 A    8 X   11 X   10 A   21 X   20 A   19 +   16 B   15  Z
18 Z   17 B   28 Z   27 B   26+   23 A   22 X   25 X   24 A

PREORDER
SY=AX+BZZBBZ+AXXAXA+BZZBZB+AXXA


ENTER EQUATION

Y=AX+BY
ERROR AT 7TH CHARACTER  Y

Y=AX+BZ
OK

Y=BZ+AX
OK

Y=XA+BZ
OK

Y=XA+ZB
OK

Y=BZ+XA
OK

Y=ZB+XA
OK

Y=ZB+AX
OK

Y=AX+ZB
OK

Y=AZ+BX
ERROR AT 4TH CHARACTER  Z

Y=AX+BX
ERROR AT 4TH CHARACTER X
```

Figure 7.18 Sample input and output of symbolic equation checker.

7.7 FORESTS

Forests are united groups of trees, usually having something in common. For example, a system of symbolic equations describing physical motion, each one represented by a tree, could be assembled into a forest. If a tree is used to describe the syntax of a sentence (a useful practice), a forest of such trees could describe the syntax of a text. A collection of check-cashing procedures, each one represented as a flow structure tree, could be formed into a forest to facilitate comparison against other check-cashing procedures. A series of related geometric patterns could be usefully represented as a forest.

Trees are transformed into forests to simplify computer operations. The forest is a single structure that can be searched, traversed, and tested for isomorphism and subisomorphism, among other things. For example, the forest of symbolic equations relates to motion, and it could be used to identify and verify all motion equations and to reject unrelated ones.

Trees are combined into forests by transforming each tree into its binary version, establishing a supraroot preceding the tree roots and treating all tree roots as siblings of the supraroot. This procedure is illustrated in Figure 7.19. The two trees in our forest are shown individually in Figure 7.19*a* with arbitrary symbols. Their binary transformations are shown in Figure 7.19*b*. Keys have been assigned here to facilitate construction. (Note these are construction keys. Any other needed keys or symbols must be held in another field.) Figure 7.19*c* is realized by first assigning a supraroot (S) and then combining the roots of each tree as the direct siblings of S. Construction keys are assigned in the usual way.

We need to relate operations on forests to operations on the individual trees within the forest. This can be done heuristically by comparing results of tree and forest operations. The reader has all the tools necessary to conduct these investigations. Here, we compare the effects of traversals on individual trees and on their forest.

Figures 7.20*a*, 7.20*b*, and 7.20*c* show the results of traversing binary versions of two multiway trees separately and concatenating the results. Figures 7.20*d*, 7.20*e*, and 7.20*f* show the results of traversing a forest formed from the two trees. The two trees and their binary versions are shown in Figures 7.19*a* and 7.19*b*, and their forest, in Figure 7.19*c*.

The most interesting result of this experiment arises from the preorder traversals. Figures 7.20*a* and 7.20*d*, preorder traversals of the trees and their forest, are identical except for the added supraroot (S). This is a general result. The preorder traversal of a forest is always equal to the concatenation of the preorder traversals of its individual (binary version) trees, provided a fixed traversal order is maintained. This is also true of the inorder traversals, but *inorder* does not always have a clear meaning for multiway trees.

The postorder results (Figures 7.20*c* and 7.20*f*) are close, but not identical. The position of the "a" differs. It lies at the end of each traversal string for the individual trees but at the end of the forest string. The root node of the first tree in the forest will always be next to the supraroot in the postorder traversal list.

7.8 SUMMARY

The multiway tree is a versatile structure that significantly extends the uses of the binary tree by eliminating the dyadic limitation. The structure can be used to establish context, to represent diagrams, and to match tasks in which new *moves*

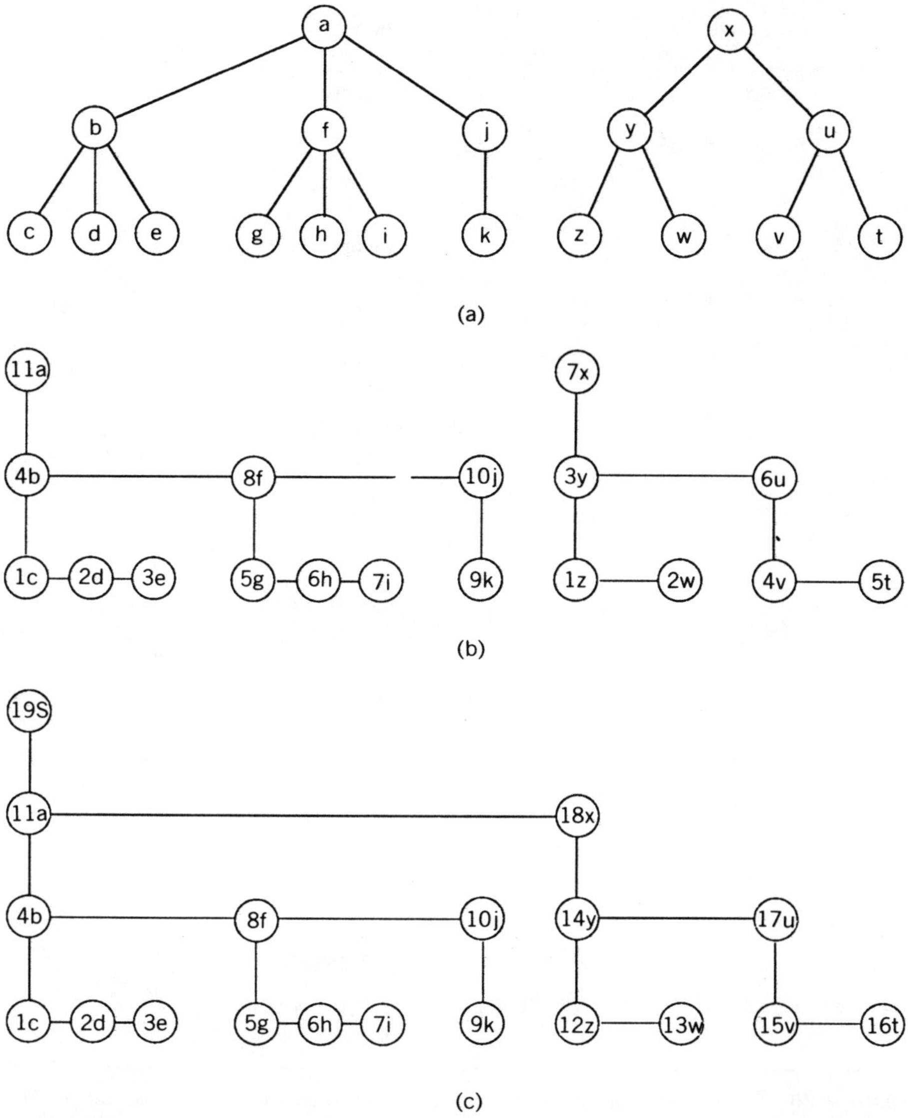

Figure 7.19 Forest construction: (a) multiway trees; (b) binary conversions; (c) forest.

are controlled by past ones (history). Examples of such tasks include a spelling checker, a symbolic equation checker, speech and symbol recognition, pattern recognition in general, among many others.

Because operations on multiway trees are dependent on the order of the tree, they are consequently complicated and nonstandardized. Therefore, it is best to

TREES

A B

PREORDER

a b c d e f g h i j k x y z w u v t

(a)

INORDER

c d e b g h i f k j a z w y v t u x

(b)

POSTORDER

e d c i h g k j f b a w z t v u y x

(c)

FOREST

PREORDER

S a b c d e f g h i j k x y z w u v t

(d)

INORDER

c d e b g h i f k j a z w y v t u x S

(e)

POSTORDER

e d c i h g k j f b w z t v u y x a S

(f)

Figure 7.20 Comparison of traversals on individual trees and their forest: (a) preorder—trees; (b) inorder—trees; (c) postorder—trees; (d) preorder—forest; (e) inorder—forest; (f) postorder—forest.

work with binary versions of the multiway tree. The binary version is easily constructed by assigning keys as shown in this section and subsequently using the methods of Chapter 6. The binary version of the tree can retain all of the parent tree information by using dummy nodes to fill all unused links.

It is not possible to describe all forms of the multiway tree in a single chapter. We have not described the indexed tree in which the number of permitted links are less than the number of permitted link directions. Nor have we discussed hedges (trees or forests composed of indexed subtrees). There are also flow structure multiway trees, lexical trees, paged (BB) trees, syntax trees, and a vast amount of unexplored possibilities. We leave further exploration of this versatile structure to our readers.

PROGRAMMING PROJECTS

7.1 A genealogy tree displays parents and their offsprings over the entire history of a family. First, compose a program that will construct and display this tree. Then, use traversals to answer questions such as: What are the names of first siblings or last siblings? Who are the sons or daughters of a specified parent? Which parents had daughters only? Which offsprings had no children? Who had the most children?. *Hint:* Use traversals to elicit information from the tree.

7.2 Compose a program to play Tic-Tac-Toe. *Hint:* Number each square. First show all starting moves of the opponent. For each starting move, show all possible responses and mark the best responses. Continue until the game is won or lost.

7.3 Compose a program to solve any maze. *Hint:* Input the maze as a diagram. Transform it into a tree, with the entrance as the root. (If there is more than one entrance, you need more than one tree.)

7.4 Compose a spelling checker. Limit the extent of this program as you wish, but make it more realistic than the text example.

7.5 Compose a disk-based database that can be efficiently searched.

7.6 Compose a program to check two geometric patterns for isomorphism or subisomorphism.

8 Stacks and Sets

8.1 STACKS

8.1.1 Concept

The stack is a simple, but widely used, data structure. It is defined as an ordered collection of items with only one accessible end. Items can be inserted into or removed from the stack at this end only. Because of this limitation, stack operations are few and simple: *insert* (STACK), and *remove* (UNSTACK). Two tests for stack condition, OVERFLOW (stack full) and UNDERFLOW (stack empty), complete the gamut of operations. This small operation set is one of the stack's most valuable characteristics.

Items contained in a stack are ordered relative to their insertion. Each newly entered item pushes all previous occupants toward the *bottom* of the stack while the newly entered item remains at the *top*. For this reason, the stack is sometimes called a *push-down list*. Because items can be removed (or inserted) only from the top of the stack, the last-entered item must always be removed first. This basic property is expressed by the acronym LIFO (Last In First Out).

The stack is often likened to the spring-loaded dish-well found in diners and other fast-food restaurants. There, the employees can remove only the topmost dish or insert new dishes from the top. This is a poor analogy. The dishes in this stack are effectively identical so that order plays no role. In the computer stack, the contained items are unique and their order is important.

A better analogy would compare the stack to a long, spring-loaded cloakroom used by soldiers entering and leaving a mess hall. The function of this stack-cloakroom is to simplify and accelerate the storage and retrieval of the soldiers' coats. It works as follows: The soldiers may enter in any order but must leave in exactly the reverse order of their entry. The first entering soldier hangs his coat on the rack and goes on to eat. The next soldier hangs his coat in front of the first one, pushing the first coat toward the rear of the cloakroom. This process continues until all soldiers have hung up their coats. On leaving, the soldier who entered last is now at the head of the line. The first coat on the rack is the last coat placed on the rack and is clearly his. The soldier who entered second from the last takes the next available coat. This is his coat since it was hung second from the last. This continues until all soldiers have retrieved their coats and the cloakroom is empty.

One essential element of the stack, *order,* is incorporated into this analogy by the maintenance of relative position within the cloakroom-cum-stack. The second essential element, *simplicity,* is demonstrated by the uncomplicated way in which the coats may be hung (insertion) and removed (retrieval). Both these elements permit the cloakroom (stack) to store and release different-sized coats (data) in a simple and efficient way.

8.1.2 Applications

Compilers are frequently required to store and retrieve data in an efficient and ordered way. The program to be run must be stored and retrieved statement by statement. The current position within the program must be retained. The status of the loop index must be known while looping. When entering a nested subprogram, the parent's variable values must be retained until the nested subprogram is terminated and restored upon returning to the parent routine. For maximum efficiency, mainframes (large computers) often interrupt one program to run part of another. The program status and the current values of all variables must be retained and restored when the interrupted program resumes. These functions are invariably performed with the aid of stacks.

Recursion provides a good example of a stack application. A typical recursive program will call itself many times. Each time it does so, the contents of the variables in the parent procedure must be stored until the parent procedure resumes. These contents are inserted and retrieved in the same way as in our cloakroom analogy. The contents of the parent variables are entered into the recursion stack in order. Before resuming the parent procedure, contents are retrieved from the stack and assigned to the parent variables in reverse order. Languages that support recursion may be required to hold variable contents from many levels of nesting and therefore need deep recursion stacks.

Stacks are useful in any task involving the monitoring of *scope* (the range over which parameters apply). For example, suppose it is necessary to make sure that within a mathematical expression every left parenthesis is balanced by a right one. (This capability is usually included in grammar-checking programs.) The following simple algorithm using the stack suggests itself. Whenever a left parenthesis is encountered, insert a copy of it within the stack; whenever a right parenthesis is encountered, remove (and discard) the left parenthesis from the stack. If, in the course of the test, the stack is found to be empty when the removal of a left parenthesis is required, or if at the end of the test the stack is not empty, the expression fails the test. If the stack is empty after all elements of the expression have been processed, the expression is correct. This test can be extended to include brackets and braces as well.

The concept of scope and scope nestings have wider applications. Anything that can be represented by levels of enclosing parenthesis can be considered *nested* and is a candidate for scope checking. A group of tasks that must be performed before their parent group can proceed is one example. Structures that are composed of nested substructures are another example. The tree is such a structure and is often represented by nested strings. (The multiway tree of Figure 7.6*a,* for example, can be represented by

```
(S(A(abcd)B(efgh)C(ijkl)D(mnop)))
```
(8.1)

where each level of parenthesis represents the level of the nodes in the tree.) A scope checker can be used to verify the integrity of such representations.

In another application, stacks are used to evaluate arithmetic and algebraic expressions. The expression should be in prefix format to eliminate parenthesis and the problems associated with them. Two stacks are required: S1 and S2. Initially the expression (in prefix format) is stacked into S1. S2 is left empty. The elements of the expression are unstacked one by one from S1 and examined. There are two types of elements: operands and operators. If the element is an operand, it is stacked into S2. If it is an operator, the two previously entered elements are unstacked from S2, and the operator is applied to them. The result is again stacked in S2. This operation is performed until S1 is empty. Then, S2 is emptied into S1, and the procedure is reapplied. This is repeated until a single result is achieved.

Figure 8.1 shows this procedure applied to the expression

```
*+baa
```
(8.2)

where a and b represent operands and * and + are operators. Figure 8.1*a* shows the initial status of the two stacks: S2 empty and the expression stacked into S1. Figure 8.1*b* shows the status after the first operator has been unstacked from S1. S2 contains the first three elements of the expression, and S1, the last. Because an operator has been unstacked from S1, the two top elements, a and b, are unstacked from S2, evaluated as (a + b)—a single result—and returned to S2 (Figure 8.1*c*). Figure 8.1*c* also shows the status of the stacks when the last element, the operator *, is unstacked from S1. The two top elements, (a+b) and a, are next unstacked from S2, evaluated, and returned to S2 (Figure 8.1*d*). Since only one element remains in S2, the expression has been successfully evaluated and the procedure is terminated. If S1 had been empty, and S2 contained more than one element, S2 would have been emptied into S1 and the procedure repeated.

Although there is no reason for high-level language users to reinvent the

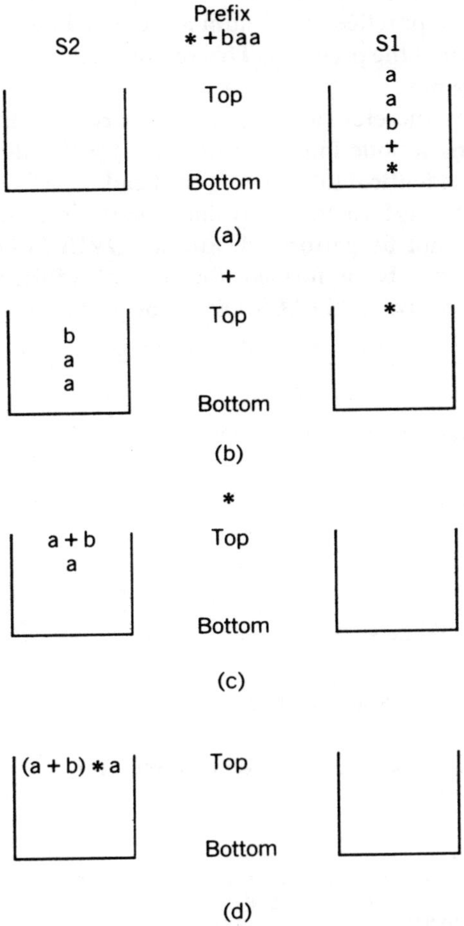

Figure 8.1 Using stacks to evaluate expressions: (a) initial status; (b) status after first operator is unstacked; (c) status after second operator is unstacked; (d) final status, evaluated result in S2.

wheel, occasions arise when analytical operators not supported by the language are required. In these cases, the preceding procedure can be used to implement any desired set of operators. This is an efficient way to extend a high-level language.

8.1.3 Stack Operations

The stack is efficiently implemented as a singly-linked list with access restricted to the head end. The chief advantage of this implementation is in memory-economy since the list is a dynamic structure adjusting its memory requirement to immediate needs. Otherwise, if the stack were implemented as a one-dimensional array, a common practice, maximum anticipated memory would have to be allocated at the start of the program. This requirement can often be extremely wasteful and troublesome.

Stack operations are therefore a subset of list operations. Insertion (STACK) is identical to inserting a node into the front of a list (head-on insertion). Retrieval (UNSTACK) is identical to removing the head node from a list. However, before a STACK can be performed, the available node list must be checked. If it is empty, STACK cannot be performed, and an OVERFLOW flag is raised. Before an UNSTACK can be performed, the contents of the stack list must be checked. If the list is empty, UNSTACK cannot be performed, and an UNDERFLOW flag is raised.

```
REM PROGRAM STACKS-- STACKS AND UNSTACKS
DIM INTEGER AVAIL(50)
DIM STRING SYMB(50)
VAR P,J,K,AVPNTR=INTEGER
VAR ST=STRING:5

PROCEDURE SAVAIL(N=INTEGER); BUILDS SOURCE NODE LIST
   VAR I=INTEGER
   FOR I=1 TO N
     AVAIL(I)=I+1 ;SETS RIGHT POINTER
   NEXT
   AVAIL(N)=0 ;TERMINATES LIST
   AVPNTR=1;POINTER TO START OF AVAIL
   END

PROCEDURE STACK(S=STRING);BUILDS SINGLY-LINKED LIST
   VAR TEMP=INTEGER
   IF AVPNTR<>0 THEN
     BEGIN
      TEMP=AVPNTR; TEMPORARY POINTER TO SOURCE LIST
      AVPNTR=AVAIL(AVPNTR); POINTS AVPNTR TO NEXT NODE IN SOURCE LIST
      AVAIL(TEMP)=P; POINTS NEW NODE TO P
      P=TEMP; POINTS P TO START OF LIST
      SYMB(TEMP)= S; PLACES STRING IN STRING ARRAY
    END
    ELSE PRINT "OVERFLOW"
END

FUNCTION UNSTACK =STRING ;UNSTACKS TOP ITEM
    VAR TEMP=INTEGER
    VAR SS=STRING
    IF P<> 0 THEN
      BEGIN
       SS=SYMB(P) ;PLACES TOP STRING ITEM IN TEMPORARY VARIABLE
       TEMP=P; TEMPORARY POINTER TO START OF LIST
       P=AVAIL(P); POINTER ADVANCED TO SECOND NODE IN LIST
       AVAIL(TEMP)=AVPNTR; DELETED NODE CONNECTED TO AVAIL LIST
       AVPNTR= TEMP; AVPNTR POINTED TO NEW NODE
      END
    ELSE SS="UNDERFLOW"
 END=SS ;PLACES RESULT IN FUNCTION
```

Figure 8.2 Declarations and STACK/UNSTACK procedures (SBASIC).

Figures 8.2 and 8.3 show SBASIC and Pascal procedures for implementing stacks. In both cases, the STACK procedure builds a singly-linked list head-on, but there are differences worth mentioning. Normally, an SBASIC list with string content inhabits a two-dimensional numeric array containing key and right pointer columns, and an associated string vector containing the content. The stack, however, has no need of keys because no internal operations are supported. Therefore, the numeric array can be replaced by the vector (AVAIL). The Pascal list is composed of nodes defined by the RECORD structure. Here, too, the key field can be eliminated, leaving a stripped-down node containing only a content and right-pointer field.

The STACK procedures also contain tests for OVERFLOW. In the SBASIC version, this is signaled by an empty source node list (AVPNTR = 0). If this condition exists, STACK is terminated, and OVERFLOW is displayed. In the Pascal case, OVERFLOW occurs when the node source, the *heap,* is empty. The number of bytes available in this heap is ascertainable. (In Turbo Pascal, this is contained in the variable MEMAVAIL.) If their are more than 12 bytes available (this is the record size), STACK proceeds; otherwise, it terminates.

UNSTACK, implemented as a function, attempts to delete the head node and

```
TYPE
 S=STRING[35];
 RP=^NODE;
 NODE = RECORD
          CONT:S;
          RIGHT:RP ;
         END;

PROCEDURE STACK(VAR P:RP;C:S);
   VAR Q:RP;
    BEGIN
       IF MEMAVAIL > 12 THEN {CHECKS FOR OVERFLOW}
         BEGIN
          NEW(Q); {RETRIEVES A SOURCE NODE FROM HEAP}
          Q^.RIGHT := P; {SETS POINTER FIELD TO P}
          Q^.CONT:=C; {FILLS CONTENT FIELD}
          P:= Q;  {POINTS P TO INSERTED NODE}
         END ELSE WRITELN('OVERFLOW');
    END;

FUNCTION UNSTACK(VAR P:RP):S;
   VAR TEMP:RP;
    BEGIN
      IF P <> NIL THEN
        BEGIN
         WRITELN('UNSTACK'); {SUCCESSFUL UNSTACK}
         UNSTACK:=P^.CONT; {ASSIGNS UNSTACKED STRING TO UNSTACK}
         TEMP:=P;
         P:=P^.RIGHT; {MOVES POINTER RIGHT}
         TEMP^.RIGHT:=NIL; {DISCONNECTS UNSTACKED NODE}
        END ELSE UNSTACK:='UNDER'; {UNSUCCESSFUL ATTEMPT}
    END;
```

Figure 8.3 STACK/UNSTACK procedures (Pascal).

to store its contents in the function name. If the list is empty (P = 0 or NIL), the operation fails, and UNDER is displayed. If successful, UNSTACK is displayed, although this is optional. In SBASIC, the deleted node is returned to the source node list, but in Pascal, the deleted node is left as *garbage* until it is subsequently reclaimed.

Figure 8.4 shows the results of several STACKS and UNSTACKS using the Pascal version. STACK(PP,'A') places A in the initially empty stack PP. The next two STACKS push B and C into the stack. Stack PP now contains CBA in top-down order. UNSTACK(PP) removes the last entered item, C, leaving BA in the stack. Subsequent UNSTACK(PP)'s remove B and A, leaving the stack empty. Another UNSTACK(PP) fails and generates an UNDER.

8.1.4 Scope Checking: An Application

The task is to check the nesting of parenthesis, brackets, and braces (delimiters) in mathematical expressions. The algorithm is straightforward. The expression is scanned from left to right. Each time a left delimiter is encountered, a copy of it is stacked. Each time a right delimiter is encountered, the top item is removed

```
STACK OR UNSTACK?
STACK(PP,'A')  (instruction)
A   (contents of stack)

STACK OR UNSTACK?
STACK(PP,'B')    (instruction)
BA (contents of stack)

STACK OR UNSTACK?
STACK(PP,'C')    (instruction)
CBA   (contents of stack)

STACK OR UNSTACK?
UNSTACK (PP)     (instruction)
C   (unstacked string)
BA (contents of stack)


STACK OR UNSTACK?
UNSTACK(PP)    (instruction)
B   (unstacked string)
A   (contents of stack)

STACK OR UNSTACK?
UNSTACK(PP)    (instruction)
A   (unstacked string)
     (contents of stack--empty)

STACK OR UNSTACK?
UNSTACK(PP)    (instruction)
UNDER (result of attempt to UNSTACK an empty stack)
```

Figure 8.4 Sample output of STACK/UNSTACK procedures.

from the stack and compared against the right delimiter. If the delimiters are correctly placed, the two should match. For example, a right parenthesis in the expression should cause a left parenthesis to be unstacked; similarly, for the other delimiters. When the expression has been completely scanned, the stack should be empty. Any other result flags an error.

Figures 8.5 and 8.6 show SBASIC and Pascal programs that perform this task. Both use the STACK and UNSTACK procedures displayed in Figures 8.2 and 8.3. These are called by a main program that makes excellent use of the CASE statement. This statement is supported by both SBASIC and Pascal, although not by many other BASICS. However, the same result can be simply achieved with IF statements.

Figure 8.5 Program to check paren, bracket, and brace balance (SBASIC).

```
REM STACKS STACKS AND UNSTACKS
DIM INTEGER AVAIL(50)
DIM STRING SYMB(50)
VAR P,J,K,AVPNTR=INTEGER
VAR ST=STRING:25

PROCEDURE SAVAIL(N=INTEGER); BUILDS SOURCE NODE LIST
    VAR I=INTEGER
    FOR I=1 TO N
      AVAIL(I)=I+1 ;FILLS POINTER VECTOR
    NEXT
    AVAIL(N)=0 ;SETS LAST POINTER TO 0
    AVPNTR=1;POINTER TO START OF AVAIL
  END

PROCEDURE STACK(S=STRING);BUILDS SINGLY-LINKED LIST
    VAR TEMP=INTEGER
    IF AVPNTR<>0 THEN
     BEGIN
      TEMP=AVPNTR; TEMPORARY POINTER TO SOURCE LIST
      AVPNTR=AVAIL(AVPNTR); POINTS AVPNTR TO NEXT NODE IN SOURCE LIST
      AVAIL(TEMP)=P; POINTS NEW NODE TO P
      P=TEMP; POINTS P TO START OF LIST
      SYMB(TEMP)= S; PLACES STRING IN STRING ARRAY
     END
     ELSE PRINT "OVER"
END

FUNCTION UNSTACK =STRING ;UNSTACKS TOP NODE
  VAR TEMP=INTEGER
  VAR SS=STRING
  IF P<> 0 THEN
     BEGIN
       SS=SYMB(P)  ;SET  OUTPUT  AND  UNDERFLOW FLAG
       TEMP=P; TEMPORARY POINTER TO START OF LIST
       P=AVAIL(P); POINTER ADVANCED TO SECOND NODE IN LIST
       AVAIL(TEMP)=AVPNTR; DELETED NODE CONNECTED TO AVAIL LIST
       AVPNTR= TEMP; AVPNTR POINTED TO NEW NODE
     END
     ELSE SS="UNDER"
  END=SS ;ASSIGNS SS TO FUNCTION
```

Figure 8.5 *(Continued)*

```
REM MAIN PROGRAM
FOR J=1 TO 50
 SYMB(J)=" "
NEXT ;INITIALIZES STRING VECTOR TO BLANKS
P=AVPNTR;  SETS STACK POINTER TO FIRST SOURCE NODE
SAVAIL 10; BUILDS SOURCE NODE VECTOR
INPUT "ENTER STRING";ST
ST=ST+"!" ;ADDS ADDITIONAL SYMBOL
FOR K= 1 TO LEN(ST); CALLS CASE FOR EACH SYMBOL
   CASE MID(ST,K,1) OF
    "(":STACK "("
    "[":STACK "["
    "{":STACK "{"
    ")":IF UNSTACK <>"(" THEN BEGIN
             PRINT "ERROR  ) UNEXPECTED AT POS";K
             STOP
             END
    "]":IF UNSTACK <>"[" THEN BEGIN
            PRINT "ERROR ] UNEXPECTED AT POS";K
            STOP
            END
    "}":IF UNSTACK <> "{" THEN BEGIN
            PRINT "ERROR } UNEXPECTED AT POS";K
            STOP
           END
   END
IF K=LEN(ST) THEN BEGIN
       IF (UNSTACK="UNDER") THEN PRINT "OK"
       ELSE PRINT "UNBALANCED"
       END ;CHECKS FOR EMPTY STACK AT END OF STRING
NEXT K
```

The CASE statement is used similarly in both programs. After the expression has been entered and the empty stack established, each element of the expression is successively processed through the CASE statement. Left delimiters are stacked. Right delimiters initiate an unstacking and comparison procedure. If the expected delimiter does not appear, an error printout giving the unexpected result and the location of the error is displayed.

Figure 8.7 shows typical output of this program (Pascal version). The first expression is correct. The second is shy a final parenthesis and displays an UNBALANCED flag. The third and fourth expressions are correct, but the fifth has a right bracket at position 13 in place of a parenthesis. The fourth has an extra terminal parenthesis.

8.1.5 Implementing New Operators: An Application

We are required to extend SBASIC and Pascal by redefining the +, *, and − operators. In anticipation of the next section, we call these new operators UNION, INTERSECTION, and DIFFERENCE. These operate on strings composed of 1's and 0's: "1101" (a) or "1011" (b), for example. UNION generates a string containing all the 1's of both strings. The UNION of "1101" and "1011"

```
PROGRAM PARENS(INPUT,OUTPUT);
TYPE
 S=STRING[100];
 RP=^NODE;
 NODE = RECORD
          CONT:S;
          RIGHT:RP ;
         END;
 LABEL STP;
 VAR I,:INTEGER;PP:RP;X,BB:S;

PROCEDURE STACK(VAR P:RP;C:S);
  VAR Q:RP;
   BEGIN
      IF MEMAVAIL > 12 THEN {CHECKS FOR OVERFLOW}
        BEGIN
         NEW(Q); {RETRIEVES A SOURCE NODE FROM HEAP}
         Q^.RIGHT := P; {SETS POINTER FIELD TO P}
         Q^.CONT:=C; {FILLS CONTENT FIELD}
         P:= Q;  {POINTS P TO INSERTED NODE}
        END ELSE WRITELN('OVERFLOW');
   END;

FUNCTION UNSTACK(VAR P:RP):S;
  VAR TEMP:RP;
   BEGIN
     IF P <> NIL THEN
       BEGIN
        WRITELN('UNSTACK'); {SUCCESSFUL UNSTACK}
        UNSTACK:=P^.CONT; {ASSIGNS UNSTACKED STRING TO UNSTACK}
        TEMP:=P;
        P:=P^.RIGHT; {MOVES POINTER RIGHT}
        TEMP^.RIGHT:=NIL; {DISCONNECTS UNSTACKED NODE}
       END ELSE UNSTACK:='UNDER'; {UNSUCCESSFUL ATTEMPT}
   END;


BEGIN {MAIN}
PP:=NIL;  {CREATES EMPTY LIST}
WRITELN('ENTER STRING');READLN(BB); {ENTERS TEST STRING}
FOR I:=1 TO LENGTH(BB) DO {FILLS AND EMPTIES STACK}
  BEGIN
    CASE BB[I] OF
      '(': STACK(PP,'(');
      '[': STACK(PP,'[');
      '{': STACK(PP,'{');
      ')': IF UNSTACK(PP)<> '(' THEN
           BEGIN ;WRITELN('ERROR IN )');GOTO STP;END;{SPOTS PAREN ERRORS}

      ']': IF UNSTACK(PP)<>'[' THEN
           BEGIN WRITELN('ERROR IN ]');GOTO STP;END;{SPOTS BRACKET ERRORS}

        '}': IF UNSTACK(PP)<>'{' THEN
             BEGIN WRITELN('ERROR IN }');GOTO STP;END;{SPOTS BRACE ERRORS}
     END;
  END;
WRITELN;
IF UNSTACK(PP)<>'UNDER' THEN WRITELN('UNBALANCED') ELSE WRITELN('OK');
STP: END.
```

Figure 8.6 Program to check paren, bracket, and brace balance (Pascal).

```
ENTER STRING
y=(a*(b+c))
OK

ENTER STRING
y=(a*(b+c)
UNBALANCED

ENTER STRING
y={a+[b*(a+c)]}
OK

ENTER STRING
y={a+[b*(a+c)]}
OK

ENTER STRING
y=(a+[b*(a+c]}
ERROR ] UNEXPECTED AT POS 13

ENTER STRING
y=(((a+b))))
ERROR ) UNEXPECTED AT POS 12
```

Figure 8.7 Output of PAREN.

(a+b) yields "1111". INTERSECTION generates a string containing only the 1's found in the same positions in both strings. The INTERSECTION of "1101" and "1011" (a*b) yields "1001". DIFFERENCE (a−b) generates a string containing only the 1's in the first string (a) that are not present in the second string (b). The DIFFERENCE, "1101" minus "1011" (a−b), yields "0100".

Instead of adding operators, languages can be extended by adding functions. For example, we could add a function UNION(A,B) that would perform the required operation. This solution, although easier to realize, is clumsy for lengthy expressions. For example, the expression in operator notation

+a−a+**bc*ac (8.3)

becomes in briefest function format

```
U(a,D(a,U(I(b,c),I(a,c))))
```
(8.4)

where U, I, and D signify UNION, INTERSECTION, and DIFFERENCE respectively.

Figure 8.8 shows the SBASIC program for redefining operators. The algorithm has already been explained. The program requires two stacks (STACK1 and STACK2); therefore, the STACK and UNSTACK routines have been coded twice. The TRANSLATE procedure stacks the actual values of the operands as well as the operator symbols into STACK1. The functions UNION, INTER, and DIFF perform the operations of UNION, INTERSECTION, and DIFFER-

Figure 8.8 Program to redefine operators (SBASIC).

```
REM PROGRAM REDEFINES OPERATORS
 DIM INTEGER AVAIL(50)
 DIM STRING SYMB(50)
 VAR J,P1,P2,AVPNTR=INTEGER
 VAR ST=STRING:10
 VAR A,B,C,Y=STRING:10

 PROCEDURE SAVAIL(N=INTEGER); BUILDS SOURCE NODE LIST
    VAR I=INTEGER
    FOR I=1 TO N
      AVAIL(I)=I+1
    NEXT
    AVAIL(N)=0
    AVPNTR=1;POINTER TO START OF AVAIL
  END

 PROCEDURE STACK1(S1=STRING);BUILDS SINGLY-LINKED LIST
    VAR TEMP=INTEGER
    IF AVPNTR<>0 THEN
     BEGIN
      TEMP=AVPNTR; TEMPORARY POINTER TO SOURCE LIST
      AVPNTR=AVAIL(AVPNTR); POINTS AVPNTR TO NEXT NODE IN SOURCE LIST
      AVAIL(TEMP)=P1; POINTS NEW NODE TO P1
      P1=TEMP; POINTS P1 TO START OF LIST
      SYMB(TEMP)= S1; PLACES STRING IN STRING ARRAY
     END
     ELSE PRINT "OVER"
 END

 PROCEDURE STACK2(S2=STRING);BUILDS SINGLY-LINKED LIST
    VAR TEMP=INTEGER
    IF AVPNTR<>0 THEN
     BEGIN
      TEMP=AVPNTR; TEMPORARY POINTER TO SOURCE LIST
      AVPNTR=AVAIL(AVPNTR); POINTS AVPNTR TO NEXT NODE IN SOURCE LIST
      AVAIL(TEMP)=P2; POINTS NEW NODE TO P2
      P2=TEMP; POINTS P2 TO START OF LIST
      SYMB(TEMP)= S2; PLACES STRING IN STRING ARRAY
     END
     ELSE PRINT "OVER"
 END
```

Figure 8.8 (Continued)

```
FUNCTION UNSTACK1 =STRING ;UNSTACKS STACK 1
 VAR TEMP=INTEGER
 VAR SS=STRING
 IF P1<> 0 THEN
    BEGIN
      SS=SYMB(P1)
      TEMP=P1; TEMPORARY POINTER TO START OF LIST
      P1=AVAIL(P1); POINTER ADVANCED TO SECOND NODE IN LIST
      AVAIL(TEMP)=AVPNTR; DELETED NODE CONNECTED TO AVAIL LIST
      AVPNTR= TEMP; AVPNTR POINTED TO NEW NODE
    END
    ELSE SS="UNDER"
 END=SS
FUNCTION UNSTACK2 =STRING ;UNSTACKS STACK2
 VAR TEMP=INTEGER
 VAR SS=STRING
 IF P2<> 0 THEN
    BEGIN
      SS=SYMB(P2)
      TEMP=P2; TEMPORARY POINTER TO START OF LIST
      P2=AVAIL(P2); POINTER ADVANCED TO SECOND NODE IN LIST
      AVAIL(TEMP)=AVPNTR; DELETED NODE CONNECTED TO AVAIL LIST
      AVPNTR= TEMP; AVPNTR POINTED TO NEW NODE
    END
    ELSE SS="UNDER"
 END=SS

PROCEDURE TRANSLATE(YY=STRING) ;CONVERTS INPUT STRING TO STACKED ELEMENTS
   VAR II=INTEGER
    FOR  II=1 TO LEN(YY) ;CALLS CASE FOR EACH CHARACTER
      CASE MID(YY,II,1) OF
        "A":STACK1 A
        "B":STACK1 B
        "C":STACK1 C
        "*":STACK1 "*"
        "+":STACK1 "+"
        "-":STACK1 "-"
      END
    NEXT II
   END

FUNCTION UNION(SET1,SET2=STRING:10)=STRING:10 ; UNION
  VAR I=INTEGER
  VAR SETR=STRING:10
  SETR=""  ;INITIALIZES RESULT STRING
  FOR I=1 TO LEN(SET1) ;APPLIES  UNION TEST
   IF (MID(SET1,I,1)="1") OR (MID(SET2,I,1)="1") THEN SETR=SETR+"1"
   ELSE SETR=SETR+"0"
NEXT I
END = SETR ;ASSIGNS RESULT TO FUNCTION

FUNCTION INTER(SET1,SET2=STRING:10)=STRING:10 ; INTERSECTION
  VAR I=INTEGER
  VAR SETR=STRING:10
  SETR="" ;INITIALIZES RESULT STRING
  FOR I=1 TO LEN(SET1) ;APPLIES INTERSECTION TEST
   IF (MID(SET1,I,1)="1") AND (MID(SET2,I,1)="1") THEN SETR=SETR+"1"
   ELSE SETR=SETR+"0"
NEXT I
END = SETR ;ASSIGNS RESULT TO FUNCTION
```

```
FUNCTION DIFF(SET1,SET2=STRING:10)=STRING:10 ; DIFFERENCE
  VAR I=INTEGER
  VAR SETR=STRING:10
  SETR="" ;INITIALIZES RESULT STRING
  FOR I=1 TO LEN(SET1) ;APPLIES DIFFERENCE TEST
   IF (MID(SET1,I,1)="1") AND (MID(SET2,I,1)="1") THEN SETR=SETR+"0"
   IF (MID(SET1,I,1)="1") AND (MID(SET2,I,1)="0") THEN SETR=SETR+"1"
   IF MID(SET1,I,1)="0" THEN SETR=SETR+"0"
 NEXT I
 END = SETR ;ASSIGNS RESULT TO FUNCTION

FUNCTION COMPUTE =STRING:10 ;PERFORMS OPERATIONS USING STACKS
VAR K=INTEGER
VAR R,X,Z,V = STRING:10
K=0 ;INITIALIZE TERMINATION VARIABLE
X=UNSTACK1
WHILE K <> 1 DO ;UNTIL FINAL RESULT IS IN STACK1
  BEGIN
   WHILE X <> "UNDER" DO ;UNTIL STACK1 IS EMPTY
     BEGIN
       IF (X="+") OR (X="*") OR (X="-") THEN ;TRUE FOR OPERATORS
         BEGIN
           Z=UNSTACK2 ;CALLS UNSTACK FUNCTION
           V=UNSTACK2 ; "          "
           IF X="+" THEN R=UNION(Z,V) ;UNION
           IF X="*" THEN R=INTER(Z,V) ;INTERSECTION
           IF X="-" THEN R=DIFF(Z,V) ;DIFFERENCE
           STACK2 R ; STACKS RESULT IN STACK 2
         END
        ELSE STACK2 X ;STACKS NON-OPERATORS IN STACK 2
        X = UNSTACK1 ;UNSTACKS NEXT ITEM FROM STACK 1
     END
        X= UNSTACK2 ;STARTS DUMP FROM STACK2 INTO STACK 1
        WHILE X <> "UNDER" DO ;UNTIL STACK2 IS EMPTY
         BEGIN
          STACK1 X ;STACK 2 ITEM PLACED IN STACK 1
          K=K+1 ;COUNTS ITEM IN STACK2
          X=UNSTACK2 ;UNSTACKS NEXT ITEM FROM STACK 2
         END
       END
      X=UNSTACK1 ;PLACES RESULT IN X
 END = X ;ASSIGNS RESULT TO FUNCTION

REM MAIN PROGRAM
 P1=0 ;INITIALIZES POINTER TO TOP OF STACK 1
 P2=0 ;"                                 " 2
 J=10 ;SET SIZE OF AVAIL
 A = "1101" ;ASSIGNS VALUES TO VARIABLES--COULD BE INPUT AT RUN-TIME
 B= "1001"
 C = "0110"
 SAVAIL J ;SETS UP SOURCE NODE LIST
 INPUT "EXPRESSION ";Y
 TRANSLATE Y  ;CONVERTS EXPRESSION TO STACK ELEMENTS
 PRINT "RESULT ";COMPUTE ;CALLS COMPUTE
```

ENCE, respectively (If other operations were required other functions would define them.)

COMPUTE implements the algorithm. The function terminates when K = 1. This means that the expression has been completely evaluated. Until then, or until STACK1 is empty, its items are unstacked one by one and examined. If they are not operators, they are stacked into STACK2 (STACK2,R statement). If they are operators, then the top two items of STACK2 are unstacked, the appropriate operation performed, and the result restacked in STACK2. The three IF statements—IF X="+" THEN R=UNION(Z,V), IF X="*" THEN R=INTER(Z,V), and IF X="−" THEN R=DIFF(Z,V)—perform these operations. After this pass is completed, STACK2 is emptied back into STACK1. If more than one item now resides in STACK1, the entire procedure is repeated. Otherwise, the function terminates, and the result is assigned to COMPUTE.

The Pascal program (Figure 8.9) differs in only a few details. Pascal makes it easy to reuse the same STACK and UNSTACK routines for more than one stack. Therefore, we escape duplicating these routines. Also, the function UNSTACK is executed whenever it is cited even in a list of arguments of another function or procedure. This makes the statements such as R = UNION(UNSTACK, UNSTACK) acceptable, each citation generating a new unstacking. (This does not occur in SBASIC.) Otherwise, the Pascal program is effectively the same as the SBASIC one.

Figure 8.10 shows the Pascal program output for several expressions. A, B, and C are given by '1101', '1011', and '1001', respectively. (Note Pascal requires single quotes to delimit a string.) The expression to be solved is input in response to the prompt EXPRESSION. (This reveals an incidental benefit, the ability to input expressions.) The result appears next to RESULT. In some programs, an intermediate display of the results may not be desired. In such cases, since the function COMPUTE contains the result, it can be used for further computation.

8.2 SETS

The set is the data structure with the least organization. It can be thought of as an unordered collection of distinguishable elements. To be useful, these elements should share some meaningful characteristic, but this is not required. For example, all positive integers between 0 and 100 form a set. This is a *finite*, or *closed*, set. (The ensemble of all integers also forms a set, but this is clearly an *infinite* one and inappropriate for computers.) The 26 letters of the alphabet form a set, as does a collection of customer's names and addresses. The set has two essential properties: its elements are distinguishable (unique), and order is unimportant.

The set is represented symbolically by enclosing the elements (members)

Figure 8.9 Program to redefine operators (Pascal).

```
PROGRAM SETOPS(INPUT,OUTPUT); {REDEFINES SET OPERATORS}
  TYPE
   S=STRING[10];
   RP=^NODE;
   NODE = RECORD
           CONT:S;
           RIGHT:RP ;
          END;
   VAR I:INTEGER;S1,S2:RP;A,B,C,D,E,F,G,Y:S;

PROCEDURE STACK(VAR P:RP;C:S);{STACKS STRING}
   VAR Q:RP;
    BEGIN
       IF MEMAVAIL > 12 THEN {CHECKS FOR OVERFLOW}
         BEGIN
          NEW(Q); {RETRIEVES A SOURCE NODE FROM HEAP}
          Q^.RIGHT := P; {SETS POINTER FIELD TO P}
          Q^.CONT:=C; {FILLS CONTENT FIELD}
          P:= Q;  {POINTS P TO INSERTED NODE}
         END ELSE WRITELN('OVERFLOW');
    END;

FUNCTION UNSTACK(VAR P:RP):S; {REMOVES STRING FROM STACK}
   VAR TEMP:RP;
    BEGIN
      IF P <> NIL THEN
        BEGIN
         UNSTACK:=P^.CONT; {ASSIGNS UNSTACKED STRING TO UNSTACK}
         TEMP:=P;
         P:=P^.RIGHT; {MOVES POINTER RIGHT}
         TEMP^.RIGHT:=NIL; {DISCONNECTS UNSTACKED NODE}
        END ELSE UNSTACK:='UNDER'; {UNSUCCESSFUL ATTEMPT}
    END;

PROCEDURE  TRANSLATE(YY:S);{CONVERTS INPUT EXPRESSION TO  STACKED ELEMENTS}
   VAR I:INTEGER;
     BEGIN
      FOR I:=1 TO LENGTH(Y) DO {CALLS CASE TO SEARCH STRING}
       CASE YY[I] OF
        'A': STACK(S1,A);
        'B': STACK(S1,B);
        'C': STACK(S1,C);
        '*': STACK(S1,'*');
        '+': STACK(S1,'+');
        '-': STACK(S1,'-');
       END;
END;


 FUNCTION UNION(SET1,SET2:S):S; {DEFINES UNION}
    VAR I:INTEGER;SETR:S;
      BEGIN
        SETR:=''; {INITIALIZES RESULT STRING}
        FOR I:=1 TO LENGTH(SET1) DO {PERFORMS UNION}
          IF (SET1[I]='1') OR (SET2[I]='1') THEN SETR:=SETR + '1'
          ELSE SETR:=SETR + '0';
        UNION:=SETR; {ASSIGNS RESULT TO FUNCTION}
      END;
```

Figure 8.9 (Continued)

```
FUNCTION INTER(SET1,SET2:S):S; {DEFINES INTERSECTION}
    VAR I:INTEGER;SETR:S;
      BEGIN
       SETR:=''; {INITIALIZES RESULT STRING}
       FOR I:=1 TO LENGTH(SET1) DO {PERFORMS INTERSECTION}
         IF (SET1[I]='1') AND (SET2[I]='1') THEN SETR:=SETR+'1'
         ELSE SETR:=SETR+'0';
       INTER:=SETR; {ASSIGNS RESULT TO FUNCTION}
 END;

FUNCTION   DIFF(SET1,SET2:S):S;{DEFINES   DIFFERENCE}
    VAR I:INTEGER;SETR:S;
      BEGIN
       SETR:=''; {INITIALIZES RESULT STRING}
       FOR I:=1 TO LENGTH(SET1) DO {PERFORMS SET DIFFERENCE}
        BEGIN
         IF (SET1[I]='1') AND (SET2[I]='1') THEN SETR:=SETR+'0';
         IF (SET1[I]='1') AND (SET2[I]='0') THEN SETR:=SETR+'1';
         IF SET1[I]='0'THEN SETR:=SETR+'0';
        END;
       DIFF:=SETR;{ASSIGNS RESULT TO FUNCTION}
      END;

FUNCTION COMPUTE:S; {COMPUTES VALUE OF INPUT STRING}
    VAR K:INTEGER;R,X:S;
     BEGIN
      K:=0; {INITIALIZES TERMINATION COUNTER}
      X:=UNSTACK(S1); {UNSTACKS TOP OF STACK}
      WHILE K<>1 DO
       BEGIN
        WHILE X<>'UNDER' DO
          BEGIN
           IF (X='+') OR (X='*') OR (X='-') THEN {SEPARATES OPERATORS}
            BEGIN
             IF X='+' THEN R:=UNION(UNSTACK(S2),UNSTACK(S2)); {UNION}
             IF X='*' THEN R:=INTER(UNSTACK(S2),UNSTACK(S2));{INTERSECTION}
             IF X='-' THEN  R:=DIFF(UNSTACK(S2),UNSTACK(S2));{DIFFERENCE}
             STACK(S2,R);{RESULT OF SET OPERATION RESTACKED IN S2}
            END
            ELSE STACK(S2,X); {NON-OPERATOR STACKED IN S2}
            X:=UNSTACK(S1); {UNSTACK NEXT ELEMENT}
         END;

     X:=UNSTACK(S2);
     WHILE X <>'UNDER' DO {STACKS S2 IN S1 TO PERMIT REPEAT OF PROCEDURE}
       BEGIN
         STACK(S1,X); K:=K+1; {STACKS S2 IN S1 AND MAINTAINS COUNT}
         X:=UNSTACK(S2); {UNSTACK NEXT ELEMENT}
       END;
   END; {ENDS OPENING WHILE LOOP}
  COMPUTE:=UNSTACK(S1); {ASSIGNS RESULT TO COMPUTE}
END;


BEGIN {MAIN}
  A:='1101';B:='1011';C:='0110'; {ASSIGNS STRINGS--COULD BE INPUT}
  S1:=NIL;S2:=NIL; {INITIALIZES STACK POINTERS}
  WRITE('EXPRESSION-- ');READ(Y);WRITELN; {ACCEPTS EXPRESSIONS}
  {--COULD BE ASSIGNED}
  TRANSLATE(Y); {CALLS TRANSLATE TO FILL S1}
  WRITELN('RESULT ',COMPUTE); {CALLS AND OUTPUTS COMPUTE}
 END.
```

```
EXPRESSION-- '+AB'

RESULT 1111


EXPRESSION-- '*AB'

RESULT 1001


EXPRESSION-- '-AB'

RESULT 0100


EXPRESSION-- '+*ABC'

RESULT 1001


EXPRESSION-- '+*AB*AC'

RESULT 1001


EXPRESSION-- '+*A-BC+AB'

RESULT 1111
```

Figure 8.10 Output of SETOPS program A = '1101', B = '1001', C = '0110'.

within braces. It is not always necessary to list all elements of a set, although this is always correct. Sets can be defined by ellipsis

$$\{1, 2, \ldots, 10\} \tag{8.4}$$

as long as sufficient information is provided to fill in the omitted elements. Sets can also be defined by equation.

$$\{x \mid 4x^2 - 16 = 0\} \tag{8.5}$$

defines the set as composed of all x's that satisfy the equation $4x^2 - 16 = 0$. Sets can as a practical matter even be described in ordinary language, *The entire male population of Alaska,* for example.

8.2.1 Set Operations

Set algebra is a well-developed mathematical discipline. Its elements are sets. Set operators and tests manipulate entire sets. Its operators consist of *union intersection* and *difference.* In addition, it supports tests for *equality, inequality,* and *inclusion* (one set contained within another). Set theory is extremely useful to programmers and provides a valuable source of algorithms. It is well worth the time and effort required to master it.

We have already implemented *union, intersection,* and *difference* for strings consisting of 1's and 0's (binary strings). Tests for equality and inequality of these strings are supported by BASIC and Pascal. Inclusion we leave to the reader. In addition, as a practical programming need, we need to know how to construct the set.

Binary strings can represent sets. We first establish a *universe.* This is an ordered list that contains all the elements of the set and establishes the position of each. Then, the set can be represented by a binary string in which the positions of the 1's and 0's reflect the presence or absence of elements. A 1 means that the element located at the same relative position in the list of elements is present; a 0 signifies absence. A set containing all 1's represents the universe set; every element is present. A set composed solely of 0's is an empty set; no elements are present. Although order is unimportant in formal sets, it is crucial in the binary string representation.

To illustrate, let us represent sets contained within the universe $\{a, b, d, g, o, e, f\}$ as binary strings. The required strings contains seven digits, either 1's or 0's. For example, the string 1100010 represents the set $\{a, b, e\}$. The string 1111001 represents the set $\{a, b, d, g, f\}$. The universe set is represented by 1111111, and the empty set by 0000000.

Using this representation, the string algebra that we have defined and implemented in the previous section is transformed into set algebra. The redefined operators of that section are now set operators, and the programs and procedures for manipulating strings now serve to manipulate sets.

8.2.2 Applications

Information Retrieval

Sets are appropriate structures for obtaining information about the contents of documents. The documents may be journal articles, books, survey responses, and so on. The only requirement is that the content of each document be reflected in a set. For example, it is now general practice to supply authors of journal articles with a list of key words from which they must select sets that reflect the contents of their article. This is also done automatically by people filling out survey forms. Their names are associated with a set of yes/no answers arranged in the same order as the questions. Obviously, the structure of this task is very general and has extremely wide potential.

After the contents of each document in the *library* (collection of documents) have been represented by a binary string, *queries* are entered as masks. A mask is a binary string containing 1's at locations that coincide with target elements. For example, a library containing documents described by the universe set {solid state theory, transistors, chips, analog, digital, devices, circuits} may contain documents described by the following key words:

Document 1	{solid state theory, chips, analog, devices} → 1011010
Document 2	{solid state theory, transistors, digital, circuits} → 1100101
Document 3	{transistors, analog, digital, devices, circuits} → 0101111
Document 4	{chips, digital, devices, circuits} → 0010111

Suppose we seek those documents dealing with the solid state theory of transistors without regard to anything else it may contain. Our query set would be {solid state theory, transistors}, and our mask would be 1100000. If we sought articles that discuss digital devices, our mask would be 0000110.

The information retrieval algorithm hinges on the test

```
IF *AB = B                                                    (8.6)
```

where A represents the binary string representation of each document, B is the mask, and * signifies *intersection.* The relation (8.6) will be true only if the mask is contained in the document string *(inclusion).* In set terms, this means that the query set is a subset of the document set. The algorithm compares each document string against the mask and identifies those that satisfy the test.

A computer analysis of a survey questionnaire would be processed by the same algorithm. Names replace document identification, and the respondees list of yes/no answers to the ordered list of questions, replace the list of key words. Statistical results can be compiled by summing responses to single questions (masks containing a single 1) or to combinations of questions (masks with multiple 1's).

In general, sets are related to *categories.* We figuratively place braces around groups of things that share significant features. Most of our thinking involves the manipulation of these categories. Therefore, the set structure is a likely candidate for tasks involving the manipulation of categories. These might include Venn diagram arithmetic, manipulation of syllogisms, investigations into artificial intelligence, and the like.

Figures 8.11 and 8.12 show programs that implement the information retrieval algorithm. Figure 8.11 is the SBASIC version, and Figure 8.12 is the Pascal one. The programs are similar. They both contain a $I INCLUDE SETPROC statement that accesses the SETPROC routine that performs the required operations on binary strings. (The SETPROC routines are the operator redefining programs of Figures 8.7 and 8.8, modified into independent functions. Their use here illustrates the convenience of building a library of such routines.) The main programs make the necessary declarations and initializa-

```
REM RETRIEVE--INFORMATION RETRIEVAL
DIM INTEGER AVAIL(50)
DIM STRING SYMB(50)
VAR KK,J,P1,P2, AVPNTR = INTEGER
VAR NN,A,B,Y = STRING:10

$INCLUDE SETPROC; RETRIEVES SETPROCESSING FUNCTION

REM MAIN PROGRAM
 P1=0; INITIALIZES POINTER TO STACK1
 P2=0; INITIALIZES POINTER TO STACK2
 J=10; SETS SIZE OF SOURCE NODE LIST
 RESTORE; READS FROM START OF DATA LIST
 10 KK=1; INITIALIZES COUNTER
 INPUT "ENTER MASK"; B
 20 READ NN,A; RECEIVES MASK
 IF NN = "END" THEN; TERMINATES PROGRAM
   BEGIN
    RESTORE; READS FROM START OF DATA LIST
    GOTO 10;  BACK FOR NEW MASK
   END
 ELSE
   BEGIN
    Y="*AB"; SEARCH EQUATION--INTERSECTION
    IF SETOP=B THEN;TESTS FOR INTERSECTION OF MASK AND SET
      BEGIN
       PRINT KK,NN; DISPLAYS FOUND SETS
       KK=KK+1; INCREMENTS COUNTER
      END
      GOTO 20; RETURNS FOR NEXT SET TO BE CHECKED
   END
 REM FOLLOWING DATA WOULD BE READ FROM A FILE IN PRACTICE
 DATA  A,110011010,B,101100111,C,001110100;
 DATA D,011111001, E,000001000,F,010000000,ND,000000000
```

Figure 8.11 Information retrieval using set operators (SBASIC).

tions and then input the desired mask. The *intersection* operation between the mask (B) and the document string (A) is set up by Y = *AB and performed by SETOP. The test is made by IF SETOP = B. For convenience, program data is contained in the program. However, this data would be much more voluminous in practice and would be stored in a magnetic file.

Figure 8.13 shows sample output of this program. The first two cases show the results for masks containing a single 1. As expected, several documents are retrieved in both cases. The second and third entries (multiple 1 masks) are more selective and retrieve only one document for each query. The last two masks match nothing in the library. The last mask represents the universe set and would retrieve documents (if any) that deal with every item in the library.

Gate Circuits

Computers and other digital devices are largely composed of solid state devices called *gates*. There are five basic gates: OR, NOR, AND, NAND, and NOT. However, we shall use only three (OR, AND, and NOT) since the action of the

```
PROGRAM SETS(INPUT,OUTPUT); {INFORMATION RETRIEVAL}
  TYPE
    S=STRING[10];
    RP=^NODE;
    NODE = RECORD
             CONT:S;
             RIGHT:RP ;
           END;
   VAR I2,I1,I:INTEGER;S1,S2:RP;A,B,C,D,E,F,G,Y:S;
       A2,A1:ARRAY[1..10] OF S;

 {$I B:SETPROC} {RETRIEVES SET OPERATOR FUNCTION FROM DISK}

BEGIN {MAIN}
 {FOLLOWING DATA WOULD BE READ FROM A FILE IN PRACTICE}
 A1[1]:='110011010';A1[2]:='101100111';A1[3]:='001110100';A1[4]:='011111001';
 A1[5]:='000001000';A1[6]:='010000000';A1[7]:='END';
 A2[1]:='A';A2[2]:='B';A2[3]:='C';A2[4]:='D';A2[5]:='E';A2[6]:='F';
 S1:=NIL;S2:=NIL; {INITIALIZES STACK POINTERS}
 WRITELN('ENTER MASK ');READLN(B);
 A:='000000000';;I1:=1;I2:=1; {INITIALIZES A AND I1}
 WHILE A<>'END' DO {SEARCH LOOP}
  BEGIN
   A:=A1[I1]; {PLACES EACH SET INTO A IN TURN}
   Y:='*AB'; {INTERSECTION EQUATION}
   IF SETOP=B THEN BEGIN WRITELN(I2,' ITEM ',A2[I1]);I2:=I2+1;END;
   {PERFORMS TEST}
   I1:=I1+1; {INCREMENTS I1 AFTER EACH PASS}
  END;
END.
```

Figure 8.12 Information retrieval using set operators (Pascal).

NOR and NOT gate can be reproduced by using the NOT gate in conjunction with the OR and AND gates. (Actually, all gates can be mimicked by systems of NOR gates alone or of NAND gates alone.)

Gates are defined by truth tables that specify all possible outputs for all possible inputs. This is feasible since the gate as a binary device accepts only four combinations of inputs. Truth tables and schematic symbols for these gates are shown in Figure 8.14. More complex gate circuits are defined by constructing overall truth tables relating output to input. However, this can be a tedious process.

There is an interesting relation between truth tables and set operations. When the range of input combinations are expressed as two paired binary strings, all truth tables can be derived analytically by appropriate set operations. For example, the inputs into all gates can be represented by the string 1100 (input A) and 1010 (input B). This is taken to mean that the input into A and B consists of a 1 into A and a 1 into B (leftmost digits of each string), a 1 into A and a 0 into B (second-from-left digits), a 0 into A and a 1 into B (third-from-left digits), or 0's (fourth digits) into both A and B. This reproduces the input conditions of the truth table. Designate the binary string into A by the letter A and the

```
ENTER MASK? 100000000

1         A

2         B

ENTER MASK? 010000000

1         A

2         D

3         F

ENTER MASK? 110011010

1         A

ENTER MASK? 011100000

1         D

ENTER MASK? 001001010

ENTER MASK? 111111111
```

Figure 8.13 Output of information-retrieval program.

string into B by B. Then, as shown in Figure 8.15, the outputs of the basic gates are given analytically by

```
+AB (OR gate)
```
(8.7)

```
*AB (AND gate)
```
(8.8)

```
-CX (NOT gate)
```
(8.9)

where C = 1111, X = A or B, and +, *, and − are the set operators.

Complex gate circuits are built by cascading gates; the outputs of preceding gates become the inputs of the succeeding one. Therefore, it is always possible to formulate an overall equation using expressions (8.7) through (8.9) to define successive input/output relations as we move through the circuit. This overall equation can then be solved by applying set algebra.

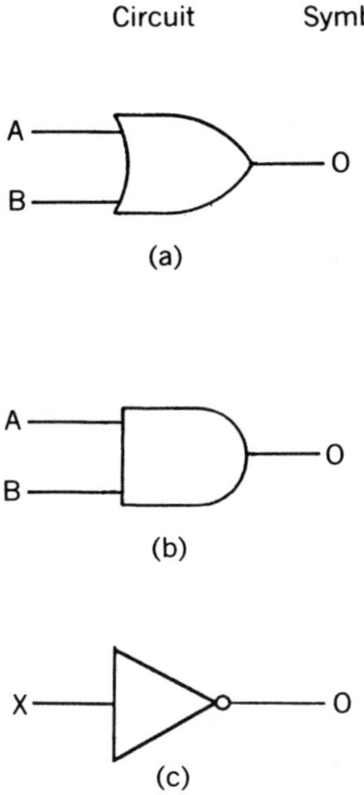

Truth Table

A	B	O
1	1	1
1	0	1
0	1	1
0	0	0

(a)

A	B	O
1	1	1
1	0	0
0	1	0
0	0	0

(b)

X	O
1	0
0	1

(c)

Figure 8.14 Gate circuit symbols and truth tables: (a) OR gate; (b) AND gate; (c) NOT gate.

Figure 8.16 shows how this procedure is applied to an exclusive OR gate (outputs a 1 when either, but not both, inputs are 1). The output of NOT gate 1, −CA, is input to AND gate 3 along with B. The output of this gate is *−CAB. Input to AND gate 4 consists of NOT gate 2 output (−CB) and A. Its output is given by *−CBA. OR gate 5 outputs the union of *−CAB and *−CBA and gives the overall relation, +*−CAB*−CBA. Solving this by computer gives the exclusive OR truth table.

Figure 8.17 shows SBASIC and Pascal programs that are used to find the overall truth tables of gate circuits. Both access the set operator routine, SETPROC via the $I INCLUDE SETPROC statements, and exploit its ability to receive expressions during run-time. Strings A and B are set at 1100 and 1010, respectively, to reproduce the entire range of gate input combinations. String C is set at 1111 (the universe-set string) to support the NOT gate formulation (−CX). Otherwise, the program is straightforward.

```
ENTER GATE SYSTEM EQUATION

+AB (OR gate)

A  1100
B  1010
O  1110


ENTER GATE SYSTEM EQUATION

-C+AB (NOR gate)

A  1100
B  1010
O  0001


ENTER GATE SYSTEM EQUATION

*AB (AND gate)

A  1100
B  1010
O  1000


ENTER GATE SYSTEM EQUATION

-C*AB (NAND gate)

A  1100
B  1010
O  0111

ENTER GATE SYSTEM EQUATION
-CA (NOT gate)
A  1100
B  1010
O  0011


ENTER GATE SYSTEM EQUATION

-CB (NOT gate)

A  1100
B  1010
O  0101
```

Figure 8.15 Output (0) of GATES program (Pascal version).

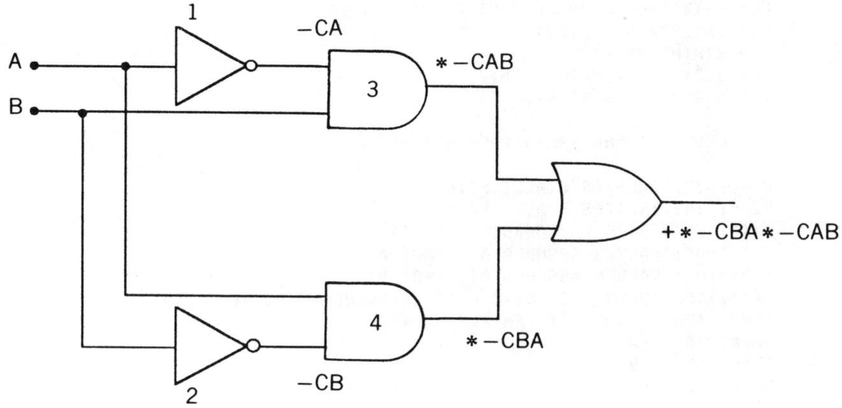

(a)

```
ENTER GATE SYSTEM

+*-CBA*-CAB

A    1100
B    1010
O    0110
```

(b)

Figure 8.16 Analysis of exclusive OR gate: (a) circuit; (b) output of GATES program.

8.3 SUMMARY

The stack, although a relatively simple structure, has wide and interesting applications. Whenever an efficient and simple way to store and retrieve data is needed, the stack is the likeliest candidate. For this reason, it is widely used in compilers for data management. Not unexpectedly, this capability also permits the stack to function effectively in algorithms involving scope nesting and operator redefinition. One essential advantage of the stack in all these applications is its compact and concise ensemble of commands and tests.

The operator-redefinition algorithms are particularly interesting. Operator redefinition provides an excellent way to extend high-level languages and is often superior to extension by adding functions and procedures. The section on set theory applications illustrates the potential of this technique.

```
REM RETRIEVE--FINDS OUTPUT OF GATE SYSTEMS
DIM INTEGER AVAIL(50)
DIM STRING SYMB(50)
VAR J,P1,P2, AVPNTR = INTEGER
VAR A,B,C,Y = STRING:30

$INCLUDE SETPROC ;RETRIEVES SETPROC FILE

P1=0; INITIALIZES STACK1 POINTER
P2=0; INITIALIZES STACK2 POINTER
J=10; SETS SIZE OF SOURCE NODE LIST
A="1100"; VALUES ASSUMED AT INPUT A
B="1010"; VALUES ASSUMED AT INPUT B
C="1111";  USED  TO  GIVE  "NOT"  VALUES--C-A GIVES NOT A
INPUT "ENTER GATE SYSTEM EQUATION";Y
PRINT "A  ";A
PRINT "B  ";B
PRINT "O  ";SETOP
```

(a)

```
PROGRAM SETOPS(INPUT,OUTPUT); {FINDS OUTPUT OF GATE SYSTEMS}
TYPE
  S=STRING[30];
  RP=^NODE;
  NODE = RECORD
           CONT:S;
           RIGHT:RP ;
         END;
 VAR I:INTEGER;S1,S2:RP;A,B,C,Y:S;

{$I B:SETPROC}; {RETRIEVES SETPROC FILE}

BEGIN {MAIN}
  S1:=NIL;S2:=NIL;{INITIALIZES STACKS POINTERS}
  A:='1100';B:='1010';{ VALUES INTO INPUT GATES}
  C:='1111'; {USED TO REPRESENT NOT GATE}
  WRITELN('ENTER GATE SYSTEM EQUATION ');
  READLN(Y);
  WRITELN('A  ',A);
  WRITELN('B  ',B);
  WRITELN('O  ',SETOP);
END.
```

(b)

Figure 8.17 Digital-gate-solving programs: (a) SBASIC; (b) Pascal.

8.4 CONCLUDING NOTES

Throughout this chapter and the preceding ones, we have attempted to show that data structuring is a vital tool for programmers, one that will significantly extend their ability to formulate sophisticated algorithms. We trust that the many realistic examples and applications have made that point.

This text has certainly not exhausted the subject and has in fact discussed only a few data structures. In reality, the discovery or formulation of data structures should be a continuing process akin to the development of mathematics. Sometimes, these discoveries will have immediate application. Other times, they will languish unused until a need arises. In any event, this process is necessary for the continued development of programming.

PROGRAMMING PROJECTS

8.1 Compose a program that will check the following punctuation items:

(a) Every sentence ends with a ".", "?", or "!".

(b) Every set of parentheses is closed.

(c) All single and double quotes are closed.

8.2 Compose a program to support complex arithmetic. (Use operator redefinition.)

8.3 Modify the information-retrieval program to permit the rejection of documents that discuss unwanted topics, even though they are otherwise acceptable.

8.4 Compose a program to support syllogistic thought: If A is a subset of B, then A satisfies the relation that exist across B. Illustrate with some conventional syllogisms.

8.5 Compose a program to support Boolean operations using "1" for TRUE and "0" for FALSE and the normal Boole-Schroeder algebra.

8.6 Select some tasks that generate lengthy Boolean equations, and solve them using the program of project 8.5.

Index